Nonprofit Governance

Law, Practices, and Trends

Nonprofit Governance

Law, Practices, and Trends

Bruce R. Hopkins and
Virginia C. Gross

WILEY

John Wiley & Sons, Inc.

Library of Congress Cataloging-in-Publication Data:
Hopkins, Bruce R.
Nonprofit governance: law, practices, and trends/Bruce R. Hopkins and Virginia C. Gross.
    p. cm.
  Published simultaneously in Canada.
  Includes index.
  ISBN 978-0-470-35804-7 (cloth)
    1. Nonprofit organizations—Law and legislation—United States.   2. Corporate governance—Law and legislation—United States.   I. Gross, Virginia C.   II. Title.
  KF1388.H64 2009
  346.73′064—dc22   2008053453

Printed in the United States of America
10 9 8 7 6 5 4 3 2 1

There is no precedential federal tax law guidance that prescribes the appropriate standards for nonprofit governance. This lack of guidance not only impairs taxpayer efforts at voluntary compliance but also creates a risk that similarly situated taxpayers may be subject to differing treatment from the Service. Without enforceable uniform standards, taxpayers who submit exemption applications or ruling requests may obtain disparate and subjective interpretations of the Service's policy, depending on the agent who happens to handle the matter. Absent published guidance on this issue, a taxpayer under examination has no context or ability to challenge the Service's findings regarding its governance practices at the examination level or within the agency's Appeals function. To ensure consistent, transparent enforcement of the federal tax laws, we respectfully request that the Treasury Department issue guidance regarding the standards for nonprofit governance.

—**Excerpts from a letter sent by Marcus S. Owens (former director of the Exempt Organizations Division) to the Department of the Treasury, January 14, 2009**

About the Authors

BRUCE R. HOPKINS is a senior partner in the law firm of Polsinelli Shughart PC, practicing in the firm's Kansas City, Missouri, and Washington, D.C., offices. He specializes in the representation of tax-exempt organizations. His practice ranges over the entirety of law matters involving exempt organizations, with emphasis on governance and the law, the formation of nonprofit organizations, acquisition of recognition of tax-exempt status for them, the private inurement and private benefit doctrines, the intermediate sanctions rules, legislative and political campaign activities issues, public charity and private foundation rules, unrelated business planning, use of exempt and for-profit subsidiaries, joint venture planning, tax shelter involvement, review of annual information returns, Internet communications developments, the law of charitable giving (including planned giving), and fundraising law issues.

Mr. Hopkins served as chair of the Committee on Exempt Organizations, Tax Section, American Bar Association; chair, Section of Taxation, National Association of College and University Attorneys; and president, Planned Giving Study Group of Greater Washington, D.C.

Mr. Hopkins is the series editor of Wiley's Nonprofit Law, Finance, and Management Series. He is the author of, in addition to co-authoring the *Nonprofit Governance* book, *The Law of Tax-Exempt Organizations, Ninth Edition; Planning Guide for the Law of Tax-Exempt Organizations: Strategies and Commentaries; IRS Audits of Tax-Exempt Organizations: Policies, Practices, and Procedures; The Tax Law of Charitable Giving, Third Edition; The Law of Fundraising, Fourth Edition; The Tax Law of Associations; The Tax Law of Unrelated Business for Nonprofit Organizations; The Nonprofits' Guide to Internet Communications Law; The Law of Intermediate Sanctions: A Guide for Nonprofits; Starting and Managing a Nonprofit Organization: A Legal Guide, Fifth Edition; Nonprofit Law Made Easy; Charitable Giving Law Made Easy; Private Foundation Law Made Easy; 650 Essential Nonprofit Law Questions Answered; The First Legal Answer Book for Fund-Raisers; The Second Legal Answer Book for Fund-Raisers; The Legal Answer Book for Nonprofit Organizations; The Second Legal Answer Book for Nonprofit Organizations;* and *The Nonprofit Law Dictionary;* and is the co-author, with Jody Blazek, of *Private Foundations: Tax Law and Compliance, Third Edition;* also with Ms. Blazek, *The Legal Answer Book for Private Foundations;* with Thomas K. Hyatt, of *The Law of Tax-Exempt Healthcare Organizations, Third Edition;* with David O. Middlebrook, of *Nonprofit Law for Religious Organizations: Essential Questions and Answers;* and with Douglas K. Anning, Virginia C. Gross, and Thomas J. Schenkelberg, of *The New Form 990: Law, Policy, and Preparation.* He also writes *Bruce R. Hopkins' Nonprofit Counsel,* a monthly newsletter, published by John Wiley & Sons.

Mr. Hopkins earned his J.D. and L.L.M. degrees at the George Washington University National Law Center and his B.A. at the University of Michigan. He is a member of the bars of the District of Columbia and the State of Missouri.

Mr. Hopkins received the 2007 Outstanding Nonprofit Lawyer Award (Vanguard Lifetime Achievement Award) from the American Bar Association, Section of

Business Law, Committee on Nonprofit Corporations. He is listed in *The Best Lawyers in America, Nonprofit Organizations/Charity Law*, 2007–2009.

VIRGINIA C. GROSS is a shareholder in the law firm of Polsinelli Shughart PC. Ms. Gross concentrates her practice in the fields of tax and nonprofit law. She represents a variety of nonprofit clients, including public charities, educational organizations, private foundations, associations, supporting organizations, healthcare and research organizations, and social welfare organizations. She works with all aspects of nonprofit law, including issues regarding the structure, governance, operations, fundraising, unrelated business income planning, joint venturing and partnering of tax-exempt entities, and use of supporting organizations and for-profit subsidiaries by exempt organizations.

Ms. Gross is a frequent writer and speaker on nonprofit issues. She is listed in *The Best Lawyers in America* for *Nonprofit Organizations/Charity Law* for 2008 and 2009. She is a co-author of *The New Form 990: Law, Policy, and Preparation* published by John Wiley & Sons and of Tax Management Portfolio's "Private Foundations—Distributions (Sec. 4942)," published by the Bureau of National Affairs. Ms. Gross earned her J.D. at the University of Texas and her B.S. at Texas A&M University.

She is a member of the bars of the District of Columbia, Missouri, Kansas, and Texas.

Contents

CONTENTS

Book Citations

Throughout this book, six books by Bruce R. Hopkins (in some instances as co-author), all published by John Wiley & Sons, are referenced in the following manner:

1. *The Law of Fundraising, Fourth Edition* (2009): *Law of Fundraising.*

2. *The Law of Tax-Exempt Organizations, Ninth Edition* (2007): *Law of Tax-Exempt Organizations.*

3. *The New Form 990: Law, Policy, and Preparation* (2009) (with Virginia C. Gross as a co-author): *New Form 990.*

4. *Planning Guide for The Law of Tax-Exempt Organizations: Strategies and Commentaries* (2004): *Planning Guide.*

5. *Private Foundations: Tax Law and Compliance, Third Edition* (2008): *Private Foundations.*

6. *The Tax Law of Charitable Giving, Third Edition* (2005): *Law of Charitable Giving.*

The first, second, fifth, and sixth of these books are annually supplemented. Also, updates on all of the foregoing subjects (plus *Nonprofit Governance: Law, Policies & Trends*) are available in *Bruce R. Hopkins' Nonprofit Counsel*, the author's monthly newsletter, also published by Wiley.

Preface

Governance seems to be the subject that is perched atop every nonprofit lawyer's worry list (and, in many instances, wish list). This is a somewhat unusual situation, for two reasons. One, a few years ago, governance would not have even made the list. Two, there is not much law on the point, particularly at the federal level. Thus, from a pure law standpoint, there is not much for the nonprofit lawyer to work with.

This absence of a legal underpinning has obviously not deterred the matter of governance in leaping to first place among today's nonprofit law issues. This ascension in importance is due in part to law created in the for-profit realm, but the true drivers propelling all of this are (1) the various organizations propounding good governance or, if you prefer, best practices, principles for public charities and other forms of nonprofit organizations, and (2) the Internal Revenue Service. (A certain United States senator from Iowa also is a force in this regard.) The IRS's role in this context is manifested in many ways these days, principally by means of the redesigned Form 990; the agency's aggressive push of certain good governance principles in the tax-exempt organizations' setting, chiefly, conflict-of-interest policies and the notion of independent boards; and the issuance of certain (questionably valid) private letter rulings.

The IRS is sending, when it comes to governance and law, mixed messages. Reading private letter rulings and watching IRS employees handle examinations of public charities and the processing of applications for recognition of exemption, one sees an agency demanding, as conditions for exemption, the adoption of certain policies and procedures. This view is somewhat reflected in the speeches of the TE/GE Commissioner, most of which are summarized in the book. One not part of the book was in a speech on November 20, 2008, at the Western Conference on Tax-Exempt Organizations; he made his view clear that the IRS is going to continue to push hard when it comes to mandated adoption of governance principles and procedures. "We intend to let the sun shine" when it comes to matters of governance, he declared.

Yet, the Commissioner of Internal Revenue, in a speech at an Independent Sector conference, on November 10, 2008, said: "We [the IRS] shouldn't supplant the business judgment of organizational leaders, and certainly shouldn't determine how a nonprofit fulfills its individual mission. That's not our role." He continued with the observation that the IRS's role in this context is to work "with you and others to promote good governance" and that the agency "want[s] to arm you with information and guidance you need to help you comply." This sounds more like education and encouragement, not dictation, when it comes to governance.

This latter view also appears reflected in the IRS Exempt Organizations work plan for fiscal year 2009, unveiled on November 25, 2008. There, the Exempt Organizations Division stated that it will develop a checklist to be used by agents in examinations of tax-exempt organizations to determine whether the organization's governance practices "impacted the tax compliance issues identified in the examination" and to educate organizations "about possible governance considerations." EO will commence a training program to educate its employees about "nonprofit governance implications" in the determinations, rulings and agreements, and education and outreach areas. EO will begin identifying Form 990 governance questions that could be used in conjunction with other Form 990 information in possible compliance initiatives, such as those involving executive compensation, transactions with interested persons, solicitation of noncash contributions, or diversion or misuse of exempt assets.

This section of the EO work plan, relating to governance, is encouraging. The forthcoming training program for IRS employees is shrouded in bureaucratize ("nonprofit governance implications"), but the hope is that agents will be taught to stop mandating conflict-of-interest policies, executive compensation policies, and independent boards as a condition of exemption. The IRS should be educating and guiding in the area of governance, not arbitrarily imposing requirements that are absent from the law. Thus, it is good to read about IRS efforts to "educate organizations about possible governance considerations."

We confront the matter of nonprofit governance constantly in our law practices. Endless hours of meditating over the new Form 990 and sifting through the many (and inconsistent) best practices principles convinced us of the need for some cohesion in the realm of nonprofit governance. Thus this book. We have done three things: Summarize the law that exists; explain and evaluate the many good governance principles that have been promulgated; and make recommendations for the adoption of policies and procedures that are appropriate and relevant for nonprofit organizations.

The book is intended as a guide, not just for lawyers, but for anyone who is facing decisions as to good governance in the nonprofit organization context and is lost in the maze of conflicting principles, ever-increasing policies and procedures, murky law, and the intensity of the IRS in insisting on adoption of various principles in the absence of legal requirements for them. (Even worse, in a way, is the manner in which the private benefit doctrine is being manipulated as the justification in law for forcing nonprofit organizations to incorporate various policies, procedures, protocols, and practices into their operations.)

Leaders and managers of nonprofit organizations, and their lawyers, accountants, and other advisors, can use this book to understand the legal backdrop for nonprofit governance, sort through the numerous good governance principles, and select the ones that most appropriately apply to the particular organization. From there, the suitable policies and procedures can be devised. Our hope is to help nonprofit organizations improve their operations and effectiveness to the extent that improved governance can contribute to those outcomes (and, not incidentally, be in a position to file, if applicable, Forms 990 that cast them in the best possible light).

Woody Allen observed that most of success in life (around 80 percent, as we recall) is achieved by just showing up. This also used to be the case with nonprofit board service. Those days are rapidly disappearing. Indeed, the fundamental concept of the role of the nonprofit board is undergoing reevaluation and interpretation, with interesting and compelling view changes as to nonprofit board members' duties, responsibilities, and liabilities. We believe that the trend will continue to be intense focus on and reshaping of nonprofit governance. Our book is intended as a guide to and through all of the governance policymaking that is unfolding, all to the end of improved management of nonprofit organizations and, yes, compliance with nonprofit governance law (to the extent it exists).

We extend our thanks to our senior editor, Susan McDermott, and our senior production editor, Natasha Andrews-Noel, for their valued help on the book.

Bruce R. Hopkins
Virginia C. Gross
May 2009

CHAPTER ONE

Federal and State Law Fundamentals

For decades, the law in the United States concerning governance of nonprofit organizations was almost solely confined to state (and, to some extent, local) law. While this state of affairs is rapidly changing, with the matter of nonprofit organizations' governance becoming a province of federal (mostly tax) law, many of the underlying fundamental principles remain those formulated (and once seemingly resolved) at the state law level.

§ 1.1 STATE LAW OVERVIEW

There are essentially seven bodies of state law concerning the organization and operations of nonprofit organizations'. Most of the state law principles pertaining to nonprofit organizations governance are found in the nonprofit corporation acts[1] and the charitable solicitation acts.[2]

(a) Types of Nonprofit Organizations

Most nonprofit organizations are formed as one of three types: corporation,[3] trust,[4] or unincorporated association.[5] It is possible to have a tax-exempt, nonprofit limited liability company.[6] Occasionally, the U.S. Congress "charters" (that is, creates by legislation) a nonprofit organization.[7]

The application for recognition of tax exemption filed by most organizations seeking to be tax-exempt charitable entities[8] (Form 1023) graphically depicts these types. It asks if the filing organization is one of the four types, then, in bold print, directs the entity to not file the application if it is not.[9]

---

1. See § 1.1(b).
2. See § 1.1(c).
3. See § 1.2(b).
4. See § 1.2(a).
5. *Id.*
6. See *Law of Tax-Exempt Organizations* § 4.4(d).
7. See, e.g., § 3.11.
8. That is, organizations that are tax exempt pursuant to Internal Revenue Code section (IRC §) 501(a) because of description in IRC § 501(c)(3). See *Law of Tax-Exempt Organizations*, Part Three.
9. Form 1023, Part II. See *Law of Tax-Exempt Organizations*, App. D, p. 1123.

Nonprofit, tax-exempt organizations, as part of the process of their establishment, prepare (and sometimes file with a state) *articles of organization*.[10] The nature of these articles will depend, in large part, on the type of nonprofit organization. If the non-profit organization wants to be tax-exempt under the federal tax law, it usually will be required to meet an *organizational test*.[11]

(b) Nonprofit Corporation Acts

Nearly every state has a *nonprofit corporation act*. The few states that do not have such a statute require nonprofit corporations to fare as best they can by using what is applicable in the statutory law applicable to for-profit business corporations. Most of the states with a nonprofit corporation act have based their law on a model nonprofit corporation act.[12]

(c) Nonprofit Trust Statutes

Nearly every state has a body of statutory law applicable to *charitable trusts*. Many private foundations, for example, are trusts. These laws frequently impose fiduciary standards and practices that are more stringent than those for nonprofit corporations and entail an annual filing requirement. A nonprofit organization that is a trust is formed by the execution of a *trust agreement* or a *declaration of trust*.

(d) Unincorporated Associations

To the uninitiated, a nonprofit corporation and a nonprofit unincorporated association look alike. An unincorporated association is formed by the preparation and adoption of a *constitution*. The contents of a constitution are much the same as those of articles of incorporation. Likewise, the bylaws of an unincorporated association are usually the same as those of a nonprofit corporation.

(e) Charitable Solicitation Acts

A majority of the states have adopted comprehensive *charitable solicitation acts* for the purpose of regulating fundraising for charitable purposes[13] in their jurisdictions. A few states have not enacted any form of charitable solicitation act. The remaining states (including the District of Columbia) have elected to regulate charitable fundraising by means of differing approaches.

The various state charitable solicitation acts are (to substantially understate the situation) diverse. The content of these laws is so disparate that any implication that it is possible to neatly generalize about their assorted terms, requirements, limitations, exceptions, and prohibitions would be misleading. Of even greater variance are

---

10. See § 1.2(a); *Law of Tax-Exempt Organizations* § 4.2.
11. *Id.* § 4.3.
12. Section III, Part 13, of Independent Sector's Panel on the Nonprofit Sector, *Strengthening Transparency, Governance and Accountability of Charitable Organizations: A Final Report to Congress and the Nonprofit Sector* (June 2005) ("Nonprofit Panel's Final Report"), includes a summary of the Revised Model Nonprofit Corporation Act (at 76-77). See § 3.12.
13. The concept of *charitable* for purposes of state charitable solicitation acts is usually substantially broader than the concept used in the federal tax law. See *Law of Fundraising* § 3.2(a).

the requirements imposed by the many regulations, rules, and forms promulgated to accompany and amplify the state statutes.[14] Nonetheless, some basic commonalities can be found in the comprehensive charitable solicitation acts.

The fundamental features of many of these charitable fundraising regulation laws are a series of definitions of various terms; registration or similar requirements for charitable organizations; annual reporting requirements for charitable organizations; exemption of certain charitable organizations from all or a portion of the statutory requirements, registration and reporting requirements for professional fundraisers; registration and reporting requirements for professional solicitors; requirements with respect to the conduct of charitable sales promotions; record-keeping and public disclosure requirements; requirements regarding the contents of contracts involving fundraising charitable organizations; a wide range of prohibited acts; registered agent requirements; rules pertaining to reciprocal agreements; investigatory and injunctive authority vested in enforcement officials; civil and criminal penalties; and other sanctions.[15]

(f)   Tax Exemption Laws

State law typically provides for tax exemption, from income or ad valorum tax, for a variety of nonprofit entities in the jurisdiction. Usually, the criteria for this exemption are identical to the federal law requirements; some states impose qualifications in addition to the federal ones. Tax exemption may also be available in connection with sales,[16] use, tangible personal property, intangible personal property, and real estate taxes.

(g)   Charitable Deduction Laws

Most states' laws provide for a charitable contribution deduction for the making of gifts of money or property to charitable organizations.[17] Usually, the criteria for this deduction are identical to the federal law requirements; some states impose qualifications in addition to the federal ones.

(h)   Other Statutory Law

In addition to the panoply of the foregoing bodies of law, nonprofit organizations may have to face other state statutory or other regulatory requirements. These include:

- A state's nonprofit corporation act, which has registration and annual reporting requirements for foreign (out-of-state) corporations that are *doing business* within the state.[18] For example, it is not clear whether, as a matter of general

---

14. An attempt has been made to resolve this problem by adoption of *uniform annual reports* in many of the states. Some states, however, have added material to the "uniform" form, thereby somewhat returning matters to the original (and confusing) state of affairs. See *Law of Fundraising* § 3.22.

15. Each of these elements in a comprehensive state charitable solicitation act is detailed in *Law of Fundraising*, Chapter 3.

16. A state sales tax exemption relates to the *payment* of these taxes, not necessarily to the *collection* of them when it is the nonprofit entity that is the seller of goods or services.

17. See, in general, *Law of Charitable Giving*.

18. See *Law of Fundraising* § 3.23.

law, the solicitation of charitable contributions in a foreign state constitutes doing business in the state.[19] Some states provide, by statute, that fundraising is the conduct of business activities in their jurisdictions. If the solicitation of charitable contributions were declared, as a matter of general law, to be a business transaction in each of the states, the compliance consequences would be enormous, considering the fact that nearly every state has a nonprofit corporation act. This type of a requirement would cause a charitable organization that is soliciting contributions in every state to register and report more than 90 times each year, not taking into account federal and local law requirements!

- A state's insurance law, which may embody a requirement that a charitable organization writing charitable gift annuity contracts[20] obtain a permit to do so and subsequently file annual statements.

- A state's *blue sky statute* regulating securities offerings, which may be applicable to offers to sell and to sales of interests in, and the operation of, pooled income funds.[21] These laws may also apply with respect to charitable remainder annuity trusts and unitrusts.[22]

- A state's law prohibiting fraudulent advertising or other fraudulent or deceptive practices.[23]

- A state's version of the Uniform Supervision of Trustees for Charitable Purposes Act, which requires a charitable trust to file, with the state attorney general, a copy of its governing instrument, an inventory of the charitable assets, and an annual report. Of similar scope and effect are the state laws that invest the state attorney general with plenary investigative power over charitable organizations.[24]

---

19. One court observed that "[i]t is doubtful . . . whether the solicitation of funds for a charitable purpose is, to use the statutory words, the 'carrying on, conducting or transaction of business' " (Lefkowitz v. Burden, 254 N.Y.S.2d 943, 944-945 (1964)). A subsequent court opinion, however, suggested that the solicitation of funds constitutes doing business in a state (Commonwealth v. Events International, Inc., 585 A.2d 1146, 1151 Pa. 1991)).

    Clearly, a charitable organization organized in one state and maintaining an office or similar physical presence in another state is doing business in the latter state. The general rule is that merely mailing charitable solicitation material into a state is not doing business in that state, although a contrary approach can be established by statute or regulation. In many states, the determination as to whether an organization is doing business in a state is under the jurisdiction of the secretary of state, whereas the registration and reporting requirements of a charitable solicitation act are administered by the attorney general. In some states (such as California), a determination that a charitable organization is doing business in the state leads to a requirement that the organization file for and receive a ruling as to its tax-exempt status in the state (or else be subject to state taxation). Thus, fundraising in a state can entail an obligation on the part of the charitable organization to file with three separate agencies in the state.

20. See *Law of Charitable Giving*, Chapter 14.
21. See *id.*, Chapter 13.
22. See *id.*, Chapter 12. In general, Horner and Makens, "Securities Regulation of Fundraising Activities of Religious and Other Nonprofit Organizations," XXVII *Stetson L. Rev.* (No. 2) 473 (Fall 1997).
23. E.g., People v. Gellard, 68 N.E. 2d 600 (N.Y.1946).
24. In addition to these state law requirements, there are hundreds of county and city charitable solicitation ordinances.

§1.2 FORMATION OF ORGANIZATION

The nature of governance of a nonprofit, tax-exempt organization is dependent in part on the type of the entity.[25] (For tax exemption to be available, there must be a separate legal entity.[26])

(a) Articles of Organization

As noted, the document by which a nonprofit organization is created is known generically in the parlance of the federal tax law as the *articles of organization*.[27] Usually, there is a separate document containing more specific rules pursuant to which the organization conducts its affairs; this document is most often termed the *bylaws*.[28] A nonprofit organization may also develop other documents governing its operations, in the form of various policies, procedures, codes, handbooks, and/or manuals.[29]

The types of articles of organization for each type of nonprofit organization are:

- Corporation: articles of incorporation
- Unincorporated association: constitution
- Trust: declaration of trust or trust agreement
- Limited liability company: agreement of members

(b) Articles of Incorporation

A typical nonprofit corporation act requires the organization that is to be incorporated to prepare and file *articles of incorporation* that address the following subjects:

- The name of the organization
- A general statement of its purposes
- A statement as to whether the organization has members
- A statement as to whether the organization can issue stock
- The name(s) and address(es) of its initial director(s)
- The name and address of its registered agent
- The name(s) and address(es) of its incorporator(s)
- Provisions reflecting any other state law requirements

Frequently, although state law does not require it, the articles of incorporation will include provisions referencing the applicable federal tax law requirements. For example, an organization intending to be a tax-exempt charitable entity[30] must have

---

25. See § 1.1(a).
26. See *Law of Tax-Exempt Organizations* § 4.1(a), text accompanied by notes 19–23.
27. See § 1.1(a).
28. See § 1.2(c).
29. See, e.g., Chapter 7.
30. See *supra* note 8.

a *dissolution clause* (that is, a provision preserving the net income and assets of the organization for charitable purposes in the event of its liquidation or dissolution).[31]

(c) Bylaws

The bylaws of an incorporated nonprofit organization will usually include provisions with respect to:

- Its purposes (these are often restated in the bylaws)
- The election (or appointment or ex officio positions) and duties of its directors
- The election and duties of its officers
- The role of its members (if any)
- Meetings of members and directors, including dates, notice rules, quorum requirements, and voting
- The role of executive and other committees
- The role of its chapters (if any)
- The function of affiliated organizations (if any), such as ex officio positions
- A conflict-of-interest policy (if not in a separate document)[32]
- The organization's fiscal year

A repeat of the provisions referencing the applicable federal tax law requirements may be included in a set of bylaws.

(d) Other Governing Instruments

The articles of organization and bylaws (if any) of a nonprofit organization that is not a nonprofit corporation may, and in some instances must, partake of elements of the articles of incorporation and bylaws of a nonprofit corporation. As noted, for example, a constitution is likely to be similar to a set of articles of incorporation.[33]

(e) Selection of Entity Form

Those in the process of establishing a nonprofit organization thus must decide which of the four forms of entity to select. The principal factors to take into account in this regard are the exposure of members of the governing body to personal liability; the answers to questions regarding management and administrative operations that may be provided by state law; general familiarity with the entity form; state law registration and reporting requirements; and federal tax law considerations.

(i) Personal Liability. The corporate and limited liability company forms are the only elements of entity that provide the advantage of shielding board members from most types of personal liability that may arise because of service on the board. Liability, if any, is generally confined to the organization; that is, it does not normally extend to those who manage it. Thus, trustees of trusts and directors of

---

31. See *Law of Tax-Exempt Organizations* § 4.3.
32. See § 6.3(b).
33. See § 1.1(d).

unincorporated associations do not have this "corporate veil" to protect them. The corporate form is likely to be preferable in this regard because of the vagaries of formation of a nonprofit organization as a limited liability company.[34]

(ii) Answers to Questions. The statutory law of a state usually provides answers to many of the questions that inevitably arise when forming and operating a nonprofit organization. These answers are most likely found in the state's nonprofit corporation act (assuming there is one) and thus are technically applicable only if the entity is a nonprofit corporation. Some examples are:

- How many directors must the organization have? What are their voting rights? How is a quorum ascertained? How is notice of meetings properly given? What is the length of their terms of office? Are there term limits?

- What officers must the organization have? What are their duties? What is the length of their terms of office? Are there term limits? Can an individual simultaneously hold more than one office?

- How frequently must the governing board meet? Must the board members always meet in person, or can the meetings be by telephone conference call or video teleconferencing? Can the board members vote by mail or by means of unanimous written consent?[35]

- If there are members, what are their rights? When must they meet? What notice of the meetings must be given?

- What issues must be decided by members (if any)? By directors?

- May there be an executive committee of the governing board? If so, what are its duties? What limitations are there on its functions?

- What about other committees? Is there an audit committee? What are the responsibilities of each committee? Does the organization have an advisory committee?

- How are the organization's governing instruments amended?

- How must any merger involving the organization occur?

- What is the process for dissolving the organization? What are the requirements for distribution of its assets and net income on the occasion of a dissolution?

If the organization is not a corporation, these and other questions are usually unanswered under state law. The unincorporated organization may make an effort to

---

34. Generally, limited liability companies are not as conducive to operation as a nonprofit entity as a corporation. Although most states have a nonprofit corporation act, they do not have statutes governing a nonprofit limited liability company. In addition, a limited liability company must be formed with members, unlike a nonprofit corporation (which often is formed without members, instead opting for a self-perpetuating board). Federal tax law considerations can be more awkward for the operation of a limited liability company as a nonprofit entity. The IRS only recently began to recognize limited liability companies as tax-exempt organizations and more closely scrutinizes the applications for recognition of exemption of these types of entities. In addition, a limited liability with more than one member must file a special election to "check-the-box" to be taxed as a corporation; otherwise, it will be taxed as a partnership with its income flowing through to its members.

35. A generally applicable rule forbids directors from voting by proxy.

add to its rules the answers to all of the pertinent questions (assuming they can be anticipated) or live with the uncertainties.

(iii) Familiarity. People are more familiar with corporations than other forms of entities. Thus, if the nonprofit organization is a corporation, more persons will understand the nature of the entity. In general, the world in which the nonprofit organization will be functioning is comfortable with the concept of a corporation. Trusts are also well known, particularly in the private foundations and other estate planning areas, although they are less known and used than corporations. Unincorporated associations are the least used (and least understood) of these entities.

(iv) Registration and Reporting. Incorporation entails an affirmative act of a state government: it "charters" the entity (by issuing a certificate of incorporation or document by a similar name). In exchange for the grant of status as a corporation, the state expects certain forms of compliance by the organization, such as adherence to its rules of operations, an initial filing fee, annual reports, annual fees, and compliance with public disclosure requirements. These costs are frequently nominal, however, and the reporting requirements usually are not extensive. Rarely are there comparable filing requirements for trusts and unincorporated associations. Although articles of incorporation and annual reports are public documents, trust documents and unincorporated association constitutions often are not. Thus, one of the principal reasons for use of the trust form is privacy.

(v) Federal Tax Law Requirements. In most instances, the federal tax law is silent as to the form of nonprofit, tax-exempt organizations; most of them can select from among the four types. In a few instances, however, a specific form of organization is required to qualify under federal law as a tax-exempt organization. As illustrations, an instrumentality of the United States[36] and a single-parent title-holding organization[37] must, pursuant to the federal tax law, be formed as corporations, while entities such as supplemental unemployment benefit organizations,[38] Black Lung benefit organizations,[39] and multiemployer plan funds[40] must be formed as trusts. A multiple-parent title-holding organization[41] can be formed as a corporation or a trust.

The trust form for a nonprofit organization is rarely the appropriate choice except for certain charitable entities (most notably, private foundations), some labor organizations, and certain funds associated with employee plans. This form is also used when creating charitable giving vehicles in the planned giving setting, such as charitable remainder trusts[42] and charitable lead trusts.[43] By contrast, for example, membership organizations are ill-suited to the trust form.

The principal problem with structuring a nonprofit organization as a trust is that most state laws concerning trusts are written for the regulation of charitable trusts. These rules are rarely as flexible as contemporary nonprofit corporation acts; the rules frequently impose fiduciary standards and practices that are more stringent than

---

36. See *Law of Tax-Exempt Organizations* § 19.1.
37. See *id.* § 19.2(a).
38. See *id.* § 18.4.
39. See *id.* § 18.5.
40. See *id.* § 18.7.
41. See *id.* § 19.2(b).
42. See *Law of Charitable Giving*, Chapter 12.
43. See *id.*, Chapter 16.

those for nonprofit corporations. The trust form may, however, provide more privacy to the founders of a trust and certainly makes amendment of the terms of the entity more difficult (often accomplished only by court order). It is unusual—although certainly permissible—for the trustee or trustees of a trust to adopt a set of bylaws.

The term *unincorporated association* employs the word *association* for a reason: these entities are usually membership-based. That is, societies and the like are often formed without the formalities of incorporation.

A nonprofit corporation and a nonprofit unincorporated association may look alike. A membership association has many of the same characteristics, whether or not incorporated. The contents of a constitution are much the same as the contents of a set of articles of incorporation. Bylaws for an unincorporated association look much like those of a nonprofit corporation.

§1.3 BOARD OF DIRECTORS BASICS

The fundamentals of the law concerning the boards of directors of nonprofit organizations include the nomenclature assigned to the group, the number of directors, the origin(s) of the director positions, the control factor, the scope of the board's authority, and the relationship to the officer positions.

(a) Nomenclature

State law generally refers to the individuals who are responsible for the affairs of nonprofit organizations as *directors*. Some tax-exempt organizations use other terms, such as *trustees* or *governors*. Generally, organizations are free to use the terminology they wish; if the entity is a corporation, however, it may have to use the term *director* in its articles of incorporation, then define it in the bylaws.

The choice of term is not usually a matter of law. Some organizations prefer to refer to their governing board as the *board of trustees*. (Technically, only a director of a trust can be a trustee, but that formality has long since disappeared.) This is particularly the case with charitable and educational institutions. Schools, colleges, and universities, for example, favor this approach.

Where organizations are related,[44] this terminology can be used to reduce confusion. For example, in an instance of a tax-exempt membership association and its related foundation, the board of the former may be termed the *board of directors* and the board of the latter the *board of trustees*.[45]

This governing board may have within it a subset of individuals who oversee the operations of the organization more closely and frequently than the full board. This group of individuals is usually termed the *executive committee*. A few exempt organizations use this term to describe the full governing board.

(b) Number

A tax-exempt organization—irrespective of form—must have one or more directors or trustees. State law typically mandates at least three of these individuals,

---

44. See *Law of Tax-Exempt Organizations*, Chapters 28, 29.
45. See, e.g., Hopkins, *The Tax Law of Associations* (Hoboken, NJ: John Wiley & Sons, 2006), Chapter 8.

particularly in the case of nonprofit corporations. Some states require only one. Some nonprofit organizations have large governing boards, often to the point of being unwieldy. (State law does not set a maximum number of directors of nonprofit organizations.) Federal law does not address this subject.[46]

The optimum size of a governing board of a nonprofit organization depends on many factors, including the type of organization involved, the nature and size of the organization's constituency, the way in which the directors are selected, and the role and effectiveness of an executive committee (if any). In some instances, particularly in the case of trusts, there may be an institutional trustee.

(c) Origin(s) of Positions

The board of directors of a nonprofit organization can be derived in several ways; in addition, these ways can be blended. The basic choices are election by the other directors (a self-perpetuating board), election by a membership, selection by the membership of another organization, selection by the board of another organization, ex officio positions, or a blend of two or more of the foregoing options.

If there are bona fide members of the organization (such as an association[47]), it is likely that these members will elect some or all of the members of the governing board of the entity. This election may be conducted by mail ballot or voting at the annual meeting. It is possible, however, for a nonprofit organization with a membership to have a governing board that is not elected by that membership.

In the absence of a membership, or if the membership lacks a vote on the matter, the governing board of a nonprofit organization may be a *self-perpetuating* board. With this model, the initial board continues with those it elects and those elected by subsequent boards.

Some boards have one or more *ex officio* positions. This means that individuals are board members by virtue of other positions they hold.[48] These other positions may be those of the organization itself, those of another organization, or a blend of the two.

In the case of many nonprofit organizations, the source of the membership of the board is preordained. Examples include the typical membership organization that elects the board (such as a trade association, social club,[49] or veterans' organization[50]); a hospital,[51] college,[52] or museum[53] that has a governing board generally reflective of the community; and a private foundation[54] that has one or more trustees who represent a particular family or corporation.

---

46. See, however, § 5.2.
47. See *Law of Tax-Exempt Organizations*, Chapter 14.
48. Despite widespread belief to the contrary, this term has nothing to do with whether the individual in the position has the right to vote. Absent a provision in the document to the contrary, those holding office in this manner have the same voting rights as others on the board.
49. See *Law of Tax-Exempt Organizations*, Chapter 15.
50. See *id.* § 19.11.
51. See *id.* § 7.6(a).
52. See *id.* § 8.3(a).
53. See *id.* § 8.3(b).
54. See *id.* § 12.1.

(d) Control Factor

With the rare exception of the stock-based nonprofit organization,[55] no one *owns* a nonprofit entity. *Control* of a nonprofit organization, however, is another matter. Certainly, the governing board of a nonprofit organization controls the organization (at least from a law standpoint).

There are, nonetheless, other manifestations of this matter of control. One is the situation where an individual or a close-knit group of individuals wants to control a nonprofit organization. This can be of particular consequence in the case of a single-purpose organization that was founded by an individual or such a group. Those who launch and grow a nonprofit organization understandably do not want to put their efforts and funds into formation and development of the organization, only to watch others assume control over it and remove them from the organization's management. Systems are available to facilitate this type of control.

The seven alternatives to achieve this end are:

1. *Trust.* Most individuals in this position assemble a board of friends and family members, and hope that trust and loyalty will prevail. Usually, they do. Occasionally, however, there is internal conflict, a new majority emerges, and the founder or founders are ousted.

2. *Superterm.* Some individuals attempt to create for themselves a term longer than that of the others. Sometimes, an effort is made to have a term for life. This approach usually is untenable under state law.

3. *One director.* A founder of a nonprofit entity can form it in a state that requires only one director, then if necessary qualify it in the state in which it will operate.

4. *Membership classes.* One technique is to have two classes of board members: Class A and Class B. Class A consists of the founders; Class B is everyone else on the board. The governing instrument is written in such a way that certain major decisions (such as expenditures in excess of a set amount or dissolution of the organization) cannot be approved without a majority vote of those in Class A.

5. *Entity membership.* Another technique is to establish the organization as a membership entity and to have only the founders as members. The member/founders have the authority to elect the board members—and to remove them.

6. *Stock.* In a few states, a nonprofit organization can issue stock. Such an entity can be formed with the founders being the sole shareholders. The shareholders would have the authority to elect and remove board members.

7. *Advisory committee.* The governing board can be confined to a select few, coupled with an advisory committee. The latter body is a group of individuals who are not on and do not substitute for the board of directors but provide policy and/or technical input in advancement of the organization's programs. Because members of an advisory committee lack voting rights, their number is governed only by what is practical. Committee members serve without the

---

55. A few states permit a nonprofit corporation to issue non-dividend-paying stock, as an ownership/control technique.

threat of personal liability that may accrue to the organization's directors and officers (assuming their role is, in fact, only advisory), and without incurring the larger set of responsibilities shouldered by the directors. Moreover, with an advisory committee, an organization can surround itself with luminaries in the field.

Those involved with nonprofit organizations will discover that techniques such as those described above in items 2 to 6 seem feasible in theory but rarely work in practice. This is because these approaches are, as a matter of group dynamics, divisive and likely to cause more difficulties than they resolve. In the end, usually the first option is selected, perhaps augmented with the seventh.[56]

(e) Scope of Authority

The directors are those who set policy for the organization and oversee its affairs; actual implementation of plans and programs and day-to-day management are left to officers and employees. In reality, however, it is difficult to mark a precise line of demarcation where the scope of authority of the board of directors stops and the authority of other managers begins. (In the parlance of the tax law, trustees, directors, officers, and key employees of an organization are *managers* of the entity.[57])

Frequently, authority of this nature is resolved in the political arena, not the legal one. It may vary, from time to time, as the culture of the entity changes. In some organizations, the directors do not have the time or do not want to take the time to micromanage; others restrain themselves from doing so (and still others do not). Often, the matter comes down to the sheer force of personalities. In some organizations, the most dominant manager is the executive director, rather than the president or chair of the board.

(f) Other Considerations

The board of directors of a nonprofit organization may decide to have a chair (or chairperson, chairman, or chairwoman) of the board. This individual presides over board meetings. The chair position is not usually an officer position (although it can be made one). The position may (but need not) be authorized in the organization's bylaws.

Some organizations find it useful to stagger the terms of office so that only a portion of the board need be elected or re-elected at any one time, thereby providing continuity of service and expertise. A model in this regard is the nine-person board with three-year terms for members; one-third of the board is elected annually.

A board of directors of a tax-exempt organization usually acts by means of in-person meetings where a quorum is present. Where state law allows, the members of the board can meet via conference call (a call where all participants can hear each other) or by unanimous written consent. These alternative procedures should be authorized in the organization's bylaws (indeed, that may be a requirement of state law).

---

56. All of this should be contrasted with the IRS's view of application of the private benefit doctrine (see § 5.21(d)).
57. See, e.g., *Law of Tax-Exempt Organizations* §§ 12.2, 21.3.

Unless there is authorization in the law (and there is not likely to be), the directors of a tax-exempt organization may not vote by proxy, mail ballot, e-mail, or telephone call (other than by a qualified conference call). Members of an organization have more flexibility as to voting than members of the board of the organization. For example, usually they can vote by mail ballot and by use of proxies.

(g) Relationship to Officers

Nearly every tax-exempt organization has officers.[58] A prominent exception is the trust, which usually has only one or more trustees. As with the board of directors, the scope (or levels) of authority of the officers of an organization is difficult to articulate. In the case of a nonprofit organization that has members, directors, officers, and employees, setting a clear distinction as to who has the authority to do what is nearly impossible. General principles can be stated but will usually prove nearly useless in practice.

For example, it can be stated that the members of the organization (if any) set basic policy and the board of directors sets additional policy, albeit within the parameters established by the membership. The officers thereafter implement the policies, as do the employees, although this is more on a day-to-day basis. Yet the reality is that, at all levels, policy is established and implemented.

The officers of a tax-exempt organization are usually elected, either by a membership or by the board of directors. In some instances, the officers of an organization are ex officio with, or are selected by, another organization. The basic choices as to the origin(s) for officer position are election by a membership; election by the directors, who are elected by the members; election by the directors, who are a self-perpetuating board; election (or appointment) by the board of another organization; or a blend of two or more of the foregoing options.

§1.4 PRINCIPLES OF FIDUCIARY RESPONSIBILITY

Out of the common law of charitable trusts has evolved the concept that a director of a tax-exempt organization, particularly a charitable entity, is a fiduciary of the organization's resources and a facilitator of its mission. Consequently, the law imposes on directors of exempt organizations standards of conduct and management that comprise *fiduciary responsibility*.

Most state laws, by statute or court opinion, impose the standards of fiduciary responsibility on directors of nonprofit organizations. A summary of this aspect of the law stated: "In many cases, nonprofit corporation fiduciary principles govern the actions of the organization's directors, trustees, and officers, and charitable trust law governs the use and disposition of the assets of the organization." This summary added: "These laws generally address issues such as the organization's purposes and powers, governing instruments (such as articles of organization and bylaws), governance (board composition, requirements for board action, and duties and standards of conduct for board members and officers), and dedication of assets for charitable uses

---

58. In general, see § 2.2.

(including a prohibition against the use of assets or income for the benefit of private individuals)."[59] Thus, personal liability can result when a director (or officer or key employee) of a nonprofit organization breaches the standards of fiduciary responsibility.[60]

One of the principal responsibilities of board members is to maintain financial accountability and effective oversight of the organization they serve. Board members are guardians of the organization's assets, and are expected to exercise due diligence to see that the organization is well managed and has a financial position that is as strong as is reasonable under the circumstances. Fiduciary duty requires board members of exempt organizations to be objective, unselfish, responsible, honest, trustworthy, and efficient. Board members, as stewards of the organization, should always act for its good and betterment, rather than for their personal benefit. They should exercise reasonable care in their decision-making, and not place the organization under unnecessary risk.

The distinction as to legal liability between the board as a group and the board members as individuals relates to the responsibility of the *board* for the organization's affairs and the responsibility of *individual board members* for their actions personally. The board collectively is responsible and may be liable for what transpires within and happens to the organization. As the ultimate authority, the board should ensure that the organization is operating in compliance with the law and its governing instruments. If legal action ensues, it is often traceable to an inattentive, passive, and/or captive board. Legislators and government regulators are becoming more aggressive in demanding higher levels of involvement by and accountability of board members of tax-exempt organizations; this is causing a dramatic shift in thinking about board functions, away from the concept of mere oversight and toward the precept that board members should be far more involved in policy-setting and review, employee supervision, and overall management. Consequently, many boards of exempt organizations are becoming more vigilant and active in implementing and maintaining sound policies.

In turn, the board's shared legal responsibilities depend on the actions of individuals. Each board member is liable for his or her acts (commissions and omissions), including those that may be civil law or even criminal law offenses. In practice, this requires board members to hold each other accountable for deeds that prove harmful to the organization.

The board of a tax-exempt organization is collectively responsible for developing and advancing the organization's mission; maintaining the organization's tax-exempt status and (if applicable) its ability to attract charitable contributions; protecting the organization's resources; formulating the organization's budget; hiring and evaluating the chief executive; generally overseeing the organization's management; and supporting the fundraising that the organization undertakes.[61]

---

59. Joint Committee on Taxation, "Description of Present Law Relating to Charitable and Other Exempt Organizations and Statistical Information Regarding Growth and Oversight of the Tax-Exempt Sector" 17 (JCX-44-04), 108th Cong., 2d Sess. (June 22, 2004).

60. See § 5.4.

61. In general, Hopkins, *Legal Responsibilities of Nonprofit Boards* (Washington, D.C.: BoardSource, 2008); Goldschmid, "The Fiduciary Duties of Nonprofit Directors and Officers: Paradoxes, Problems, and Proposed Reforms," 23 *J. Corp. L.* 631 (Summer 1998).

§1.5 DUTIES OF DIRECTORS

The duties of the board of directors of a tax-exempt organization essentially are the duty of care, the duty of loyalty, and the duty of obedience. Defined by case law, these are the legal standards against which all actions taken or not taken by directors are measured. They are collective duties adhering to the entire board; the mandate is active participation by all of the board members. Accountability can be demonstrated by showing the effective discharge of these duties.

(a) Duty of Care

The duty of care requires that directors of a tax-exempt organization be reasonably informed about the organization's activities, participate in decision-making, and act in good faith and with the care of an ordinarily prudent person in comparable circumstances. In short, the duty of care requires the board—and its members individually—to pay attention to the organization's activities and operations.

The duty of care is satisfied by attendance at meetings of the board and appropriate committees; advance preparation for board meetings, such as reviewing reports and the agenda prior to meetings of the board; obtaining information, before voting, to make appropriate decisions; use of independent judgment; periodic examination of the credentials and performance of those who serve the organization; frequent review of the organization's finances and financial policies; and compliance with filing requirements, particularly annual information returns.

(b) Duty of Loyalty

The duty of loyalty requires board members to exercise their power in the interest of the tax-exempt organization and not in their personal interest or the interest of another entity, particularly one with which they have a formal relationship. When acting on behalf of the exempt organization, board members are expected to place the interests of the organization before their personal and professional interests.

The duty of loyalty is satisfied when board members disclose any conflicts of interest; otherwise adhere to the organization's conflict-of-interest policy; avoid the use of corporate opportunities for the individual's personal gain or other benefit; and do not disclose confidential information concerning the information.

Conflicts of interest are not inherently illegal. Indeed, they can be common, because board members are often simultaneously affiliated with several entities, both for-profit and nonprofit. The important factor is the process by which the board copes with these conflicts. A conflict-of-interest policy can help protect the organization and its board members by establishing a procedure for disclosure and voting when situations arise where a board member may potentially derive personal or potential benefit from the organization's activities.

(c) Duty of Obedience

The duty of obedience requires that directors of a tax-exempt organization comply with applicable federal, state, and local laws; adhere to the organization's governing documents; and remain guardians of the organization's mission. The duty of obedience is complied with when the board endeavors to be certain that the organization is

■ 15 ■

in compliance with applicable regulatory requirements, complies with and periodically reviews all documents governing the operations of the organization, and makes
decisions in advancement of the organization's mission and within the scope of the
entity's governing documents.[62]

§1.6 BOARD COMPOSITION AND FEDERAL TAX LAW

Generally, the federal statutory tax law, the federal tax regulations, or the rulings
from the Internal Revenue Service (IRS) have little to say about the composition of the
governing board of a nonprofit, tax-exempt organization; it is, as noted, essentially a
state law matter.[63] Basically, then, as a matter of law,[64] those forming and operating a
nonprofit organization are free to structure and populate its board in any manner
they determine.

(a) Doctrine of Private Inurement

A federal tax law doctrine that is directly relevant to the matter of nonprofit governance is the doctrine of *private inurement*. The federal law of tax exemption for charitable and other exempt organizations requires that each of these entities be organized
and operated so that "no part of . . . [its] net earnings . . . inures to the benefit of any
private shareholder or individual." Literally, this means that the profits of an exempt
organization may not be passed along to individuals or other persons in their private
capacity. In fact, the private inurement proscription, as expanded and amplified by
the IRS and the courts, today means much more.

The contemporary meaning of the thoroughly antiquated statutory private inurement provision is scarcely reflected in its literal form and transcends the nearly 100-
year-old formulation. What the doctrine means is that none of the income or assets of
a tax-exempt organization that is subject to the inurement rule (and most types are)
may be permitted to directly or indirectly unduly benefit an individual or other person who has a close relationship with the organization, when he, she, or it is in a position to exercise a significant degree of control over it.

The essence of the private inurement concept is to ensure that a nonprofit organization, particularly a charitable one, is serving public, not private, interests. To be tax-
exempt, a nonprofit organization must establish that it is not organized and operated
for the benefit of private interests—designated individuals, the creator of the entity or
his or her family, shareholders of the organization, persons controlled (directly or
indirectly) by private interests, or any persons having a personal and private interest
in the activities of the organization. For the private inurement doctrine to apply, the
transaction or other arrangement must involve an *insider* with respect to the organization, such as its trustees, directors, officers, and key employees, and their family
members and controlled entities.

---

62. In general, Sasso, "Searching for Trust in the Not-For-Profit Boardroom: Looking Beyond the Duty of
    Obedience to Ensure Accountability," 50 *U.C.L.A. L. Rev.* 1485 (August 2003); Cherry, "Update: The
    Current State of Nonprofit Director Liability," 37 *Duq. L. Rev.* 557 (Summer 1999); Sparks, III & Hamer-
    mesh, "Common Law Duties of Non-Director Corporate Officers," 48 *Bus. Law.* 715 (Nov. 1992).
63. There are four exceptions to this statement; they are the subject of § 5.3(a).
64. As opposed to the IRS's application of the law (see § 5.21(e), (f)).

Private inurement has a multitude of manifestations. For a transaction to entail private inurement, however, the economic benefit to the insider must be excessive or unreasonable; benefits to insiders that are reasonable are permissible. The most common form of private inurement is excessive compensation. Other private inurement transactions are rental arrangements, loans, and provision of certain services or certain uses of an organization's assets.

The sanction for violation of the private inurement doctrine is loss or denial of recognition of the organization's tax-exempt status. The general expectation is that the IRS will first apply the intermediate sanctions rules, invoking private inurement principles only in egregious cases. Nonetheless, it is possible for the IRS to apply both bodies of law, thus penalizing the insider or insiders who obtained the excess benefit and the tax-exempt organization that provided it.[65]

(b) Doctrine of Private Benefit

The private benefit doctrine is somewhat the same as the private inurement doctrine; indeed, nearly every transaction or arrangement that constitutes private inurement simultaneously amounts to private benefit. The principal dissimilarities between the two sets of rules are that application of the private benefit doctrine does not require the involvement of an insider and the private benefit doctrine tolerates insubstantial private benefit. Technically, the private benefit doctrine applies only with respect to exempt charitable entities. The sanction for violation of the private benefit doctrine also is loss or denial of recognition of tax-exempt status.

The private benefit doctrine, created largely by the courts, is more sweeping than the private inurement doctrine. In recent years, the private benefit doctrine has emerged as a potent force in the law concerning charitable organizations. Private benefit can occur, for example, in connection with various types of joint ventures. The IRS, from time to time, finds impermissible private benefit conferred by charitable entities on other types of tax-exempt organizations, such as social welfare organizations and associations.[66]

The IRS is applying the private benefit doctrine in an attempt to achieve certain objectives in the nonprofit governance setting. Although the doctrine is supposed to be applied as a sanction—that is, only when some form of unwarranted benefit actually occurs[67]—today's IRS asserts that the doctrine is applicable where, on the basis of revenue agents' speculation, private benefit *might* or *could* occur.[68]

(c) Board Composition and Courts

The courts have constructed certain presumptions in the private inurement and private benefit contexts. Particularly with respect to the private inurement doctrine, an arrangement involving insiders often gives rise to a higher scrutiny of the facts and potential for violation of the doctrine. For example, the U.S. Tax Court expressed the view that ''where the creators [of an organization] control the affairs of the organization, there is an obvious opportunity for abuse, which necessitates an open and

---

65. The private inurement doctrine is the subject of Chapter 20 of *Law of Tax-Exempt Organizations*; the intermediate sanctions rules are summarized in *id.*, Chapter 21.
66. The private benefit doctrine is the subject of *id.*, § 20.11.
67. See § 1.6(c).
68. See § 5.21(e).

candid disclosure of all facts bearing upon the organization, operation, and finances so that the Court can be assured that by granting the claimed exemption it is not sanctioning an abuse of the revenue laws."[69] The court added that, where this disclosure is not made, the "logical inference is that the facts, if disclosed, would show that the [organization] fails to meet the requirements" for tax-exempt status.[70]

In another case, where all of the directors and officers of an organization were related, the Tax Court could not find the "necessary delineation" between the organization and these individuals acting in their personal and private capacity.[71] Earlier, a court of appeals concluded that the fact that a married couple comprised two of three members of an organization's board of directors required a special justification of certain payments by the organization to them.[72] Before that, an appellate court decided that an individual who had "complete and unfettered control" over an organization has a special burden to explain certain withdrawals from the organization's bank account.[73]

In still another setting, a court considered an organization with three directors, consisting of the founder, his wife, and their daughter; they were part of the membership base totaling five individuals. The small size of the organization was held to be "relevant," with the court finding private inurement and private benefit because of the "amount of control" the founder exercised over the organization's operations and the "blurring of the lines of demarcation between the activities and interests" of the organization.[74] The court observed, nonetheless, that "[t]his is not to say that an organization of such small dimensions cannot qualify for tax-exempt status."[75]

Private inurement was also the basis for revocation of the tax-exempt status of a private school.[76] The individual who was the founder, president, chief executive officer, and executive director of the school used the school's funds for personal purposes. There was no documentation of any loans to or repayments by this individual. The state where the school was located revoked the school's charter, in part because this individual had "unfettered discretion to direct and manage the operation" of the school and "its financial affairs."[77] The court wrote that factors "emerging repeatedly [in the law] as indicative of prohibited inurement and private benefit include control by the founder over the entity's funds, assets, and disbursement; use of entity moneys for personal expenses; payment of salary or rent to the founder without any accompanying evidence of analysis of the reasonableness of the amounts; and purported loans to the founder showing a ready private source of credit."[78]

---

69. United Libertarian Fellowship, Inc. v. Comm'r, 65 T.C.M. 2175, 2181 (1993).
70. *Id.* Identical phraseology was used by the court in a prior proceeding (Bubbling Well Church of Universal Love, Inc. v. Comm'r, 74 T.C. 531, 535 (1980), *aff'd*, 670 F.2d 104 (9th Cir. 1981)).
71. Levy Family Tribe Found., Inc. v. Comm'r, 69 T.C. 615, 619 (1978).
72. Founding Church of Scientology v. United States, 412 F.2d 1197 (Ct. Cl. 1969), *cert. den.*, 397 U.S. 1009 (1970).
73. Parker v. Comm'r, 365 F.2d 792, 799 (8th Cir. 1966), *cert. den.*, 385 U.S. 1026 (1967).
74. Western Catholic Church v. Comm'r, 73 T.C. 196, 213 (1979).
75. *Id.* In Blake v. Comm'r, 29 T.C.M. 513 (1970), an organization of similar dimensions was ruled to be tax-exempt; private inurement and private benefit were not at issue in the case. In comparable circumstances, the IRS refused to grant recognition of exemption to an organization, although private inurement was not in evidence, because the agency suspected private inurement would occur in the future (Priv. Ltr. Rul. 200535029).
76. Rameses School of San Antonio, Texas v. Comm'r, 93 T.C.M. 1092 (2007).
77. *Id.* at 1093.
78. *Id.* at 1095.

(d) Board Composition and the IRS

Some in the IRS who process applications for recognition of tax exemption or otherwise review the operations of tax-exempt organizations are not well trained in the law of tax-exempt organizations. These individuals have a tendency to substitute their view as to what the law is (or should be) for the actual legal requirements and demand that the organizations do something (or refrain from doing something) as a condition of exemption. In this regard, they usually are in error. Nowhere is this regrettable phenomenon more prevalent than in the case of the composition of the board of tax-exempt organizations.

Following are positions of IRS reviewers that tax-exempt organizations, most likely charitable ones, and their representatives may encounter:

- *Public board.* The governing board of a tax-exempt organization must be reflective of the public. An IRS specialist asserted that "[u]nrelated individuals selected from the community you serve should control the non-profit." One applicant was directed to "expand your board at this time, so control no longer rests with related individuals." Another was told that the entity needs to enlarge its board "to remove the close control issue." Still another IRS specialist articulated the thought that the "structure [of the board] must be changed to allow members of the general public to control the non-profit organization."

- *Control by a for-profit organization.* An IRS specialist wrote: "No for-profit should have control of a non-profit organization."[79]

- *Conflicts.* An IRS specialist asserted that a majority of an exempt organization's board may not be related to salaried personnel or to parties providing services to the organization.

- *One director.* An IRS law specialist was of the view that a tax-exempt organization could not have only one director, state law notwithstanding. This fact was seen by the specialist as a violation of the doctrine of private inurement. The specialist wrote that this individual "stands in a relationship" with the organization, "which offers him the opportunity to make use of the organization's income or assets for personal gain."

- *Experience.* An IRS reviewer asked an organization for a statement as to the board members' "experience" in serving on the board of a nonprofit organization.

- *Participation.* An IRS law specialist demanded that an applicant organization produce a statement, signed by each director, that the directors will "take an active part" in the operations of the organization.

- *Intermediate sanctions.* An IRS law specialist tried to force an applicant organization to provide a statement, signed by each director, that they were aware of and would abide by the intermediate sanctions rules in their service to the organization.[80]

---

79. Were this the law, a for-profit corporation could not have a related private foundation.
80. To compound the foolishness, the applicant organization was a private operating foundation (see *Law of Tax-Exempt Organizations* § 12.1(b)), so the intermediate sanctions rules did not apply in the first instance.

These assertions as to the state of the law, practices, and required statements have an element in common: they are nonsense. None of this is the law; none of this is required. The lawyer or other representative of the organization should stand up to these IRS exempt organization law "specialists," explain to them (politely, of course) why they are flat wrong, make it abundantly clear that their demands are going to be disregarded, and state that if they persist with their position(s), the matter will be referred to the IRS National Office for resolution. They usually will back down, particularly in the face of an assertion that they are merely (and erroneously) inserting their personal views into the case. A problem in this regard arises when an applicant organization has made the filing without the services of a tax-exempt organizations professional, or is using the services of a professional who is not sufficiently proficient in this area of the law, and innocently believes that it must comply with the specialist's demand(s)—and does.

The IRS traditionally has been more measured on these points in its private letter rulings, relying more (as do the courts) on presumptions than absolute declarations. In one instance, the agency's lawyers wrote that when an organization is "totally controlled" by its founder and his or her immediate family, the entity "bears a very heavy burden to be forthcoming and explicit about its plans for the use of [its] assets" for charitable purposes, and warned that this structure lacks "institutional protections," that is, a board of directors consisting of "active, disinterested persons."[81] Thus, this rule was articulated: "Small, closely controlled exempt organizations—and especially those that are closely controlled by members of one family— . . . require thorough examination to [e]nsure that the arrangements serve charitable purposes rather than private interests."[82] The IRS's lawyers conceded, nonetheless, that "[t]here is nothing that precludes an organization that is closely controlled . . . from qualifying, or continuing to qualify, for exemption."[83]

Consequently, while there is nothing specific in the operational test[84] concerning the size or composition of the governing board of a charitable or other tax-exempt organization, the courts and the IRS have grafted onto the test a greater burden of proof standard when the organization has a small board of directors and/or is dominated by an individual.[85]

---

81. IRS Technical Advice Memorandum (Tech. Adv. Mem.) 200437040.
82. *Id.*
83. *Id.*
84. See *Law of Tax-Exempt Organizations* § 4.5(a).
85. In general, Gary, "Regulating Management of Charities: Trust Law, Corporate Law, and Tax Law," 21 *Haw. L. Rev.* 593 (Winter 1999).

CHAPTER TWO

Board Members: Responsibilities and Liability

The overarching trend in the law of corporate governance of nonprofit organizations is an expectation—by legislators, regulators, and other formulators of good governance principles—of considerable expansion of the role and scope of authority of the governing board of these organizations. The concept of the board of a nonprofit organization as a group of overseers and policymakers is being replaced by the view that the duties and responsibilities of these individuals include far more in the way of direct management and other hands-on involvement in the organization's operations. With this increase in duties and responsibilities comes the potential for more personal liability.

§2.1 BOARD OF DIRECTORS GOVERNANCE PRINCIPLES

Despite the assertion of the IRS that there are commonly "accepted standards of good governance,"[1] that is not the case. The standards-setters cannot even agree on what a contemporary board of directors of a charitable or other type of nonprofit organization is expected to do[2] or, for that matter, how many of them there should be.[3] Nonetheless, here is one effort at distilling the common elements of the responsibilities of today's nonprofit board.

(a) Statement of Purpose/Mission Statement

The board of trustees or directors of a nonprofit organization is expected to formulate, revisit from time to time, and, if necessary, restate the organization's purposes. This statement of purposes may be in a formal organizing document, such as articles of incorporation, or in a separate mission statement. While there will likely be differences of opinion as to the length of this statement, it should accurately describe the reason for and objectives of the organization. Once the statement is formulated, the board should reexamine the text of it from time to time for relevance and accuracy. Thus, the Evangelical Council for Financial Accountability's (ECFA's) inventory of best practices includes the recommendation that the organization develop a

---

1. See Chapter 5, note 1.
2. See § 5.4.
3. See § 5.2.

mission statement, "putting into words why the organization exists and what it hopes to accomplish," "[r]egularly reference" this statement to be certain it is being "faithfully followed," and "[h]ave the courage to refocus the mission statement, if appropriate."[4] The principles of the Panel on the Nonprofit Sector state that the board "sets the vision and mission for the organization and establishes the broad policies and strategic direction that enable the organization to fulfill its charitable purpose."[5]

The Standards for Excellence Institute's standards provide that an organization's "purpose, as defined and approved by the board of directors, should be formally and specifically stated." These standards add that an organization "should evaluate whether the mission needs to be modified to reflect societal changes, its current programs should be revised or discontinued, or new programs need to be developed."[6]

There are differences of opinion as to the degree of formality of this process. The mildest of the recommendations is from the American National Red Cross Governance Modernization Act, which includes, as one of the board's responsibilities, the review and approval of the organization's mission statement;[7] followed in this regard by the Treasury Department's voluntary best practices, which call for the organization's governing instruments to delineate the organization's basic goal(s) and purpose(s).[8] The Standards for Excellence Institute standards include the rule that the board of an organization "should engage in short-term and long-term planning activities as necessary to determine the mission of the organization, to define specific goals and objectives related to the mission, and to evaluate the success of the organization's programs toward achieving the mission."[9] The Senate Finance Committee staff paper states that the board should "[e]stablish, review, and approve program objectives and program measures."[10] The draft of best practices devised by the IRS states that the board of directors of an organization should adopt a "clearly articulated mission statement," which should "explain and popularize the charity's purpose and serve as a guide to the organization's work."[11] A "well-written mission statement shows why the charity exists, what it hopes to accomplish, and what activities it will undertake, where, and for whom."[12] The Panel on the Nonprofit Sector's good governance principles provide that an organization must have a governing body that is "responsible for reviewing and approving the organization's mission and strategic direction."[13]

The Better Business Bureau (BBB) Wise Giving Alliance standards state more formally that an organization should have "defined, measurable goals and objectives in place" and a process that "identifies ways to address any deficiencies."[14] These standards add that an organization should "[h]ave a board policy of assessing, no less than every two years, the organization's performance and effectiveness and of

---

4. See § 3.3(d)(vi).
5. See § 3.12(b).
6. See § 3.3(e)(i).
7. See § 3.11.
8. See § 3.6.
9. See § 3.3(e)(ii).
10. See § 3.5(a).
11. See § 3.10(a).
12. Id.
13. See § 3.12(b).
14. See § 3.3(c)(ii).

determining future actions required to achieve the mission."[15] The Panel on the Non-profit Sector's good governance principles include a similar rule, in that the board should "set strategic goals and review them annually" and "should establish and review regularly the organization's mission and goals and should evaluate, no less frequently than every five years, the organization's programs, goals and [other] activities to be sure they advance its mission and make prudent use of its resources."[16] The Standards for Excellence Institute standards provide that an organization "should periodically revisit its mission (e.g., every 3 to 5 years) to determine if the need for its programs continues to exist."[17]

An element that directly devolves from the thought that an organization should have an up-to-date and accurate mission statement is the matter of measuring progress in achieving the mission.[18] This, of course, is far more difficult to achieve than formulating goals. The BBB standards, for example, state that an organization "should regularly assess its effectiveness in achieving its mission" and have a "defined process in place to evaluate the success and impact of its program(s) in fulfilling the goals and objectives of the organization."[19] These standards add that the board of an organization should receive, "for its approval, a written report that outlines the results of the aforementioned performance and effectiveness assessment and recommendations for future actions."[20] The Panel on the Nonprofit Sector, observing that "[b]ecause organizations and their purposes differ, it is incumbent on each organization to develop its own process for evaluating effectiveness," took a less rigorous approach, noting that "interim benchmarks can be identified to assess whether the work is moving in the right direction."[21]

The Standards for Excellence Institute standards are the most expansive on this point. There it is stated that a nonprofit organization "should have defined, cost-effective procedures for evaluating, both qualitatively and quantitatively, its programs and projects in relation to its mission." These procedures "should address programmatic efficiency and effectiveness, the relationships of these impacts to the cost of achieving them, and the outcomes for program participants." Evaluations, which "should include input from program participants," should be "candid, be used to strengthen the effectiveness of the organization and, when necessary, be used to make programmatic changes."[22]

Evolving from the notion that a board of a nonprofit organization should periodically evaluate the organization is the idea that, from time to time, the board should evaluate itself. This rule, infrequently invoked in the standards, is articulated in the Panel on the Nonprofit Sector's principles: board members "should evaluate their performance as a group and as individuals no less frequently than every three years, and should have clear procedures for removing board members who are unable to fulfill their responsibilities." The Panel noted that a "regular process of evaluating

---

15. *Id.*
16. See § 3.12(b).
17. See § 3.3(e)(i).
18. These two elements are often combined. Thus, the BBB standards reference "defined, *measurable* goals and objectives" (see § 3.3(c)(ii)).
19. See § 3.3(c)(ii).
20. *Id.*
21. See § 3.12(b).
22. See § 3.3(e)(i).

the board's performance can help to identify strengths and weaknesses of its processes and procedures and to provide insights for strengthening orientation and educational programs, the conduct of board and committee meetings, and interactions with board and staff leadership."[23] The ECFA best practices state that there should be an annual monitoring of "individual board performance against the board members' service commitments."[24] There it is also stated that board member participation should be evaluated "before extending terms" and board member evaluation should be used to "ensure that the organization is only served by effective members."[25] Further, the board should use "routine and periodic board self-evaluation to improve meetings, restructure committees, and address individual board member performance."[26] The Standards for Excellence Institute standards call for evaluation every two years of its performance by the board.[27]

(b) Supervision of Officers and Key Staff

It is generally recognized that one of the responsibilities of the board of a nonprofit organization is supervision of the organization's officers and senior (or key) executive staff. Thus, the BBB Wise Giving Alliance standards state that the board must provide "adequate oversight of the charity's operations and staff," including "regularly scheduled appraisals of the CEO's performance."[28] The ECFA standards provide that an organization must "exercise the management . . . controls necessary to provide reasonable assurance that all resources are used (nationally and internationally) in conformity with applicable federal and state laws and regulations to accomplish the exempt purposes for which they are intended;"[29] presumably this exercise is headed by the organization's board. The ECFA's best practices add that the organization should ensure, "by collaborating with the board and the CEO, Executive Director, or President (or similar position), that the organization has a clear financial plan that is aligned with strategic, operating, and development plans."[30] These practices also state that the board should "[a]nnually and formally evaluate the CEO, Executive Director, or President (or similar position)."[31] Similarly, the standards of the Standards for Excellence Institute and the draft best practices published by the Committee for Purchase provide that the board or a board committee should hire an executive director and evaluate, at least annually, the executive's performance.[32] The American National Red Cross Governance Modernization Act principles state that the board of the organization should select and evaluate the organization's chief executive officer; should evaluate the performance of the senior leadership team and provide for management succession; and should hold management accountable for performance.[33]

---

23. See § 3.12(b).
24. See § 3.3(d)(ii).
25. *Id.*
26. *Id.*
27. See § 3.3(e)(ii).
28. See § 3.3(c)(i).
29. See § 3.3(d)(i).
30. *Id.*
31. See § 3.3(d)(ii).
32. See §§ 3.3(e)(ii), 3.7.
33. See § 3.11.

The Panel on the Nonprofit Sector's good governance principles include the rule that the board should "hire, oversee, and annually evaluate the performance of the chief executive officer of the organization, and should conduct such an evaluation prior to any change in that officer's compensation," unless a multiyear contract is in force or the change consists solely of routine adjustments for inflation or the cost of living.[34] The Panel added that the organization's governing documents should require the full board to evaluate the executive's performance.

(c) Oversight of Finances

The BBB Wise Giving Alliance standards state that the board, in providing "adequate oversight of the charity's operations," should approve the organization's budget, have "disbursement controls" in place, and establish "accounting procedures sufficient to safeguard charity finances."[35] The ECFA best practices state that the board should "understand the organization's financial health," and should "approve the annual budget and key financial transactions, such as major asset acquisitions, that can be realistically financed with existing or attainable resources."[36] The American National Red Cross Governance Modernization Act principles call for the board to oversee the financial reporting and audit process, and provide oversight of the financial stability of the organization.[37] The Panel on the Nonprofit Sector stated that an organization's board is responsible for reviewing and approving the organization's "annual budget and key financial transactions, . . . and fiscal and governance policies."[38]

The standards of the Standards for Excellence Institute require that an organization "operate in accordance with an annual budget that has been approved by the board of directors. Accurate financial reports should be maintained on a timely basis. Internal financial statements "should be prepared no less frequently than quarterly, should be provided to the board of directors, and should identify and explain any material variation between actual and budgeted revenues and expenses."[39] It is repeated that the board "annually should approve the organization's budget and periodically should assess the organization's financial performance in relation to the budget." As part of this annual budget process, the board "should review the percentages of the organization's resources spent on program, administration, and fundraising."[40] The board "should also approve the findings of the organization's annual audit and management letter and plan to implement the recommendations of" that letter.[41]

The Senate Finance Committee staff paper states that the board should "[r]eview and approve the organization's budget and financial objectives as well as significant investments, joint ventures, and business transactions," and should "[r]eview and approve the auditing and accounting principles and practices used in preparing the organization's financial statements."[42] The Treasury Department's voluntary best practices state that an organization should have an annual budget approved and

34. See § 3.12(b).
35. See § 3.3(c)(i).
36. See § 3.3(d)(ii).
37. See § 3.11.
38. See § 3.12(b).
39. See § 3.3(e)(v).
40. See § 3.3(e)(ii).
41. See § 3.3(e)(ii).
42. See § 3.5(a).

overseen by its board; a board-appointed financial/accounting officer who is responsible for day-to-day management of the charity's assets; and, generally, an audit of
the finances of the organization by an independent certified public accounting firm.[43]
The Committee for Purchase's proposed best practices provide that the board should
approve the findings of the organization's annual audit and management letter.[44] The
Internal Revenue Service's (IRS's) draft good governance principles state that directors "must be good stewards of a charity's financial resources" and that a charitable
organization "should operate in accordance with an annual budget approved by the
board of directors." The board "should ensure that financial resources are used to
further charitable purpose[s] by regularly receiving and reading up-to-date financial
statements including Form 990, auditor's letters, and finance and audit committee
reports."[45]

The board should see to it that the organization, if an appropriate size, annually
procures audited financial statements. Thus, the ECFA best practices state that an organization generally must obtain an annual audit performed by an independent certified public accounting firm, including a financial statement prepared in accordance
with generally accepted accounting principles.[46] Also, pursuant to these practices,
the organization should ensure that "all material related-party transactions are disclosed in the financial statements."[47]

ECFA makes provision for a type of organization that does not require audited
financial statements, in which case the organization must have financial statements
that are compiled or reviewed by an independent certified public accounting firm.[48]
The approach taken by the Standards for Excellence Institute is that an organization
with annual revenue in excess of $300,000 should have its financial reports audited by
an independent certified public accountant.[49] The Department of the Treasury's voluntary best practices follows a similar approach, setting the threshold at $250,000.[50]
Organizations that are subject to California's Nonprofit Integrity Act and that have
gross revenues of at least $2 million must have annual financial statements prepared
and audited by an independent certified public accountant.[51] The IRS's draft of good
governance practices calls for an annual audit where the charity has "substantial
assets or annual revenue."[52]

Standards vary as to rotation of accounting firms. The Sarbanes-Oxley Act makes
it unlawful for an accounting firm to provide audit services to a company if the lead
(or coordinating) audit partner, or the audit partner responsible for reviewing the
audit, has performed audit services for that company in each of the company's five
previous fiscal years.[53] This rule is reflected in the Senate Finance Committee staff
paper, where it is provided that the board should hire an independent auditor and

---

43. See § 3.6.
44. See § 3.7
45. See § 3.10(h).
46. See § 3.3(d)(iii).
47. *Id.*
48. *Id.*
49. See § 3.3(e)(iv).
50. See § 3.6.
51. See § 3.4(a).
52. See § 3.10(h).
53. See § 3.2(b)(viii).

an auditor could not be retained for more than five years.[54] Similarly, the IRS's draft of good governance principles stated that the auditing firm "should be changed periodically (e.g., every five years) to ensure a fresh look at the financial statements."[55]

(d) Oversight of Compensation

Current thinking in this area has it that the board of a nonprofit organization should be directly involved in the organization's compensation practices concerning officers and other key employees. Thus, the Evangelical Council for Financial Accountability's best practices state that the board should "[a]pprove and document annually and in advance the compensation and fringe benefits of the CEO, Executive Director, or President (or similar position) unless there is a multi-year contract in force and there is no change in the compensation and fringe benefits except for an inflation or cost-of-living adjustment."[56] The Committee for Purchase's proposed best practices state that the board of an organization should periodically review the "appropriateness of the overall compensation structure" of the organization, should monitor compensation paid to the chief executive officer/president and "highly compensated individuals, and should approve all compensation packages for these individuals through a process to determine the reasonableness of the compensation.[57]

Likewise, the Standards for Excellence Institute standards provide that the board or a board committee "should hire the executive director, set the executive's compensation, and evaluate the director's performance at least annually." Where a committee performs this role, details should be reported to the board. The board "should periodically review the appropriateness of the overall compensation structure of the organization."[58] Similarly, charitable organizations that are subject to California's Nonprofit Integrity Act must have their governing board, or a designated committee of the board, review and approve the compensation of the organization's president, chief executive officer, chief financial officer, and treasurer. There must be a determination that this compensation, including benefits, is "just and reasonable." This review and approval must occur at the time of initial hiring, when a term is renewed or extended, and when the compensation is modified.[59] Further, according to the Committee for Purchase's proposed best practices, the board should establish the executive's compensation and should periodically review the "appropriateness of the overall compensation structure" of the organization.[60]

The draft of good governance practices published by the IRS (and then withdrawn) provided that a "successful charity pays no more than reasonable compensation for services rendered." Also, charities "may pay reasonable compensation for services provided by officers and staff."[61] The IRS LifeCycle Educational tool likewise states that a charity "may not pay more than reasonable compensation for services rendered" and that the IRS "encourages charities to rely on the rebuttable

---

54. See § 3.5(a).
55. See § 3.10(h).
56. See § 3.3(d)(ii).
57. See 3.7.
58. See § 3.3(e)(ii).
59. See § 3.4(c).
60. See § 3.7.
61. See § 3.10(i).

presumption.''[62] The American National Red Cross Governance Modernization Act principles state that an organization's board should determine the level of compensation of the entity's chief executive officer and establish the compensation of the senior leadership team.[63] The Panel on the Nonprofit Sector's principles state that ''[o]ne of the most important responsibilities of the board . . . is to select, supervise and determine a compensation package that will attract and retain a qualified chief executive.''[64]

(e) Accommodating Conflicts of Interest

No topic in the field of governance of nonprofit organizations has garnered more attention in recent years than conflicts of interest and conflict-of-interest policies.[65] This fact permeates the various standards and best practices that have emerged. Sometimes the focus is on prohibitions of conflicts; in other instances the emphasis is on disclosure of conflicts.

The BBB Wise Giving Alliance standards forbid ''transaction(s) in which any board or staff members have material conflicting interests with the charity resulting from any relationship or business affiliation.'' Factors that are considered in determining whether a transaction entails a *conflict of interest*, and if so, whether the conflict is *material*, include ''any arm's length procedures established by the charity; the size of the transaction relative to like expenses of the charity; whether the interested party participated in the board vote on the transaction; if competitive bids were sought [;] and whether the transaction is one-time, recurring or ongoing.''[66]

Pursuant to the Evangelical Council on Financial Accountability standards, organizations are to ''avoid conflicts of interest.'' This apparently means make a reasonable effort to not become entangled in a conflict relationship or arrangement, rather than a prohibition, because the standards continue with criteria as to when transactions with related parties are permissible. These transactions may occur, according to these standards, when (1) a material transaction is fully disclosed in the audited financial statements of the organization, (2) the related party is excluded from the discussion and approval of the transaction, (3) a competitive bid or comparable valuation exists, and (4) the organization's board has demonstrated that the transaction is in the best interest of the entity.[67] The ECFA best practices include the rules that a conflict-of-interest policy relating to the governing board and key executives be adopted; that the board and key executives should annually document any potential related-party transactions; and that all significant related-party transactions should be initially approved and, if continuing, reapproved annually by the board.[68]

The standards of the Standards for Excellence Institute state that a nonprofit organization should have a written conflict-of-interest policy. This policy ''should be applicable to all board members and staff, and to volunteers who have significant independent decision making authority regarding the resources of the organization.'' The policy ''should identify the types of conduct or transactions that raise conflict of

---

62. See § 3.14(e).
63. See § 3.11.
64. See § 3.12(b).
65. See §§ 5.17, 6.3(b).
66. See § 3.3(c)(i).
67. See § 3.3(d)(v).
68. *Id.*

interest concerns, should set forth procedures for disclosure of actual or potential conflicts, and should provide for review of individual transactions by the uninvolved members of the board of directors."[69]

These standards add that an organization "should provide board members, staff, and volunteers with a conflict of interest statement that summarizes the key elements of the organization's conflict of interest policy." This statement "should provide space for the board member, employee, or volunteer to disclose any known interest that the individual, or a member of the individual's immediate family, has in any business entity which transacts business with the organization." The statement should be provided to and signed by board members, staff, and volunteers, "both at the time of the individual's initial affiliation with the organization and at least annually thereafter."[70]

The Senate Finance Committee staff paper states that an organization should establish a conflict-of-interest policy, "which would be required to be disclosed with the [Form] 990, and require a summary of conflicts determinations made during the 990 reporting year."[71] The Treasury Department's voluntary best practices for charitable organizations engaged in international grantmaking and activities state that an organization should "establish a conflict-of-interest policy for board members and employees."[72] The Committee for Purchase's proposed best practices includes requirement of a conflict-of-interest policy that identifies the types of conflict or transactions that raise conflict-of-interest concerns, sets forth procedures for disclosure of actual or potential conflicts, and provides for review of individual transactions by the "uninvolved" members of the board of directors.[73]

The IRS's draft of good governance principles called for a conflict-of-interest policy, predicating the requirement on the fundamental standard that a director of a charity "owe[s] it a duty of loyalty."[74] This duty requires a director to, in the words of the IRS, "act in the interest of the charity rather than in the personal interest of the director or some other person or organization." In this connection, the duty of loyalty "requires a director to avoid conflicts of interest that are detrimental to the charity." To that end, the board of directors of a charitable organization "should adopt and regularly evaluate an effective conflict of interest policy" that "requires directors and staff to act solely in the interests of the charity without regard for personal interests;" includes "written procedures for determining whether a relationship, financial interest, or business affiliation" results in a conflict of interest; and prescribes a "certain course of action in the event a conflict of interest is identified." Directors and staff "should be required to disclose annually in writing any known financial interest that the individual, or a member of the individual's family, has in any business entity that transacts business with the charity."[75]

The Panel on the Nonprofit Sector's good governance principles include a requirement that an organization "adopt and implement policies and procedures to ensure that all conflicts of interest, or the appearance thereof, within the organization

---

69. See § 3.3(e)(iv).
70. *Id.*
71. See § 3.5(a).
72. See § 3.6.
73. See § 3.7.
74. See § 1.5(b).
75. See § 3.10(e).

and the board are appropriately managed through disclosure, recusal, or other means." A conflict-of-interest policy "must be consistent with the laws of the state in which the nonprofit is organized and should be tailored to specific organizational needs and characteristics." This policy "should require full disclosure of all potential conflicts of interest within the organization" and "should apply to every person who has the ability to influence decisions of the organization, including board and staff members and parties related to them."[76]

The IRS's redesigned Form 990 includes a question as to whether the filing organization has adopted a conflict-of-interest policy.[77] In addition, an organization must state whether the officers, directors, trustees, and key employees are required to annually disclose interests giving rise to conflicts.[78] The organization must indicate on the return whether and if so how it makes its conflict-of-interest policy available to the public, such as by having copies available in its office or posted on a Web site.[79]

(f) Development of Policies

It goes without saying that one of the responsibilities of a board of a nonprofit organization is to establish the entity's *policies* (and/or *procedures*). In this era of intense focus on good governance principles for charitable and other nonprofit organizations, a plethora of policies are being bandied about. For the most part, the law does not require any of these policies. A nonprofit board thus must decide which, if any, of the following 30 policies (or procedures)[80] it will adopt:

1. A policy concerning the organization's mission statement[81]
2. A conflict-of-interest policy[82]
3. A whistleblower policy[83]
4. A document retention and destruction policy[84]
5. A code of ethics[85]
6. An investment policy[86]
7. A policy concerning fundraising[87]
8. A policy concerning documentation of meetings[88]
9. A policy concerning review of annual information return[89]

---

76. See § 3.12(a).
77. See § 6.3(b).
78. See § 4.2(a).
79. See § 3.13(b).
80. These policies are in addition to policies embodied in an organization's articles of organization or bylaws (such as size of the board, term limits, preparation of minutes, and an audit committee).
81. See § 6.3(a).
82. See §§ 2.1(e), 5.17, 6.3(b).
83. See §§ 5.18, 6.3(c).
84. See §§ 5.19, 6.3(d).
85. See § 6.3(t).
86. See § 6.3(p).
87. See §§ 5.20, 6.3(q).
88. See § 6.3(g).
89. See § 6.3(i).

10.   A gift-acceptance policy[90]

11.   A policy concerning allowable expense reimbursements[91]

12.   A policy concerning donor confidentiality[92]

13.   A stewardship philosophy statement[93]

14.   An executive compensation policy[94]

15.   A procedure as to program effectiveness evaluation[95]

16.   A policy as to advocacy[96]

17.   A policy as to chapters and/or similar affiliates[97]

18.   A policy as to related organizations[98]

19.   A policy as to use of disregarded entities[99]

20.   A policy as to involvement in joint ventures[100]

21.   A policy as to safeguarding of tax-exempt status[101]

22.   Procedures as to compliance with law[102]

23.   Procedures concerning liability[103]

24.   A policy as to domestic and/or international grantmaking[104]

25.   A policy as to conservation easements[105]

26.   A charity care policy[106]

27.   A community benefit policy[107]

28.   A debt collection policy[108]

29.   A tax-exempt bond compliance policy[109]

30.   A policy as to assessment of the board's performance[110]

---

90. See § 6.3(j).
91. See §§ 6.3(r).
92. See § 5.20.
93. See § 3.3(d).
94. See §§ 3.3(d), 6.3(e).
95. See § 5.6.
96. See § 6.5.
97. See § 6.3(h).
98. See § 6.5.
99. *Id.*
100. See § 6.3(f).
101. See § 6.5.
102. See § 5.12.
103. See § 6.5.
104. See § 6.3(l).
105. See § 6.3(k).
106. See § 6.3(m).
107. See §§ 6.3(m), 6.3(n).
108. See § 6.3(o).
109. See § 6.3(s).
110. See § 5.6.

(g) Fundraising Responsibilities

Inasmuch as these good governance principles are directed principally at public charities, there is considerable emphasis on fundraising practices and procedures.[111] Boards of directors of these charitable organizations are thus importuned to, as the Philanthropic Advisory Service standards stated, "establish and exercise controls" over the fundraising process as undertaken by officers, employees, volunteers, consultants, and other contractors.[112] This includes the type or types of fundraising engaged in by the organization, the records kept, compliance with federal and state fundraising law, and the like.

Many of these standards address the quality of the solicitation materials; organizations may not always regard this as the province of the board. For example, the BBB Wise Giving Alliance standards require that an organization's solicitation and other informational materials be "accurate, truthful, and not misleading."[113] Likewise, the Evangelical Council for Financial Accountability standards state that representations of fact, description of the organization's financial condition, or narrative about events must be "current, complete, and accurate;" "material omissions or exaggerations of fact" are not permitted.[114] Similarly, the Standards for Excellence Institute standards provide that solicitation materials "should be accurate and truthful and should correctly identify the organization, its mission, and the intended use of the solicited funds."[115]

The draft of the IRS's good governance principles stated that "[s]uccess at fundraising requires care and honesty." The board of directors of a charitable organization "should adopt and monitor policies to ensure that fundraising solicitations meet federal and state law requirements and [that] solicitation materials are accurate, truthful, and candid."[116] The American National Red Cross Governance Modernization Act principles call for the members of the board to assist with fundraising on behalf of the organization.[117]

The good governance principles formulated by the Panel on the Nonprofit Sector state that solicitation materials and other communications addressed to prospective donors "must clearly identify the organization and be accurate and truthful." The Panel stated that a prospective donor "has the right to know the name of anyone soliciting contributions, the name and location of the organization that will receive the contribution, a clear description of its activities, the intended use of the funds to be raised, a contact for obtaining additional information, and whether the individual requesting the contribution is acting as a volunteer, employee of the organization, or hired solicitor."[118]

Thus, to satisfy this panoply of standards, a board of a fundraising charitable organization should endeavor to be certain that the solicitation materials involved are

---

111. Much of this aspect of the topic is the subject of § 5.20.
112. See § 3.3(b)(iv).
113. See § 3.3(c)(iv).
114. See § 3.3(d)(vi).
115. See § 3.3(e)(ix).
116. See § 3.10(g).
117. See § 3.11.
118. See § 3.12(d).

accurate, candid, current, complete, honest, and truthful; and that they are not exaggerative, do not have material omissions, and are not misleading.

§ 2.2   ROLE OF OFFICERS

As noted, the role of directors of a nonprofit organization is defined in part by the roles of the organization's officers. (A prominent exception to this point is the trust, which usually has only one or more trustees.)

(a)   Scope of Authority

As is the case with the board of directors, generalizations about the scope (or levels) of authority of the officers of a nonprofit organization are difficult to formulate. In instances of nonprofit organizations that have members, directors, officers, and employees (key or otherwise), setting a clear distinction as to who has the authority to do what is nearly impossible. General principles can be articulated but will usually prove nearly useless in practice.

For example, it can be stated that the members of the organization (if any) set basic policy and the members of the board of directors set additional policy, albeit within the parameters established by the membership. The officers thereafter implement the policies, as do the employees, although this is more on a day-to-day basis. Yet, the reality is that policy is established and implemented at all levels.

In a typical nonprofit organization, who decides what programs will be undertaken, who is hired and fired as employees, the nature of the compensation arrangements, who the lawyers and accountants for the organization will be, the type of fundraising program, the format of the journal, or the organization's physical location(s)? Depending on the circumstances, the answers may be the members, the board, the executive committee, the chair of the board, the president, the (or a) vice president, the executive director, and/or any number of others.

(b)   Positions and Duties

As a general proposition, the officers of a nonprofit organization, and their respective duties and responsibilities, are as follows:

(i) President. The president is the principal executive officer of the organization and in general supervises and controls all of the business and affairs of the entity. He or she presides at meetings of the governing board (unless there is a chair of the board). The president signs, often with one other officer of the organization (usually the secretary), any contracts (including leases) or other documents required to be executed on behalf of the organization (such as mortgages, deeds, or bonds). The bylaws of the organization should provide that the president is to perform all duties "generally incident to" the office of president.

(ii) Vice President. In the absence of the president, or in the event of the president's inability or refusal to act, the vice president performs the duties of the president. A nonprofit organization may have more than one vice president. The nature of the scope of a vice president's responsibility may be reflected in the individual's title (such as Vice President for Community Relations or Vice President for Government Relations).

(iii) Treasurer. The treasurer has charge and custody of and is responsible for all funds, securities, and perhaps other property of the organization. He or she receives and gives receipts for money due and payable to the organization, and deposits such money in the name of the organization in the banks, trust companies, or other depositories selected by the organization. The treasurer may make investments, pursuant to an overall investment policy developed by the organization's board.[119] The bylaws of the organization should provide that the treasurer is to perform all duties "generally incident to" the office of treasurer. If required by the board, the treasurer has to provide a bond (at the organization's expense) for the faithful discharge of the treasurer's duties in such sum and with such surety or sureties as the board determines.

(iv) Secretary. The secretary is responsible for preparation of the minutes of the meetings of the board of the organization. He or she has the responsibility to give all notices in accordance with the organization's bylaws or as required by law. The secretary is custodian of the record and of the seal (if any) of the organization. The secretary is to keep a register of the addresses of each member of the board of the organization (and perhaps each member of the organization). The secretary may be required to sign certain documents, along with the president. The bylaws of the organization should provide that the secretary is to perform all duties "generally incident to" the office of secretary.

(c)   Origins

The officers of a nonprofit organization are usually elected, either by a membership or by the organization's board of directors. In some instances, the officers of a nonprofit organization are ex officio with, or are selected by, another organization. The basic choices are:

- Election by a membership
- Election by the directors, who have been elected by members
- Election by the directors, who are a self-perpetuating board
- Election (or appointment) by the board of another organization
- A combination of two or more of the foregoing options

(d)   Governing Instruments

The governing instruments of a nonprofit organization (usually the bylaws) should identify the officers of the organization, and state the duties and responsibilities of each position,[120] provide for the manner of their election (or other selection),[121] state the terms of the offices, and address the matter of reelections to office (including any term limits).

---

119. See *supra* note 86.
120. See § 2.2(b).
121. See § 2.2(c).

For the most part, the law allows a nonprofit organization to use whatever governing structure it wants. In most states, a nonprofit corporations law contains rules (some mandatory, some optional) concerning officers, terms of office, and the like.

Particularly if the nonprofit organization is a corporation, state law usually requires at least certain officers. In general, the same individual can hold more than one office; the positions of secretary and treasurer are commonly combined. The president and secretary, however, should not be the same individual. (The law in many states prohibits this duality.) Frequently, legal documents will require these two officers' separate signatures.

Officers are officers of the organization. They are not officers of the board of directors. An exception to this can be the chair of the board; this individual may be considered an "officer" of the board.

§ 2.3 KEY EMPLOYEES

The law, including the federal tax law, recognizes that an individual can have significant duties and responsibilities with respect to a nonprofit organization and not be a trustee, director, or officer. A *key employee* is an employee of the organization that has powers and responsibilities that are *similar to* those of a trustee, director, or officer.[122] There often are special reporting requirements for these individuals.[123] Also, they are usually disqualified persons for purposes of the intermediate sanctions rules[124] and the private foundation self-dealing rules,[125] and insiders for purposes of the doctrine of private inurement.[126] An obvious example of a key employee of a nonprofit organization is the executive director; other key employees are likely to include the chief operating officer and chief financial officer (where they are not formally officers).

§ 2.4 MANAGEMENT COMPANIES

A nonprofit organization may use the services of a management company. This type of company does not supplant the need for directors and officers of the organization, although it may obviate the necessity of one or more employees.

There is nothing inherently inappropriate about use of a management company by a nonprofit organization. Nonetheless, the IRS tends to accord these arrangements particular scrutiny.[127] For example, if members of the board of the management company also serve as members of the board of the nonprofit organization, or there are other business and/or family ties between the two entities, the agency is likely to be acutely sensitive to the potential for private inurement, private benefit, self-dealing, and/or excess benefit transactions.[128] In some instances, the IRS may be inclined to characterize a management company–nonprofit organization relationship as a joint venture, often with adverse (to the nonprofit organization) tax law consequences.[129]

---

122. See *Planning Guide*, pages 193, 200–201.
123. E.g., Form 990, Schedule J.
124. See *Law of Tax-Exempt Organizations* § 21.3.
125. See *id*. § 12.2.
126. See *id*. § 20.3.
127. E.g., Form 1023, Part II, question 10a. Form 990.
128. See *Law of Tax-Exempt Organizations*, Chapters 20, 21, and § 12.4(a).
129. See *id*., § 30.1(c).

§2.5 BOARD MEMBER RESPONSIBILITIES

In today's litigious society, avoidance of a lawsuit—in any context—cannot be guaranteed. Rules prohibiting frivolous suits are rarely enforced; litigation can seemingly ensue over just about anything. There are, however, a number of steps that members of the board of a nonprofit organization can take to minimize (or perhaps even eliminate) the likelihood of a lawsuit against the organization—and against themselves.

(a) Understand Organization's Form

Every member of the board of a nonprofit organization should understand the form of the entity.[130] The board member should also know what is required to maintain that form—and see to it that the necessary action (or actions) is taken. For example, an organization that is incorporated can lose its corporate status if it fails to timely file annual reports with the state in which it is incorporated.

Moreover, if the nonprofit organization is not incorporated, it is incumbent on the board member to understand why that is the case. If the entity is to remain unincorporated, the board member should be satisfied by being provided (by a lawyer) at least one good reason for this status. An unincorporated organization almost always can become incorporated.[131]

(b) Understand Organization's Purposes/Mission

The board member should understand and be able to articulate the nonprofit organization's mission. The scope of this understanding entails knowledge of the organization's *purposes*. For this, the individual should contemplate the statement of purposes contained in the entity's articles of organization. If the purposes are not understood, the board member should obtain a suitable explanation. There may be a mission statement that, as noted, is in addition to, and perhaps more expansive than, the statement of purposes. The board member should be satisfied that the statement of purposes and the mission statement are consistent.

Statements of purpose and mission statements are not intractable. The board member should be satisfied with the language of both, particularly the statement of purposes. It may be that the statement should be updated (articles amended). The organization may have a statement of purposes that is not adequately reflective of its contemporary goals and objectives.

(c) Understand Activities

Just as the board member should understand the nonprofit organization's purposes, he or she should also understand and remain informed as to each of the organization's *activities*.[132] The member should be able to explain what they are and why they

---

130. See § 1.2(e).
131. An entity organized as a trust may have to obtain court approval to convert to a corporation. Change of form means, by definition, that a new legal entity has been created, with resultant legal consequences, such as the need to seek a ruling from the IRS as to the tax-exempt status (if any) of the organization (see *Law of Tax-Exempt Organizations* § 27.1(b)).
132. See, e.g., Form 990, Part III.

are conducted and should know the connection between the organization's operations and furtherance of its purposes.

The nonprofit organization's activities may include lobbying. If so, the board member should be satisfied that the lobbying is appropriate for the organization and that it is not jeopardizing its tax-exempt status.[133] The same is true with respect to any political campaign activities.[134]

If the nonprofit organization engages in fundraising activities, the board member should understand what they are. The member should make some effort to be satisfied that the organization is using the types of fundraising that are suitable for it and its objectives. Fundraising is not program, however; rather, it is a means to advance program and should be kept in that perspective.

The nonprofit organization may conduct one or more unrelated businesses.[135] There is nothing inherently wrong with unrelated activity, but the board member should know why the business is being conducted, be certain it does not detract from program undertakings, and be satisfied that the organization's tax-exempt status is not being endangered.

(d) Understand Articles of Organization

The board member of a nonprofit organization should understand each article of the entity's articles of organization[136]—what it means and why it is in the document. Of particular importance are the statement of purposes and any dissolution clause.

Other provisions to review and understand are those describing the organization's membership (if any) and provisions in the document that are reflective of federal tax law requirements and limitations.

(e) Understand Structure/Bylaws

The board member of a nonprofit organization should understand the tax-exempt organization's bylaws. This document spells out (or should spell out) the entity's basic governance and operational structure.[137] The following should be checked: (1) the origin, composition, and stated duties of the organization's directors; (2) the origins and duties of the organization's officers; (3) the qualification and functions of any members; (4) the rules as to conduct of meetings (such as notice, quorum, voting); (5) the organization's committee structure; (6) provisions as to any indemnification (although state law may require that the provisions be in the articles); and (7) provisions as to any immunity (again, the language may have to be in the articles).

(f) Understand Other Documents

The board member of a nonprofit organization should understand the reason for, and the content of, other documents published by and/or prepared for the organization. These include annual reports, promotional materials (brochures, pamphlets), fundraising materials, newsletters, and journals. Of course, if a program activity of the

---

133. See *Law of Tax-Exempt Organizations,* Chapter 22.
134. See *id.,* Chapter 23.
135. See *id,* Chapter 24.
136. See § 1.2(a).
137. *Id.*

organization is publishing, it is not necessary that the board member read every book or other publication of the organization.

There are other documents—those that have some import in the law—that the board member should understand. They include any documents that are required to be filed with a state, such as annual reports and reports filed pursuant to one or more charitable solicitation acts. The board member should understand the organization's conflict-of-interest policy (if any)[138] and have at least a general familiarity with its insurance policies. Employment contracts should also be understood.

There are other documents of considerable importance that each board member should review in draft. These are the annual financial statement (if any), the annual information return filed with the IRS,[139] and any unrelated business income tax return[140] filed with that agency. If the board member does not understand material in these documents, questions should be asked. If the organization is not required to file an annual information return, the member should know why (such as the organization is small or is a church).[141]

(g) Related Entities

A nonprofit organization often is not a solitary entity; it may be a part of a cluster of entities. For example, a membership association may have a related foundation, a political action committee, and/or a for-profit subsidiary.[142] A charitable organization may have a separate organization that functions as a "lobbying arm" or an advocacy organization may have a related educational foundation.[143] The board member should understand why these discrete entities exist, what their functions are, and how the relationships are structured.

Other entities that may be involved are partnerships, limited liability companies, and/or other forms of joint ventures.[144] In the case of multiple related entities, what has been said above may be true for all of them. For example, the board member may be well advised to review and understand the documents pertaining to each of these entities.

(h) Doing Business Requirements

The board member of a nonprofit organization should know the jurisdiction(s) in which the entity *does business*. (That term, while it sounds as though it applies only with respect to commercial enterprises, also applies with respect to nonprofit organizations.) Certainly, the organization is doing business in the state in which its offices are located.

A nonprofit organization, however, may also be doing business in one or more other jurisdictions. An obvious illustration of this is an office or some other manifestation of a physical presence in another state. The precepts in law as to what constitutes *doing business* vary from state to state, however; an organization can be considered to

---

138. See *supra* note 82.
139. See *Law of Tax-Exempt Organizations* § 27.2.
140. See *id.* § 27.7.
141. See *id.* § 27.2(b).
142. See *id.*, Chapters 28, 29.
143. *Id.*
144. See *id.*, Chapter 30.

be doing business in a state where there is less of a presence than a formal office.[145] If the organization is doing business in other jurisdictions, the board member should be advised of those locations and understand why the organization is being deemed engaged in business.

(i) Public Charity Status

If the nonprofit organization is a charitable one, the board member should know whether it is a public charity or a private foundation.[146] If it is a public charity, the board member should know the organization's classification for this purpose. The choices are (1) one of the *institutions*, such as a school, college, university, hospital, other healthcare provider, medical research organization, church, or the like; (2) a *publicly supported organization*, with the required amount of its support derived from gifts, grants, and/or exempt function (program service) revenue; or (3) a *supporting organization*.

Much of the law pertaining to private foundations focuses on transactions with, or in relation to, disqualified persons. In many instances, however, it is necessary that a public charity understand who the disqualified persons are with respect to it. The most obvious example of this is the intermediate sanctions rules.[147] Each board member should know who the organization's disqualified persons are.

(j) Perspective

The premise of the foregoing is that the member of the board of directors of a nonprofit organization who understands the foregoing legal aspects of the organization's structure and operations is far less likely to attract legal liability than the board member who acts (or fails to act) with lack of knowledge of these points.

§2.6 PROTECTIONS AGAINST PERSONAL LIABILITY

Actions by or on behalf of a nonprofit organization can give rise to personal liability. The term *personal liability* means, in this context, that one or more managers of a nonprofit organization (its trustees, directors, officers, and/or key employees) may be found personally liable for something done (commission) or not done (omission) while acting in the name of the organization.

Some of this exposure can be limited, or perhaps eliminated, by one or all of the following:

- Incorporation
- Indemnification
- Insurance
- Immunity

---

145. See *Planning Guide*, Chapter 1, pages 23–24.
146. See *Law of Tax-Exempt Organizations* §§ 12.1, 12.3.
147. See *id*, Chapter 21.

(a) Incorporation

The matter of incorporation is discussed above, in the context of choice of form.[148] To reiterate, a corporation is regarded in the law as a separate legal entity that can attract legal liability. This liability is generally confined to the organization and thus does not normally extend to those who set policy for or manage it. (This is one of the principal reasons a nonprofit organization should be a corporation.)

(b) Indemnification

Indemnification occurs (assuming it, or the scope of it, is legal under state law) when the organization agrees (usually by provision in its bylaws) to pay the judgments and related expenses (including legal fees) incurred by those who are covered by the indemnity, when those expenses are the result of a misdeed (commission or omission) by those persons while acting in the service of the organization. This indemnification cannot extend to criminal acts; it may not cover certain willful acts that violate civil law.

Because an indemnification involves the resources of the organization, the efficacy of it depends on the economic viability of the organization. In times of financial difficulties for a nonprofit organization, with little in the way of assets and revenue flow, an indemnification of its directors and officers can be a classic "hollow promise."

(c) Insurance

Insurance (directors' and officers' (D&O) insurance) has features somewhat comparable to indemnification. Instead of shifting the risk of liability from the individuals involved to the nonprofit organization (indemnification), however, with insurance the risk of the liability is shifted to an independent third party—an insurance company. Certain risks, such as criminal law liability, cannot be shifted by means of insurance (because it would be contrary to public policy). The insurance contract will likely exclude from coverage certain forms of civil law liability, such as defamation, employee discrimination, and/or antitrust matters.[149]

Even where adequate insurance coverage is available, insurance can be costly. Premiums can easily be thousands of dollars annually, even with a sizable deductible.

A nonprofit organization can purchase insurance to fund one or more indemnities it has made of its directors and officers.

(d) Immunity

Immunity is available when the law provides that a class of individuals, under certain circumstances, is not liable for a particular act or set of acts or for failure to undertake a particular act or set of acts. Several states have enacted immunity laws for directors and officers of nonprofit organizations, protecting them in the case of asserted civil law violations, particularly where these individuals are functioning as volunteers.

---

148. See §§ 1.2(a), (d).
149. Caution should be exercised here; the contents of the exclusions portion of the insurance contract may render the proposed coverage essentially useless.

§ 2.7 MINIMIZING BOARD MEMBER LIABILITY

The board member who is knowledgeable about the nonprofit organization's programs and other operations is a board member who is not likely to do (or not do) or
say something that will result in legal liability, either for the organization or personally. Here are some practical steps the board members can take to enhance this
knowledge and minimize the prospects of legal liability.

(a) Creation of Board Book

Each board member of a nonprofit organization should have, and keep up to date, a
board book. It need not be particularly formal or fancy; a simple three-ring binder
will suffice. In this book should be, at a minimum, the following documents: the
board address list,[150] the organization's articles of organization, its bylaws, any other
documents with legal overtones (such as a mission statement or conflict-of-interest
policy), recent board meeting minutes, a copy of any ruling from the IRS recognizing
the organization as a tax-exempt entity, the most recently filed state report, the most
recent financial statement, and the most recent three annual information returns.

  Other documents that may be included are recent committee reports, a copy of
the organization's application for recognition of tax exemption, and the most recent
unrelated business income tax return (if any).

(b) Board Address List

Each member of the board of a nonprofit organization should have and keep in the
board book a current list of the organization's board members. This list should contain each individual's mailing address, telephone numbers (office, home, cell, car,
pager), fax number, and e-mail address.

(c) E-mail Communications System

There should be a system by which the board members of a nonprofit organization
can communicate by e-mail. Each member should have a group listing of all of the
board members. These individuals should communicate by e-mail to the extent practicable, although e-mail messaging is not a substitute for formal board meetings.

  Board members should be careful as to what is said in e-mail messages; every-
thing should be written from the perspective that it may someday become public.
(E-mail messages can be used in civil and criminal cases as evidence.[151]) Matters that
have confidential aspects (such as the processing of ethics cases) should be discussed
cautiously (if at all) by e-mail.

(d) Minutes

Careful consideration should be given to board meeting minutes.[152] There should be
minutes of every board meeting. (Committee meetings also should be the subject of
minutes.) Minutes should be prepared with a heavy dose of common sense and

---

150. See § 2.5(b).
151. From a lawyer's perspective, *e-mail* means *evidence-mail* or *exhibit-mail*.
152. See *Planning Guide*, Chapter 1, pages 17–18.

perspective. These documents are not transcripts of the proceedings but summaries of important actions, often including resolutions.

It is difficult to generalize about the length and contents of board meeting minutes. Usually, whether something should have been in the minutes and is not, or whether something should not have been stated in the minutes and is, is determined in hindsight. The best practice is to be certain that all material decisions and actions are reflected, and be careful that nothing damaging to the organization is in the document.[153]

If a board member opposes a majority board action on a matter and is sufficiently concerned about the seriousness of the issue, he or she should be certain that this opposition is reflected in the minutes, perhaps coupled with an explanation of the board member's position.

A good practice is for the secretary to provide a draft of the minutes to legal counsel for review and, if necessary, revision before they are circulated to the board members for their review and adoption. In general, solid and current minutes are one of the most important of the "corporate" formalities to observe.

(e) Attendance at Meetings

It is critical that the board members of a nonprofit organization attend each of the meetings of the board. There will obviously be schedule conflicts; if the board member cannot attend a meeting, the minutes should reflect that fact and why. A board member cannot exercise the requisite degree of fiduciary responsibility without attending meetings and interacting with the other members.

The director should actively participate in the decision-making process. Silence is deemed to be concurrence. If a director is opposed to an action to be undertaken by the organization at the behest of the board, the director should speak up and, as noted, be certain to have his or her dissent noted in the minutes.

(f) Understanding What Is Going On

A summary of the aspects of a nonprofit organization's structure and operations, involving legal matters, that a board member should know is provided elsewhere.[154] This understanding needs to be ongoing, as purposes are revised or expanded, programs change, and documents are amended. It is essential that the board member know these basics and build on that base of knowledge as the organization evolves.

(g) Asking Questions

Probably one of the worst nonactions of a board member of a nonprofit organization is failure to ask questions. The board member who merely pretends to understand what is taking place is only fooling himself or herself, and is placed in a position to cause harm—to the organization or to himself or herself.

Questions may be asked of other board members, the organization's officers, and/or staff. Questions may be posed during the course of a board meeting or on

---

153. From a lawyer's perspective, minutes should be written with the assumption that, someday, the document will be an exhibit in a trial.
154. See Chapter 8.

other occasions. Inquiries can be made by e-mail, although caution should be exercised as to how those messages are framed.[155] Questions can be asked of lawyers and other professionals.

Some boards of nonprofit organizations do not meet without the organization's lawyer present. Others make decisions, conditioned on the procurement of favorable legal advice.

(h) Oversight of Staff

The board of a nonprofit organization should oversee the activities of the organization's staff. The board should not micromanage yet should have sufficient knowledge of the role of each staff member and a general understanding as to their performance.

How this works in practice will vary considerably. If the organization has an executive director, most of this information should be provided by that individual. (Again, questions should be asked.) Some boards prefer to meet only when the organization's executive director is present. (Indeed, in some instances, the executive director is a member of the board, perhaps a nonvoting member.) Others do that but reserve some time to meet without that individual (or other staff) present.

(i) Conflict-of-Interest Policy

While for the most part it is not required as a matter of law, a nonprofit organization—particularly a charitable one—should give serious consideration to adoption of a conflict-of-interest policy.[156] For one thing, the IRS is pushing this as a condition of recognition of tax-exempt status. More importantly, this type of policy enables a nonprofit organization to identify its insiders/disqualified persons and know at the time whether it is entering into transactions with them.

(j) Intermediate Sanctions Compliance

Board members of most nonprofit organizations certainly should be aware of the intermediate sanctions rules.[157] This is the case, if only because the penalties for violation of these rules are imposed, not on the organization, but on the disqualified persons with respect to the organization. The disqualified persons with respect to the organization almost certainly will include members of the organization's board.

(k) Reading Materials about Nonprofit Boards

There is an immense amount of literature concerning the role of members of the board of nonprofit organizations, plus material on the operations of exempt organizations as such.[158] Board members are advised to read as much of this literature as possible.

---

155. See § 2.7(c).
156. See *supra* note 82.
157. See *Law of Tax-Exempt Organizations*, Chapter 21.
158. See, e.g., Hopkins, *Starting and Managing a Nonprofit Organization: A Legal Guide, Fifth Edition* (Hoboken, NJ: John Wiley & Sons, 2009).

(l) Attending Seminars

Seminars that are of considerable utility to individuals in their capacity as board members of nonprofit organizations are presented. Just as publications are recommended, so, too, are seminars of this nature—at least one annually.

(m) Retreats

The board of directors of a nonprofit organization should consider having a periodic—perhaps annual—board retreat. This is an opportunity for the board members to escape their employment and family responsibilities, and focus—if only for a few hours—on the contemporary mission and goals of the organization. This experience can help place the nonprofit organization's activities in perspective and help the board member understand more fully its structure and operations.

At this retreat, various outside consultants can make their appearance, share their expertise, give the board members the opportunity to ask questions, and provide the board with a sense of the state of the organization. The board should consider use of a consultant for this purpose, to enhance the retreat with an outside perspective and facilitate a more directed focus.

(n) Overall Authority

The board of a nonprofit organization should not exceed its authority. The members of the board serve as overseers. Their role is to make extraordinary, not ordinary, decisions. Day-to-day management of the organization should be left to the officers and the executive staff.

CHAPTER THREE

Nonprofit Organizations' Governance Principles

Regulators, lawmakers, and other policymakers at the federal and state level are intensely focusing on the subject of the principles of governance of nonprofit, tax-exempt organizations, with an emphasis on public charities. Among the manifestations of these analyses are the emergence and refinement of a variety of written policies.

§3.1 GOVERNANCE PHILOSOPHY IN GENERAL

In some quarters, the philosophy underlying the concept of governance of nonprofit organizations is changing. The traditional roles of the nonprofit board have been oversight of the organization's operations and policy determination; historically, the implementation of policy and management have been the responsibilities of the officers and key employees. An emerging view, sometimes referred to as *best practices*, imposes on the nonprofit board greater responsibilities and functions (and thus potentially greater liability), intended to immerse the board more deeply in management. This new view is nicely reflected in the characterization of the nonprofit board in the American National Red Cross Governance Modernization Act: the "governance and strategic oversight board."[1]

The origins of this shift of view regarding the appropriate role of the governing board of a nonprofit organization are difficult to find. There has been the occasional scandal in the nonprofit management context, such as that involving the United Way of America;[2] these scandals in the nonprofit realm have increased somewhat in recent years, due in large part to greater focus by the media on charitable organizations and the various investigations conducted by the staff of the Senate Finance Committee.[3] These incidents alone, however, do not account for the contemporary magnitude of

---

1. See § 3.11.
2. E.g., Glaser, *The United Way Scandal: An Insider's Account of What Went Wrong and Why* (New York: John Wiley & Sons, 1994)
3. Entities that have been and are the subject of these inquiries include the American National Red Cross, American University, the Nature Conservancy, the Smithsonian Institution, and the Statue of Liberty Foundation, along with, in general, tax-exempt hospitals, colleges, and universities (particularly as to student athletics and use of endowment funds) and evangelical church ministries. See Chapter 7.

interest in nonprofit organization governance. Certainly, a major factor contributing to this phenomenon is the raft of recent scandals in the for-profit sector and the resulting enactment of the Sarbanes-Oxley Act, which has had an enormous impact on the evolution, over the past few years, of nonprofit organization governance principles and practices.

§3.2 SARBANES-OXLEY ACT

Historic federal accounting reform and for-profit corporate responsibility legislation—the Sarbanes-Oxley Act—was signed into law in 2002.[4] This measure is focused on publicly traded companies and large accounting firms. The emergence of this law, however, raises a number of questions for nonprofit organizations as to the applicability of the Act's principles to them; the leadership of these organizations often voluntarily adopts many of its precepts.

(a) Terminology

There are certain terms that are essential to understand for appreciation of the scope of this body of law as it relates to tax-exempt organizations.

An *audit committee* is a committee established "by and amongst" the board of directors of an issuer (see below) for the purpose of overseeing the accounting and financial reporting processes of the issuer and audits of the financial statements of the issuer.

An *audit report* is a document prepared following an audit performed for purposes of compliance by an issuer with the securities laws, and in which a public accounting firm either states the opinion of the firm regarding a financial statement, report, or other document, or asserts that such an opinion cannot be expressed.

A *code of ethics* means standards that are reasonably necessary to promote honest and ethical conduct, including the handling of conflicts of interest; full, fair, accurate, timely, and understandable disclosure in reports of an issuer; and compliance with applicable governmental rules and regulations.

A *financial expert* is an individual who has an understanding of generally accepted accounting principles and financial statements and experience in the application of these principles, the preparation or auditing of financial statements, and internal accounting controls, as well as an understanding of audit committee functions.

An *issuer* is a for-profit corporation, the stock of which is registered pursuant to the federal securities laws, that is otherwise required to comply with those laws, including the filing of reports (also known as a *public company*).

Nonaudit services means any professional services provided to an issuer by a registered public accounting firm other than those provided to an issuer in connection with an audit or review of the financial statements of an issuer.

A *public accounting firm* is a legal entity (such as a corporation or partnership) that is engaged in the practice of public accounting or preparing or issuing audit reports. A *registered public accounting firm* is a public accounting firm that is registered with the Oversight Board (see below).

---

4. Pub. L. No. 107-204, 116 Stat. 745 (2002).

(b) Principal Features of Act

(i) Public Company and Accounting Oversight Board. The Public Company and Accounting Oversight Board (Board), the members of which are appointed by the Securities and Exchange Commission (SEC), was established. The Board has five full-time members with five-year terms; two of the members may be certified public accountants. These members must be "prominent," possess "integrity and reputation," have a "demonstrated commitment to the interests of investors and the public," and have an "understanding of the responsibilities for and nature of the financial disclosures required of issuers under the securities laws and the obligations of accountants with respect to the preparation and issuance of audit reports with respect to such disclosures."

The purpose of this Board is to "oversee the audit of public companies that are subject to the securities laws, and related matters, in order to protect the interests of investors and further the public interest in the preparation of informative, accurate, and independent audit reports for companies the securities of which are sold to, and held by and for, public investors." The Board is required to submit an annual report to the SEC.

The Board is not part of the federal government but, rather, is a District of Columbia nonprofit corporation. However, only Congress can dissolve it. It is empowered to accept contributions. The statute is silent as to the tax-exempt status of the Board (the Act is not tax legislation).

The Board's duties include (1) registration of public accounting firms that prepare audit reports for issuers; (2) adoption of auditing, quality control, ethics, independence, and other standards relating to the preparation of audit reports for issuers; (3) conducting of inspections of registered public accounting firms; (4) conducting of investigations and disciplinary proceedings concerning, and imposing sanctions on, registered public accounting firms and persons associated with these firms; (5) other promotion of "high professional standards among, and improve[ment of] the quality of audit services offered by, registered public accounting firms and associated persons thereof"; and (6) enforcement of compliance with this law, the rules of the Board, and related securities laws.

(ii) Board Funding. The Board established an "annual accounting support fee" for purposes of establishing and maintaining the Board. These fees (and fees to fund an accounting standards setting body) are paid by and allocated among issuers.

Funds collected by the Board from the assessment of penalties are used to fund a "merit scholarship program" for undergraduate and graduate students enrolled in accredited accounting degree programs. The Board or an entity selected by it administers this program.

(iii) Registration with Board. It is unlawful for a person that is not a registered public accounting firm to prepare or issue, or to participate in the preparation or issuance of, an audit report with respect to an issuer. The legislation detailed the contents of the application for registration, which includes a listing of clients (issuers) and the fees paid by them for audit and other services. These applications generally are publicly available. Each registered public accounting firm pays a registration fee and an annual fee.

(iv) Standards. The Board established "auditing and related attestation standards, . . . quality control standards, and . . . ethical standards" used by registered public accounting firms in the preparation and issuance of audit reports.

These rules include a seven-year records retention requirement, a rule as to second partner review of audit reports, and rules describing in each audit report the scope of the auditor's "internal control structure and procedures of the issuer."

In this connection, the Board may establish advisory groups. It is to "cooperate on an ongoing basis" with these groups and with professional groups of accountants.

(v) Inspections. The Board conducts a "continuing program of inspections" to assess compliance by registered public accounting firms (and associated persons) with this law, rules of the SEC and the Board, or professional standards, in connection with its performance of audits, issuance of audit reports, and related matters.

If a firm regularly provides audit reports for more than 100 issuers, the inspection must be done annually. Otherwise, the review must be at least once every three years. The Board can adjust this inspection schedule and conduct special inspections.

(vi) Investigations. The Board established "fair procedures" for the investigation and disciplining of registered public accounting firms (and associated persons). These investigations pertain to alleged violations of this law, Board rules, and securities laws pertaining to the preparation and issuance of audit reports.

The statute detailed the procedures these investigations are to follow, including disciplinary procedures, sanctions, and suspensions.

(vii) Nonaudit Services. The law amended the securities laws to generally make it unlawful for a registered public accounting firm that performs an audit for an issuer to provide to that issuer, contemporaneously with the audit, any nonaudit service. The Board has the authority to grant exemptions.

These services include bookkeeping services, financial information systems design and implementation, appraisal services, fairness opinions, actuarial services, internal audit outsourcing services, investment adviser services, and legal services.

(viii) Audit Partner Rotation. The statute amended the securities laws to make it unlawful for a registered public accounting firm to provide audit services to an issuer if the lead (or coordinating) audit partner, or the audit partner responsible for reviewing the audit, has performed audit services for that issuer in each of the five previous fiscal years of the issuer.

The statute provides for a study of mandatory rotation of registered public accounting firms.

(ix) Audit Committees. The law in essence mandated the creation and functioning of audit committees of issuers. This is done, in part, by requiring the SEC to in turn direct the national securities exchanges and associations to prohibit the listing of the securities of issuers who fail to establish and use these committees.

The audit committee of an issuer must be directly responsible for the appointment, compensation, and oversight of the work of a registered public accounting firm employed by the issuer for the purpose of preparing or issuing an audit report or related work. Each such registered public accounting firm must report directly to the audit committee.

Each member of an audit committee must be a member of the board of directors of the issuer involved. He or she may not accept any consulting, advisory, or other compensation from the issuer.

The SEC issued rules to require each issuer to disclose whether or not, and if not why not, the audit committee of the issuer is comprised of at least one member who is a financial expert.

(x) Corporate Responsibility. The law requires the principal executive officer and principal financial officer of an issuer to certify each annual or quarterly report filed by the issuer in compliance with the securities laws. This includes certification that the report does not contain any untrue statement of a material fact or failure to state a material fact "necessary in order to make the statements made . . . not misleading."

If an issuer is required to prepare an accounting restatement due to the "material noncompliance" of the issuer, as a result of misconduct, with a financial reporting requirement under the securities laws, the chief executive officer and chief financial officer of the issuer must reimburse the issuer for any bonus or other incentive-based or equity-based compensation received by that individual from the issuer during a prior 12-month period. This disgorgement rule can also encompass profits realized from the sale of stock of the issuer.

It is generally unlawful for an issuer to extend or maintain credit in the form of a personal loan to or for any director or executive officer of that issuer. This includes the use of a subsidiary for this purpose.

Corporations are required to provide protection to employees and others who are whistleblowers, and this law imposes criminal penalties for destruction of documents and other evidence in the face of a government investigation.

A person who is the beneficial owner of more than 10% of any class of a registered equity security must file a statement with the SEC. This includes nonprofit organizations.

The SEC issued rules requiring each issuer to disclose whether or not, and if not why not, the issuer has adopted a code of ethics for senior financial officers.

(xi) Lawyers. The SEC, in accordance with this statute, issued rules setting forth minimum standards of professional conduct for lawyers practicing before the SEC. These rules require a lawyer to report evidence of a "major violation of securities law or breach of fiduciary duty or similar violation by the company" to the chief legal counsel or the chief executive officer of the company.

If there is not an appropriate response to the evidence presented, including remedial measures, the lawyer is to report the evidence to the audit committee of the issuer or another committee of the board.

(xii) Disgorgement Funds. If the SEC obtains a disgorgement order against a person for violation of the securities laws, and that includes a civil penalty, the penalty is to be added to and become part of a disgorgement fund for the benefit of the victims of the violation.

The SEC is authorized to accept and utilize gifts, bequests, and devises for one or more of these funds. (The law does not address the point but these contributions are deductible as charitable gifts.)

(xiii) Real-Time Disclosures. This law amended the securities to require reporting issuers to disclose to the public, on a "rapid and current basis," additional information concerning material changes in the financial condition or operations of the issuer, in "plain English." This type of disclosure may include "trend and qualitative information and graphic presentations."

(xiv) Other Provisions. The SEC, pursuant to this law, issued rules for the disclosure of material off-balance-sheet transactions. An accountant who conducts an audit of an issuer is required to maintain all audit or review workpapers for five years. A criminal law provision concerns the knowing destruction or falsification of corporate records with intent to impede or influence a federal investigation.[5]

(c) Import of Act for Nonprofit Organizations

This body of law does not, as noted, apply to nonprofit organizations (other than protection of whistleblowers and the criminal law rule concerning destruction of evidence). Again, it generally applies to, and with respect to, issuers and public accounting firms. Nonetheless, Sarbanes-Oxley standards for corporate governance parallel in many ways the fiduciary principles applicable to exempt organizations; developments with respect to the Act will inevitably help shape corporate governance standards for exempt organizations.[6]

Those who manage tax-exempt organizations, and perhaps those who make contributions to them, may want to give consideration to some or all of the following: whether (1) the accounting firm retained by an exempt organization should be a registered public accounting firm; (2) an exempt organization should have an audit committee or similar body;[7] (3) an exempt organization should develop a code of ethics for its senior officers (this would go beyond a conflict-of-interest policy); (4) an exempt organization should require certification of its financial statements and/or annual information returns by its executive; (5) an exempt organization should have a policy of prohibiting loans to its senior executives; (6) in an instance of a need for an accounting restatement by an exempt organization, due to some form of misconduct, any bonuses and/or the like to executive personnel should be reimbursed; (7) an exempt organization should follow the rules as to audit partner rotation; (8) an exempt organization should separate audit and nonaudit service providers; (9) an exempt organization's lawyers should be required to report breaches of fiduciary responsibility to its president or similar executive officer; and (10) there should be a rule requiring real-time disclosures by tax-exempt organizations.[8] Given the increasing focus on compensation matters,[9] an exempt organization, particularly a charitable entity, may want to consider establishing a compensation committee.[10]

---

5. In general, Kim, "Sarbanes-Oxley Act," 40 *Harv. J. on Legis.* 235 (Winter 2003).
6. In general, Fairfax, "The Sarbanes-Oxley Act: Confirmation of Recent Trends in Director and Officer Fiduciary Obligations," 76 *St. Johns L. Rev.* 953 (Fall 2002).
7. In general, Vanderwarren, "Financial Accountability in Charitable Organizations: Mandating an Audit Committee," 77 *Chi.-Kent L. Rev.* 963 (2002).
8. In general, Anft and Williams, "Redefining Good Governance," XVI *Chron. Of Phil.* (No. 21) 6 (August 10, 2004).
9. See *Law of Tax-Exempt Organizations* § 20.4.
10. In general, Peregrine, DeJong, and Cotter, "New EO Focus—The Board Compensation Committee," 43 *Ex. Org. Tax Rev.* (No. 3) 265 (March 2004).

Congress may enact corporate responsibility legislation applicable to tax-exempt organizations. Also, corporate responsibility principles applicable to exempt entities are embedded, directly or indirectly, in the application for recognition of exemption filed by charitable organizations[11] and the annual information return.[12] The recent revisions of these documents reflect corporate responsibility concepts, such as the adoption of conflict-of-interest policies and governing board practices as to the setting and review of compensation arrangements with senior executives. Enactment of the Act has, at a minimum, reinforced the existence and the importance of the common-law duties imposed on directors.[13]

§ 3.3   WATCHDOG AGENCIES' STANDARDS

Charitable organizations, particularly those that are engaged in fundraising, often become subject to standards set and enforced by a watchdog agency. Watchdog agencies, while not promulgators of law, can have a powerful impact on the public perception of a charitable organization and its ability to successfully generate gifts and grants. Indeed, watchdog agencies have long been in the forefront of standards-setting for nonprofit organizations.[14]

Charitable organizations that are caught up in watchdog agencies' standards enforcement and public rankings often believe they are powerless to offset the reviews and ratings of these agencies, yet in fact they have certain rights with respect to the standards themselves and the manner in which they are applied.

(a)   Watchdog Standards and Charities' Rights

For the most part, however, these rights cannot rise to the level of constitutional law protections, such as those accorded pursuant to the principles of due process enunciated in the Fifth and Fourteenth Amendments to the U.S. Constitution and in comparable provisions in the constitutions of the states. This is because due process rights are generally granted only with respect to actions by a government. The *state action doctrine*, however, can mandate adherence to due process requirements by a nongovernmental organization when there is sufficient entanglement between government and the nongovernmental group, such as in the form of support or activities in tandem.[15]

Nonetheless, where a nongovernmental organization promulgates and enforces standards, there are two situations where the law requires that the standards and the application of them be *fair*.

---

11. Form 1023. See *Law of Tax-Exempt Organizations* §§ 25.1–25.3.
12. Form 990. See *Law of Tax-Exempt Organizations* § 27.2.
13. See § 5.3(b).
14. See *Law of Fundraising*, Chapter 9.
15. E.g., Brentwood Academy v. Tennessee Secondary School Athletic Association, 531 U.S. 288 (2001); McGlotten v. Connally, 388 F. Supp. 488 (D.D.C. 1972). In general, *Law of Tax-Exempt Organizations* § 4.9. Thus, the state action doctrine could mandate applicability of due process standards to action by a watchdog agency where it is shown that, for example, an organization's status in relation to the standards is relied on by a state governmental agency in reaching a determination, under the state's charitable solicitation act, about the charitable organization.

The first of these situations is the presence of a significant economic factor. That is, where the power of the standards enforcement agency becomes so great as to cause adverse economic consequences to the charity that is ranked as not meeting standards, the courts can intervene to rectify the application of unfair standards or the unfair application of standards.[16] The test in either circumstance is whether the standards and/or the administration of them are *fair* or *reasonable*.[17] There is no question that the ratings of and reports on charitable organizations by watchdog agencies have economic consequences to the affected charities: individual and corporate donors rely on the listings to determine which organizations are to receive their gifts; private foundations and other grantors similarly rely on these listings to determine their grantees; state governmental agencies take the status of charities in relation to the independent agencies' standards into account in determining the status of charities under the states' charitable solicitation acts; and the IRS from time to time relies on the rankings of these agencies.[18] Moreover, the watchdog agencies readily provide information to the media, and the resulting publicity can cause one or more of the same three results to occur.

The second of these situations is when the agency's ratings power is in an area of public concern.[19] Again, there is little doubt that these agencies envision themselves as operating in the public interest, forcing disclosure of information to the public and otherwise acting for the benefit of prospective donors. Public reliance on the watchdog agencies' pronouncements has become so great as to make a national organization's fundraising success significantly dependent on a favorable rating, or to divert gifts from a national organization that receives a negative rating. A positive rating accorded a charity by a watchdog agency may well confer on the charity a significant "competitive" advantage in relation to one or more organizations that receive an adverse rating.

The foregoing two principles have been succinctly stated: "Self regulation programs should be based on clearly defined standards that plainly indicate what is considered proper and improper. Vague standards invite arbitrary action," and "[s]tandards once set also should be administered in a reasonable manner."[20]

The setting and application of standards by the watchdog agencies are squarely subject to both of these threshold tests, and fundamental fairness dictates that their enforcement of standards be on the basis of processes that are reasonable.

(b) Philanthropic Advisory Service Standards

The Philanthropic Advisory Service (PAS) was the division of the Council of Better Business Bureaus (CBBB) that monitored and reported on charitable organizations that solicit, nationwide, contributions and grants.[21] The primary goal of the division,

---

16. E.g., Falcone v. Middlesex County Medical Society, 170 A.2d 791 (N.J. 1961).

17. E.g., Higgins v. American Society of Clinical Pathologists, 238 A.2d 665 (N.J. 1968).

18. As noted (*supra* note 15), these latter two circumstances may likely trigger the state action principle in which the panoply of due process responsibilities would be visited upon the watchdog agency.

19. E.g., Marjorie Webster Junior College v. Middle States Association of Colleges & Secondary Schools, 302 F. Supp. 459 (D.D.C. 1969), *rev'd*, 432 F.2d 650 (D.C. Cir. 1970), *cert. denied*, 400 U.S. 963 (1970).

20. MacArthur, *Associations and the Antitrust Laws* 53, 54 (1976).

21. Although PAS focused mainly on charitable organizations, it also developed and distributed information on some lobbying and social welfare organizations described in IRC § 501(c)(4) and business membership groups described in IRC § 501(c)(6). See *Law of Tax-Exempt Organizations*, Chapters 13, 14.

which began substantive operations in 1971, was to promote ethical standards of business practices and protect consumers through self-regulation and monitoring activities. The PAS standards, which have been superseded by the Wise Giving Alliance standards,[22] are recounted here because of their historical significance as being one of the first efforts to disseminate and enforce a set of nonprofit governance principles.

PAS evaluated charitable organizations according to the "CBBB Standards for Charitable Solicitations."[23] These standards covered five basic areas: public accountability, use of funds, solicitations and informational materials, fundraising practices, and governance.

(i) Public Accountability. PAS required that a charity provide, on request, an annual report that included various items of information about the charity's purposes, current activities, governance, and finances. Additionally, a charity was required to provide on request a complete annual financial statement, including an accounting of all income and fundraising costs of controlled or affiliated entities.

A charity also was required to "present adequate information [in financial statements] to serve as a basis for informed decisions." According to the PAS, information needed as a basis for informed decisions included items such as significant categories of contributions or other income, expenses reported in categories corresponding to major programs and activities, a detailed description of expenses by "natural classification" (e.g., salaries, employee benefits, and postage), accurate presentation of fundraising and administrative costs, the total cost of multipurpose activities, and the method used for allocating costs among the activities.

Organizations that receive a substantial portion of their income as the result of fundraising activities of controlled or affiliated entities were required to provide, on request, an accounting of all income received by and fundraising costs incurred by these entities.

(ii) Use of Funds. PAS required that a charity spend a "reasonable percentage" of total income on programs, as well as a "reasonable percentage" of contributions on activities that are in accordance with donor expectations. In this context, PAS defined a "reasonable percentage" to mean "at least" 50%. Charities were also expected to ensure that their fundraising costs were "reasonable." In this context, fundraising costs were reasonable if those costs did "not exceed" 35% of related contributions. In the area of total fundraising and administrative costs, PAS standards also provided that these costs be "reasonable." In this latter context, these costs were reasonable if they did "not exceed" 50% of total income. A charity was expected to establish and exercise "adequate controls" over its disbursements.

Soliciting organizations were to substantiate, on request, their application of funds, in accordance with donor expectations, to the programs and other activities described in solicitations.

---

22. See § 3.3(c).
23. It produced other publications, including *PAS Reports on National Nonprofit Organizations; Tips on Charitable Giving;* "Give But Give Wisely," which was published bimonthly and listed the national charities generating the most inquiries to PAS; and the *Annual Charity Index,* which was a reference book featuring program descriptions and financial information on many national charities.

(iii) Solicitations and Informational Materials. PAS standards in this area required that the solicitation and informational materials be "accurate, truthful and not misleading, both in whole or in part." These terms were not defined. Solicitation materials also were required to include a "clear description" of the program and other activities for which funds were requested. Solicitations that described an issue, problem, need, or event but did not clearly describe the programs or other activities for which funds were requested did not meet the standard for accuracy and truthfulness.

Direct contact solicitations (including telephone appeals) were required to identify the solicitor and his or her relationship to the benefiting organization, the benefiting organization or cause, and the programs or other activities for which funds were requested. Solicitations in conjunction with the sale of goods, services, or admissions had to identify, among other things, the "actual or anticipated portion" of the sales or admission price that would benefit the charitable organization or cause.

(iv) Fundraising Practices. PAS standards for fundraising practices provided that soliciting organizations must "establish and exercise controls" over fundraising activities by their officers, employees, volunteers, consultants, and contractors, including the use of written contracts and agreements. Organizations were required to establish and exercise "adequate controls" over the contributions they received. Donor requests for confidentiality were to be honored, including requests that a donor's name not be exchanged, rented, or sold. Fundraising was to be conducted "without excessive pressure"; examples of this type of pressure included solicitations in the guise of invoices, harassment, intimidation, coercion, threats of public disclosure or economic retaliation, and "strongly emotional appeals which distort the organization's activities or beneficiaries."

(v) Governance. The PAS standards required three elements of governance. First, an "adequate governing structure" was required. This meant that the governing instruments must set forth the organization's goals and purposes, define the organization's structure, and identify the body having authority over policies and programs (including the authority to amend the governing instruments). A governing structure was considered inadequate if any policymaking decisions of the governing body or executive committee were made by "fewer than three persons."

Second, there had to be an "active governing body." To meet this standard, the governing body was required, among other things, to meet formally "at least three times annually, with meetings evenly spaced over the course of the year, and with a majority of the members in attendance (in person or by proxy) on average." If the full board met only once annually, there had to be at least two additional, evenly spaced executive committee meetings during the year.

Third, adequate governance required that there be an "independent governing body." Organizations did not meet this standard if "directly and/or indirectly compensated board members constitute more than one-fifth (20%) of the total voting membership of the board or of the executive committee." (The ordained clergy of a "publicly soliciting church," however, were excepted from this 20% limitation.) Organizations failed to meet this third standard if board members had material conflicting interests resulting from any relationship or business affiliation.

(c) Better Business Bureau Wise Giving Alliance Standards

The BBB (Better Business Bureau) Wise Giving Alliance (Alliance) was formed in 2001, the product of the merger of the National Charities Information Bureau (another of the early watchdog agencies) into the CBBB Foundation and the PAS. The Alliance is affiliated with the CBBB.

According to its web site, the Alliance "collects and distributes information on hundreds of nonprofit organizations that solicit [contributions] nationally or have national or international program services." It "routinely asks such organizations for information about their programs, governance, fund raising practices, and finances when the charities have been the subject of inquiries." The Alliance "selects charities for evaluation based on the volume of donor inquiries about individual organizations." The organization serves "donors' information needs" and helps donors "make their own decisions regarding charitable giving."

The Alliance developed its "Standards for Charity Accountability," to "assist donors in making sound giving decisions and to foster public confidence in charitable organizations." One of the purposes of these standards is to "promote ethical conduct" by charitable organizations. The BBB states that these standards are "voluntary."[24]

(i) Governance and Oversight. These standards state that the governing board "has the ultimate oversight authority for any charitable organization." The standards seek to ensure that the "volunteer board is active, independent and free of self-dealing." A board must provide "adequate oversight of the charity's operations and staff." This type of oversight is indicated by factors such as "regularly scheduled appraisals of the CEO's performance, evidence of disbursement controls such as board approval of the budget, fund raising practices, establishment of a conflict of interest policy, and establishment of accounting procedures sufficient to safeguard charity finances."

A board is to be comprised of a "minimum of five voting members." There is to be a "minimum of three evenly spaced meetings per year of the full governing body with a majority in attendance, with face-to-face participation," although this standard is immediately somewhat tempered with the observation that a "conference call of the full board can substitute for one of the[se] three meetings."

The standards provide that no more than one or 10% (whichever is greater) "directly or indirectly compensated person(s) [may] serv[e] as voting member(s) of the board." Further, "[c]ompensated members shall not serve as the board's chair or treasurer." The standards forbid "transaction(s) in which any board or staff members have material conflicting interests with the charity resulting from any relationship or business affiliation." Factors that are considered in determining whether a transaction entails a *conflict of interest* and if so whether the conflict is *material* include "any arm's length procedures established by the charity; the size of the transaction relative to like expenses of the charity; whether the interested party participated in the board vote on the transaction; if competitive bids were sought[;] and whether the transaction is one-time, recurring or ongoing."

(ii) Measuring Effectiveness. The standards provide that an organization "should regularly assess its effectiveness in achieving its mission." An organization should have "defined, measurable goals and objectives in place and a defined process in

---

24. Statements from BBB Web site.

place to evaluate the success and impact of its program(s) in fulfilling the goals and objectives of the organization" and a process that "identifies ways to address any deficiencies."

An organization should "[h]ave a board policy of assessing, no less than every two years, the organization's performance and effectiveness and of determining future actions required to achieve the mission." There should be a submission to the board, "for its approval, a written report that outlines the results of the aforementioned performance and effectiveness assessment and recommendations for future actions."

(iii) Finances. These standards require that an organization "[s]pend at least 65% of its total expenses on program activities,"[25] "[s]pend no more than 35% of related contributions on fund raising," avoid unwarranted accumulation of funds, disclose the organization's annual financial statements, and have a board-approved annual budget.

(iv) Fundraising and Informational Materials. The standards require that an organization's solicitation and other informational materials be "accurate, truthful, and not misleading"; that an organization prepare an annual report that is available to the public; that an organization post its annual information returns on its Web site; that the charity disclose how it benefits from a cause-related marketing campaign; and that an organization promptly respond to an inquiry from the BBB.[26]

(d)   Evangelical Council for Financial Accountability Standards

Religious organizations have established watchdog agencies that focus only on religious entities. Among them is the Evangelical Council for Financial Accountability (ECFA), which states that it is an "accreditation agency dedicated to helping Christian ministries earn the public's trust through adherence to seven Standards of Responsible Stewardship." ECFA states that these standards, "drawn from Scripture, are fundamental to operating with integrity." In addition to these standards, ECFA has developed a series of best practices that are intended to "encourage [its] members to strive for the highest levels of excellence." Founded in 1979, ECFA states that its constituency comprises more than 2,000 evangelical Christian organizations. An organization that cannot comply with one or more of the standards is ineligible for membership in ECFA.[27]

(i) Use of Resources. Every member of ECFA must "exercise the management and financial controls necessary to provide reasonable assurance that all resources are used (nationally and internationally) in conformity with applicable federal and state laws and regulations to accomplish the exempt purposes for which they are intended." According to one of the best practices, a member organization should ensure, "by collaborating with the board and the CEO, Executive Director, or

---

25. An organization does not spend expenses.
26. Of all the watchdog agency standards, the Alliance's standards are the only ones that make failure to comply with an agency inquiry itself a violation of the standards.
27. This information about ECFA is based on material on its Web site. Its standards are titled "Standards and Best Practices."

President (or similar position), that the organization has a clear financial plan that is aligned with strategic, operating, and development plans."

(ii) Board of Directors. A "responsible" board must, according to the ECFA standards, govern member organizations. These boards must have at least five individuals, a majority of whom must be "independent."[28] The board must meet at least semiannually to "establish policy and review its accomplishments." The board, or a committee consisting of a majority of independent members, must "review the annual financial statements and maintain direct communication between the board and the independent certified public accountants."

The ECFA best practices guidelines as to board members include the following:

- Board members should "annually pledge to carry out in a trustworthy and diligent manner their duties and obligations as a board member."

- The board "should understand the organization's financial health."

- In "linking budgeting to strategic planning," the board "should approve the annual budget and key financial transactions, such as major asset acquisitions, that can be realistically financed with existing or attainable resources."

- Board time "should be spent on governance, not on management issues."

- The board should "utilize a committee, whose members have financial expertise, totally comprised of independent members to annually review the financial statements."

- This committee should "[c]onduct at least a portion of the committee meeting to review the financial statements with the accounting firm in the absence of staff"; if the board "handles the financial review function, staff should be recused from a portion of the meeting with the representative(s) from the accounting firm."

- The board should "[r]equest the periodic rotation of the lead or review partners, if this is feasible for the accounting firm."

- The board should obtain "competitive fee quotes every few years." If, however, the accountants are "independent, providing quality service at competitive fees, it is generally wise to continue with the current accounting firm."

- The board should "[a]pprove and document annually and in advance the compensation and fringe benefits of the CEO, Executive Director, or President (or similar position) unless there is a multi-year contract in force and there is no change in the compensation and fringe benefits except for an inflation or cost-of-living adjustment."[29]

---

28. ECFA does not define the word *independent*, although in its best practices "independent-minded" board members are referenced as "those with the ability to place the organization's interests first, apart from the interests of the staff and other board members."

29. These best practices provide that the reasonableness of the compensation for these positions should be based on "appropriate data regarding comparable compensation under IRS regulations;" this is a reference to the rebuttable presumption found in the intermediate sanctions rules (Reg. § 53.4958-6(c)(2)) (see *Law of Tax-Exempt Organizations* §§ 20.4(b), 21.9). The data the IRS thinks are important in this context are spelled out in the college and university compliance check questionnaire (see § 6.4).

- The board should "[a]nnually and formally evaluate the CEO, Executive Director, or President (or similar position)."

- The board should "[r]outinely compare board actions and corporate bylaws."

- The board should "[p]eriodically review organizational and governing documents."

- If the organization files an annual information return (usually Form 990),[30] a "board committee should annually review the form." If the full board "handles the financial statement review responsibilities, Form 990 should be reviewed by the full board or an appropriate board committee."

- There should be "adequate communication to board members between board meetings."

- The board should "[d]etermine and adjust the optimal board size by assessing organizational needs."

- The board should "[s]tructure board membership and the board's voting with *more* than a *mere* majority of independent board members" (emphasis in original).

- The board meetings should be conducted "with *more* than a *mere* majority of independent board members in attendance" (emphasis in original).

- There should be an annual monitoring of "individual board performance against the board members' service commitments."

- The board should develop an "effective process to plan ahead for recruiting new board members."

- There should be a process for "[p]roperly orient[ing] new board members for their board service and provid[ing] ongoing education to ensure that the board carries out its oversight functions and that individual members are aware of their legal and ethical responsibilities."

- An organization should establish "clear policies and procedures on the length of terms and on the removal of board members."

- Board member participation should be evaluated "before extending terms"; board member evaluation and/or term limits should be used to "ensure that the organization is only served by effective members."

- Board members "should generally serve without compensation for board service other than reimbursement for expenses incurred to fulfill their board duties."[31] If compensation is paid to board members, however, "information on the compensation should be provided by the charity, upon request, to allow an evaluation of the reasonableness of the compensation."

- Board members "should understand clearly if they are expected to participate in stewardship activities and individual giving."

---

30. See *Law of Tax-Exempt Organizations* § 27.2.
31. An expense reimbursement generally is not *compensation*. See § 6.3(r).

- The board should use "routine and periodic board self-evaluations to improve meetings, restructure committees, and address individual board member performance."

- The board should "[f]ind opportunities to keep valuable individuals connected with the organization after their board terms expire."

(iii) Financial Statements. Every organization that is an accredited member of ECFA must obtain an annual audit performed by an independent certified public accounting firm, including a financial statement prepared in accordance with generally accepted accounting principles. ECFA may provide for an alternative category of membership that does not require audited financial statements, in which case the organization must have financial statements that are compiled or reviewed by an independent certified public accounting firm.

An ECFA best practice has the organization ensuring that "all material related-party transactions are disclosed in the financial statements."

(iv) Financial Disclosure. Every member must provide a copy of its current financial statements (including audited financial statements if required) on written request and provide other disclosures "as the law may require."[32] A member "must provide a report, on written request, including financial information, on any specific project for which it is soliciting gifts."

One of the ECFA best practices recommendations is that the organization post its most recent annual financial statement and annual information return (Form 990) (if the organization files such a return) on its Web site.

(v) Conflicts of Interest. ECFA member organizations are to "avoid conflicts of interest." Nonetheless, members may engage in transactions with related parties if (1) a material transaction is fully disclosed in the audited financial statements of the organization, (2) the related party is excluded from the discussion and approval of the transaction, (3) a competitive bid or comparable valuation exists, and (4) the organization's board has demonstrated that the transaction is in the best interest of the entity.

The ECFA best practices include the following:

- "A conflict-of-interest policy relating to the governing board and key executives should be adopted."

- "The governing board and key executives should document annually any potential related-party transactions."

- "All significant related-party transactions should be initially approved and, if continuing, reapproved annually by the governing board."

---

32. The federal tax law requires several disclosures (see *Law of Tax-Exempt Organizations* §§ 27.7 (disclosure of unrelated business income tax returns by public charities), 27.9 (disclosure of annual information return), 27.10 (information or services disclosure), and 27.11 (fundraising disclosure), 27.12 (reporting as to certain insurance); *Law of Charitable Giving* §§ 21.1 (substantiation and receipt requirements), 21.2 (appraisal requirements), 21.3 (reporting requirements), 22.1 (disclosure by charitable organizations in general), 22.2 (quid pro quo contribution rules), and 22.3 (disclosure by noncharitable organizations).

(vi) Policies and Procedures. According to the ECFA best practices, the following should be done:

- The organization should "[p]roperly document the proceedings of all board and board committee meetings in order to protect the organization." Board minutes "should identify all voting board members as present or absent to clearly document a quorum."

- The organization should develop a mission statement, "putting into words why the organization exists and what it hopes to accomplish." This statement should be "[r]egularly reference[d]" to ensure that it is being "faithfully followed." The organization should "[h]ave the courage to refocus the mission statement, if appropriate."

- The organization should adopt a "stewardship philosophy statement."

- The organization should adopt an "executive compensation philosophy statement."

- The organization should adopt "appropriate policies," such as policies with respect to:
  - Conflicts of interest (including annual approval of all significant related-party transactions)
  - Whistleblowing
  - Accountable expense reimbursements
  - Record retention
  - Board confidentiality
  - Donor confidentiality
  - Ownership of intellectual property

- Board policies should be regularly reviewed to determine whether revisions are needed.

- The organization's compliance with board policies should be monitored.

- All board policies should be maintained in a policy manual.

- The organization should develop a "vision statement communicating a compelling and inspirational hope for the future of the organization."

(vii) Fundraising. ECFA has several requirements in the area of fundraising. Representations of fact, description of the organization's financial condition, or narrative about events must be "current, complete, and accurate"; "material omissions or exaggerations of fact" are not permitted. Member organizations "must not create unrealistic donor expectations of what a donor's gift will actually accomplish within the limits of the organization's ministry." Organizations are asked to make every effort to "avoid accepting a gift from or entering into a contract with a prospective donor which would knowingly place a hardship on the donor, or place the donor's future wellbeing in jeopardy." When dealing with donors regarding commitments on "major estate assets," organizations must "seek to guide and advise donors so they have adequately considered the broad interests of the family and the various ministries they are currently supporting before they make final decisions."

These standards state that compensation of outside fundraising consultants or a member's employees, based directly or indirectly on a percentage of charitable contributions raised, is prohibited. ECFA standards also state that officers and directors may not receive any royalties for any product that is used for fundraising or promotional purposes by the organization. The ECFA member must honor all statements it made in its fundraising appeals about the use of the gift.

The ECFA best practices state that an organization should "[g]enerate compensation arrangements for development personnel (internal and external) based on merit." These practices add: "Pay-for-performance plans may be structured if it [sic] avoids compensation based on [a] percentage of gift amounts."

(viii) Other Practices. The ECFA's best practices state that an organization should spend a "reasonable percentage" of its annual expenditures "on programs in pursuance of the organization's mission." An organization should "[p]rovide sufficient resources for effective administration and, if the organization solicits contributions, for appropriate fundraising activities."

An organization should "[e]stablish and implement policies that provide clear guidance for paying or reimbursing expenses incurred when conducting business or traveling on behalf of the organization, including listing the types of expenses that can be paid for or reimbursed and the documentation required." An organization should "[a]void loans or the equivalent to executives or board members."

(e)   Standards for Excellence Institute Standards

The Standards for Excellence Institute (Institute) is a membership organization of charitable entities that claims, in its marketing material, to uphold standards that are higher "than the minimal requirements imposed by local, state and federal laws and regulations." This program was launched to "strengthen nonprofit governance and management, while also enhancing the public's trust in the nonprofit sector." This organization "promotes widespread application of a comprehensive system of self-regulation in the nonprofit sector." These standards are based on "fundamental values" such as "honesty, integrity, fairness, respect, trust, compassion, responsibility and accountability," and provide guidelines for how nonprofit organizations should act to be "ethical and accountable in their programs operations, governance, human resources, financial management and fundraising."[33]

(i) Mission and Program. The Institute's standards provide that an organization's "purpose, as defined and approved by the board of directors, should be formally and specifically stated." The organization's "activities should be consistent with its stated purpose."

A nonprofit organization "should periodically revisit its mission (e.g., every 3 to 5 years) to determine if the need for its programs continues to exist." An organization "should evaluate whether the mission needs to be modified to reflect societal changes, its current programs should be revised or discontinued, or new programs need to be developed."

---

33. These standards are titled "An Ethics and Accountability Code for the Nonprofit Sector," and are available at www.standardsforexcellenceinstitute.org/public/html/explore_b.html.

A nonprofit organization "should have defined, cost-effective procedures for evaluating, both qualitatively and quantitatively, its programs and projects in relation to its mission." These procedures "should address programmatic efficiency and effectiveness, the relationship of these impacts to the cost of achieving them, and the outcomes for program participants." Evaluations, which "should include input from program participants," should be "candid, be used to strengthen the effectiveness of the organization and, when necessary, be used to make programmatic changes."

(ii) Board Responsibilities and Conduct. The board of an organization "should engage in short-term and long-term planning activities as necessary to determine the mission of the organization, to define specific goals and objectives related to the mission, and to evaluate the success of the organization's programs toward achieving the mission." The board "should establish policies for the effective management of the organization, including financial and, where applicable, personnel policies."

The board "annually should approve the organization's budget and periodically should assess the organization's financial performance in relation to the budget." As part of this annual budget process, the board "should review the percentages of the organization's resources spent on program, administration, and fundraising." The full board "should also approve the findings of the organization's annual audit and management letter and plan to implement the recommendations of" that letter.

The board or a board committee "should hire the executive director, set the executive's compensation, and evaluate the director's performance at least annually." Where a committee performs this role, details should be reported to the board. The board "should periodically review the appropriateness of the overall compensation structure of the organization." The board should approve written personnel policies and procedures "governing the work and actions of all employees and volunteers of the organization."

The board "is responsible for its own operations, including the education, training and development of board members, periodic (i.e., at least every two years) evaluation of its own performance, and[,] where appropriate, the selection of new board members." The board "should establish stated expectations for board members, including expectations for participation in fundraising activities, committee service, and program activities." The board "should meet as frequently as is needed to fully and adequately conduct the business of the organization"; the board should, at a minimum, meet four times a year.

The organization "should have written policies that address attendance and participation of board members at board meetings." These policies "should include a process to address noncompliance." Written meeting minutes "reflecting the actions of the board, including reports of board committees when acting in the place of the board, should be maintained and distributed to board and committee members."

(iii) Board Composition. The Institute's standards state that the governing board of an organization "should be composed of individuals who are personally committed to the mission of the organization and possess the specific skills needed to accomplish the mission."

An organization's governing board should, under these standards, have at least five unrelated directors; seven or more directors are preferable. Where an employee of the organization is a voting member of the board, there must be assurance that that individual will "not be in a position to exercise undue influence."

There should be term limits for the service of board members. Board membership should reflect the "diversity of the communities" served by the organization. Board members should serve without compensation for their service as board members; they "may only be reimbursed for expenses directly related to carrying out their board service."

(iv) Conflict of Interest. The Institute's standards state that a nonprofit organization should have a written conflict-of-interest policy. This policy "should be applicable to all board members and staff, and to volunteers who have significant independent decision making authority regarding the resources of the organization." The policy "should identify the types of conduct or transactions that raise conflict of interest concerns, should set forth procedures for disclosure of actual or potential conflicts, and should provide for review of individual transactions by the uninvolved members of the board of directors."

A nonprofit organization "should provide board members, staff, and volunteers with a conflict of interest statement that summarizes the key elements of the organization's conflict of interest policy." This statement "should provide space for the board member, employee or volunteer to disclose any known interest that the individual, or a member of the individual's immediate family, has in any business entity which transacts business with the organization." The statement should be provided to and signed by board members, staff, and volunteers, "both at the time of the individual's initial affiliation with the organization and at least annually thereafter."

(v) Financial Accountability. The Institute's standards require that an organization "operate in accordance with an annual budget that has been approved by the board of directors." Accurate financial reports should be maintained on a timely basis. Internal financial statements "should be prepared no less frequently than quarterly, should be provided to the board of directors, and should identify and explain any material variation between actual and budgeted revenues and expenses." The accuracy of the financial reports of an organization with annual revenue in excess of $300,000 should be audited by a certified public accountant.

Organizations "should provide employees a confidential means to report suspected financial impropriety or misuse of organization resources and should have in place a policy prohibiting retaliation against persons reporting improprieties." They "should have written financial policies adequate for the size and complexity of their organization governing: (a) investment of the assets of the organization[,] (b) internal control procedures, (c) purchasing practices, and (d) unrestricted current net assets."

(vi) Legal Compliance and Accountability. Organizations must be "aware of and comply with all applicable Federal, state, and local laws." These laws include those pertaining to fundraising, licensing, financial accountability, document retention and destruction, human resources, lobbying and political advocacy, and taxation.

Organizations "should periodically assess the need for insurance coverage in light of the nature and extent of the organization's activities and its financial capacity." A decision to forego general liability or directors' and officers' liability insurance coverage "shall only be made by the board of directors and shall be reflected in" the appropriate board minutes. An organization "should periodically conduct an internal review" of its compliance with "legal, regulatory and financial reporting requirements"; a summary of the results of this review should be provided to the organization's governing board.

(vii) Openness. The Institute's standards require an organization to "prepare, and make available annually to the public, information about the organization's mission, program activities, and basic audited (if applicable) financial data." This report should also "identify the names of the organization's board of directors and management staff."

An organization "should provide members of the public who express an interest in the affairs of the organization with a meaningful opportunity to communicate with an appropriate representative of the organization." An organization "should have at least one staff member who is responsible to assure that the organization is complying with both the letter and the spirit of Federal and state laws that require disclosure of information to members of the public."

(viii) Public Education and Advocacy. The Institute's standards state that a nonprofit organization "should assure that any educational information provided to the media or distributed to the public is factually accurate and provides sufficient contextual information to be understood." An organization "should have a written policy on advocacy defining the process by which the organization determines positions on specific issues." The standards add that nonprofit organizations "engaged in promoting public participation in community affairs shall be diligent in assuring that the activities of the organization are strictly nonpartisan."[34]

(ix) Fundraising. The Institute's standards as to fundraising state that an organization's fundraising costs "should be reasonable over time." That is, on average, over a five-year period, a charity should realize revenue from development activities that is "at least three times the amount spent on conducting them." Organizations with a fundraising ratio of less than 3:1 "should demonstrate that they are making steady progress toward achieving this goal, or should be able to justify why a 3:1 ratio is not appropriate for the individual organization."

Solicitation and program materials "should be accurate and truthful and should correctly identify the organization, its mission, and the intended use of the solicited funds." All statements made by a charitable organization in its fundraising appeals "about the use of a contribution should be honored." A charitable organization "must honor the known intentions of a donor regarding the use of donated funds."

Charitable organizations should respect the privacy of donors and "safeguard the confidentiality of information that a donor reasonably would expect to be private." Charities should provide donors with an opportunity to make anonymous gifts. They should provide donors the opportunity to have their names removed from any mailing lists that are sold, rented, or exchanged. Charities should honor requests by a donor to curtail repeated mailings or telephone solicitations from in-house lists.

---

34. Presumably, this admonition is directed at charitable organizations. There are, however, other types of nonprofit (and tax-exempt) organizations, such as social welfare (IRC § 501(c)(4)) entities, that can lawfully (from a federal tax law standpoint) engage in partisan activities (see *Law of Tax-Exempt Organizations* § 23.5-23.8).

Solicitations should be "free from undue influence or excessive pressure," and be "respectful of the needs and interests of the donor or potential donor."

A charitable organization should have policies governing the acceptance and disposition of charitable gifts, including procedures to determine any limits on individuals or entities from which the organization will accept a gift, the purposes for which donations will be accepted, the type of property that will be accepted, and whether an "unusual or unanticipated" gift will be accepted in view of the organization's "mission and organizational capacity."

Fundraising personnel, whether employees or consultants, should not be compensated on the basis of a "percentage of the amount raised or other commission formula." When using the services of a paid professional fundraising counsel or professional solicitor, a charitable organization should only contract with those persons who are "properly registered with applicable regulatory authorities." Organizations should exercise control over any staff, volunteers, consultants, other contractors, businesses, or other organizations that solicit contributions on their behalf.

(f) American Institute of Philanthropy Standards

The American Institute of Philanthropy (AIP) is, according to its Web site, a "nationally prominent charity watchdog service whose purpose is to help donors make informed giving decisions." It provides ratings of charities, using letter grades A–F.

(i) Fundraising Expenses. Like all of the watchdog agencies, AIP believes fundraising costs should be reasonable. In this organization's view, this means that a charity should expend at least 60% of its outlays for charitable purposes. The balance, of course, is to be allocated to fundraising and administration. Fundraising expenses should not exceed 35%. These percentages are based on related contributions, not total income (thereby usually making the fundraising cost ratio higher). AIP sometimes takes it on itself to adjust an organization's fundraising expense ratio, such as where it is allocating a portion of its expenses to program in the context of direct mail fundraising.

(ii) Asset Reserves. In the view of AIP, a reserve of assets to enable an organization to function without fundraising for less than three years is reasonable. Organizations with "years of available assets" of more than five years are considered the "least needy." (This fact earns an organization the grade of "F" irrespective of other considerations.)

(g) Other Watchdog Agencies

Other charity watchdog organizations have come into being. One observer concluded that the number of them has "proliferated" and that each of them has its "own approach and mission."[35] These recent entrants into the field include Charity Navigator and Ministry Watch. Another organization, the Philanthropy Group, provides customized research about charitable organizations for a fee.[36]

---

35. Wilhelm, "Charity Under Scrutiny," XV *Chron. Of Phil.* (No. 4) 22 (Nov. 28, 2002).
36. *Id.*, at 22–26.

These groups do not focus on governance issues; their emphasis is on program and fundraising. For example, Charity Navigator rates public charities on the basis of their *organizational efficiency* and *organizational capacity*. As to organizational efficiency, this rating process analyzes four categories of performance: program expenses, administrative expenses, fundraising expenses, and fundraising efficiency. (A charity that spends less than one-third of its annual revenue on program is automatically given an organizational efficiency score of zero.) Organizational capacity is rated on the basis of primary revenue growth, program expenses growth, and working capital ratio. Charities that are rated by Charity Navigator receive zero (exceptionally poor) to four (exceptional) stars.[37]

§3.4 CALIFORNIA'S NONPROFIT INTEGRITY ACT

The state of California has the most extensive set of rules concerning governance of nonprofit organizations; these provisions were enacted in 2004 in the form of the Nonprofit Integrity Act.[38] This legislation contains laws concerning governance of and fundraising by charitable organizations doing business in the state.

(a) Financial Audits

Charitable corporations that have gross revenues of at least $2 million and are required to register and file reports with the state's attorney general must have annual financial statements prepared, audited by an independent certified public accountant. The CPA must, in this regard, follow generally accepted auditing standards; the statements must be prepared in accordance with generally accepted accounting principles. If the accounting firm and CPA performing the audit also provide nonaudit services to the charitable organization, they must follow independence standards promulgated by the U.S. Comptroller General. The audited financial statements must be made available for inspection by the attorney general and the public no later than nine months after the close of the fiscal year covered by the financial statement.

(b) Audit Committees

Charitable corporations with gross revenues of at least $2 million, and that are required to register and file reports with the state's attorney general must establish and maintain an audit committee.[39] This audit committee, which must be appointed by the organization's governing board, may include individuals who are not board members. The committee, however, cannot include members of the organization's

---

37. Information about Charity Navigator was derived from its Web site (www.charitynavigator.org).
38. California Nonprofit Integrity Act of 2004, Senate Bill 1262, amending Section 17510.5 of the California Business and Professional Code, and amending Sections 12581–12586, 12599, and 12599.1 of, and adding Sections 12599.3, 12599.6, and 12599.7 to, the California Government Code.
39. In applying this rule and the same one in § 3.4(a), grants from government agencies are not included in computing this $2 million threshold if the grantee is obligated to provide an accounting of the funds to the grantor.

staff or the organization's president, chief executive officer, treasurer, or chief financial officer. If the organization has a finance committee, members of that committee may serve on the audit committee, although those individuals cannot comprise more than one-half of the members of the audit committee.

The audit committee, under the supervision of the organization's board, is responsible for making recommendations to the board as to the hiring and dismissal of independent certified public accountants. The audit committee can negotiate the CPA firm's compensation, on behalf of the board. This committee must confer with the auditor to satisfy committee members that the financial affairs of the charitable organization are in order, review the audit and decide whether to accept it, approve nonaudit services by the CPA firm, and ensure that the nonaudit services conform to the standards issued by the U.S. Comptroller General.

(c)   Executive Compensation

Charitable organizations, including trusts, must have their governing board, or a designated committee of the board, review and approve the compensation of the organization's president, chief executive officer, chief financial officer, and treasurer. There must be a determination that this compensation, including benefits, is "just and reasonable." This review and approval must occur at the time of initial hiring, when a term is renewed or extended, and when the compensation is modified.

(d)   Fundraising Regulation

A fundraising counsel and a commercial fundraiser must notify the California attorney general before starting a solicitation campaign for a charitable organization and must have a written contract with the charity. This law dictates the elements to be included in these contracts. Charitable organizations and commercial fundraisers are prohibited from engaging in misrepresentation and certain other acts when soliciting contributions. Commercial fundraisers must retain records of solicitation campaigns for at least 10 years.[40]

§3.5   SENATE FINANCE COMMITTEE STAFF PAPER

The Senate Committee on Finance, in 2004, held a hearing on a range of subjects pertaining to nonprofit, tax-exempt organizations.[41] In connection with that hearing, the staff of the committee prepared a paper as a discussion draft that contained a variety of proposals, including a section on "strong governance and best practices" for exempt organizations.[42]

---

40. In general, Silk & Fei, "California's Nonprofit Integrity Act of 2004," 7 *Int'l J. of Not-for-Profit Law* (no. 2) 66 (Feb. 2005).
41. "Charity Oversight and Reform: Keeping Bad Things from Happening to Good Charities," Hearing before the Senate Committee on Finance, U.S. Senate, June 24, 2004 [Senate Hearing 108-603], 108th Cong., 2nd Sess. (2004).
42. This paper is available at www.finance.senate.gov/hearings/testimony/2004test/062204stfdis.pdf. The nonprofit governance policies are in Part G of this paper.

(a) Board Duties

This paper stipulated that a charitable organization must be "managed" by its board of directors or trustees. The paper stated that, in performing board duties, a board member "has to perform his or her duties in good faith; with the care an ordinarily prudent person in a like position would exercise under similar circumstances; and in a manner the director reasonably believes to be in the best interests of the mission, goals, and purposes of the corporation." The paper added that an individual who has "special skills or expertise has a duty to use such skills or expertise" in his or her board service. Federal law liability for breach of these duties was recommended.

The paper stated that any compensation consultant providing services to a charitable organization must be hired by and report to the board; the consultant must be independent. Compensation for all management positions would have to be approved by the board in advance and annually (unless there is no change in compensation other than an inflation adjustment). Compensation arrangements would have to be "explained and justified and publicly disclosed (with such explanation) in a manner that can be understood by an individual with a basic business background."

This paper asserted that the governing board of a charitable organization must:

- "[E]stablish basic organizational and management policies and procedures of organization and review any proposed deviations."

- "[E]stablish, review, and approve program objectives and performance measures and review and approve significant transactions."

- "[R]eview and approve the auditing and accounting principles and practices used in preparing the organization's financial statements and must retain and replace the organization's independent auditor." An independent auditor would have to be hired by the board; each auditor could be retained for no more than five years.

- "[R]eview and approve the organization's budget and financial objectives as well as significant investments, joint ventures, and business transactions."

- "[O]versee the conduct of the corporation's business and evaluate whether the business is being properly managed."

- "[E]stablish a conflicts[-]of[-]interest policy which would be required to be disclosed with the [Form] 990, and require a summary of conflicts determinations made during the 990 reporting year."

- "[E]stablish and oversee a compliance program to address regulatory and liability concerns."

- "[E]stablish procedures to address complaints and prevent retaliation against whistleblowers."

In general, all of these requirements would have to be "confirmed" on the organization's annual information return (Form 990).

(b) Board Composition

Boards of charitable organizations would have to be comprised of at least three members, with a maximum of 15 members. No more than one board member could be directly or indirectly compensated by the organization. A compensated board member could not serve as the chair of the board or treasurer of the organization. In the case of public charities, at least one board member or one-fifth of the board would have to be independent; a "higher number of independent board members might be required in limited cases." An *independent* board member would be defined as an individual who is "free of any relationship with the corporation or its management that may impair or appear to impair the director's ability to make independent judgments."

(c)   Board/Officer Removal

In this paper, the Committee staff proposed that an individual who is not permitted to serve on the board of a publicly traded company, because of a law violation, be barred from serving on the board of a tax-exempt organization. A criminal conviction would preclude an individual from serving as a director or officer of an exempt organization for a five-year period following the conviction. An individual who has been convicted of a crime under a law enforced by the Federal Trade Commission, U.S. Postal Service, or state attorney general for actions related to service as an officer or director of an exempt organization (or where the crime arose from an organization that falsely presented itself as an exempt organization) could not serve as an officer or director of an exempt organization for five years. An organization, or its officers or members, that knowingly retained an individual who is not permitted to serve the organization, pursuant to one or more of these rules, would be subject to a penalty.

A proposal would accord the IRS the authority to require the removal of a board member, officer, or employee of a tax-exempt organization who violated self-dealing rules, conflict-of-interest standards, excess benefit transaction rules,[43] private inurement rules,[44] or charitable solicitation laws.[45] The IRS would be able to require that such an individual not serve on any other exempt organization's board for a period of years. An organization that knowingly retained an individual who is not permitted to serve, pursuant to one or more of these rules, would have its exempt status revoked or be subject to a penalty.

(d)   Tax Court Equity Authorities

This paper proposed that the U.S. Tax Court be invested with equity powers to remedy any detriment to a charitable organization resulting from a violation of the substantive rules, and to ensure that the organization's assets are preserved for exempt purposes and that violations of the substantive rules would not occur in the future. These powers would include the power to rescind transactions, divest assets, surcharge and/or substitute trustees and directors, order accountings, appoint receivers, and enjoin activities.

In the event that appropriate state authorities institute action against a charitable organization or individuals based on acts that constitute a violation of substantive rules of law applicable to the organization, the Tax Court, where a federal civil action

---

43. See *Law of Tax-Exempt Organizations*, Chapter 21.
44. See *id.*, Chapter 20.
45. See *Law of Fundraising*, Chapter 3.

involving the organization is instituted or pending, would be required to defer action on any equitable relief for protection of the organization or preservation of its assets for its charitable purposes until conclusion of the state court action. At the conclusion of the state court action, the Tax Court could consider the state action to be adequate or provide additional equitable relief, consistent with the state action, as the law warranted. An action by a state court, however, could not defer or abate the imposition of initial federal excise tax penalties for the violations.

The IRS, or a trustee or director, could seek, before the Tax Court, removal of a board member or officer of a charitable organization. The Tax Court could remove the director or officer if the court found that the director or officer (1) engaged in fraudulent or dishonest conduct, or gross abuse of authority or discretion, with respect to the organization or (2) failed to perform his or her duties in good faith, with the care an ordinarily prudent individual in a like position would exercise under similar circumstances, and in a manner the director or officer reasonably believes to be in the best interests of the organization. The court would have to find that removal is in the best interest of enabling the organization to meet its "goals and purpose." The court would be able to bar the director or officer from serving on the board or any board for a time period prescribed by the court.

(e) Government Encouragement of Best Practices

In determining whether a tax-exempt organization may be the recipient of a federal government grant and contract, the government agency involved would be required to "give favorable consideration" to organizations that are "accredited" by IRS-designated entities that establish best practices for exempt organizations. The IRS would annually determine these organizations, with a "preference" for organizations that "perform an independent review of accredited organizations and that audit applications for accreditation." The IRS would have the authority to "base charitable status or authority of a charity to accept charitable donations on whether an organization is accredited."

The IRS, in consultation with the Office of Personnel Management, would establish "best practices/governance requirements/accreditation" for charities participating in the Combined Federal Campaign (CFC). The IRS would ensure that the best practices/governance requirements for the CFC are "uniform nationwide in order to encourage charities to participate in the CFC."

§3.6 U.S. TREASURY DEPARTMENT'S VOLUNTARY BEST PRACTICES

The Treasury Anti-Terrorist Financing Guidelines[46] provide that a charitable organization's governing instruments should (1) delineate the organization's basic goal(s) and purpose(s); (2) define the structure of the charity, including the composition of the board, how the board is selected and replaced, and the authority and responsibilities of the board; (3) set forth requirements concerning financial reporting,

---

46. U.S. Department of the Treasury Anti-Terrorist Financing Guidelines: Voluntary Best Practices for U.S. Based Charities (2006), available at www.ustreas.gov/press/releases/reports/0929%20finalrevised. pdf.

accountability, and practices for the solicitation and distribution of funds; and (4) state that the charity shall comply with all applicable federal, state, and local law.

These guidelines state that the board of directors of a charitable organization is responsible for the organization's compliance with relevant laws, and should (1) be an "active governing body"; (2) oversee implementation of the governance practices to be followed by the organization; (3) exercise "effective and independent" oversight of the charity's operations; (4) establish a conflict-of-interest policy for board members and employees; (5) establish procedures to be followed if a board member or employee has a conflict, or perceived conflict, of interest; and (6) maintain records of all decisions made, with these records available for inspection by the appropriate regulatory and law enforcement authorities.

The guidelines contain other governance practices, including (1) an annual budget approved and overseen by the board; (2) a board-appointed financial/accounting officer who is responsible for day-to-day management of the charity's assets; (3) an audit of the finances of the organization, when annual gross income is in excess of $250,000, by an independent certified public accounting firm, with the audited financial statement available for public inspection; (4) accounting for all funds received and disbursed in accordance with generally accepted accounting principles, including the name of each recipient of funds, the amount disbursed, and the date of the disbursement; (5) the prompt deposit of all funds into an account maintained by the charity at a financial institution; and (6) the making of disbursements by check or wire transfer, rather than in currency, whenever that is reasonably feasible.

Pursuant to these guidelines, charities should (1) maintain and make publicly available a current list of their board members and the salaries they are paid; (2) maintain records (while fully respecting individual privacy rights) containing additional identifying information about their board members, such as home addresses, Social Security numbers, and citizenship; and (3) maintain records (while respecting individual privacy rights) identifying information about the board members of any subsidiaries or affiliates receiving funds from them. As to key employees, charities should (1) maintain and make publicly available a current list of their five highest paid or most influential employees and the salaries and/or other direct or indirect benefits they are provided; (2) maintain records (while respecting privacy rights) containing identifying information about their key, non-U.S. employees working abroad; and (3) maintain records (while respecting individual privacy rights) identifying information about the key employees of any subsidiaries or affiliates receiving funds from them.

Moreover, pursuant to these guidelines, charitable organizations should (1) maintain and make publicly available a current list of any branches, subsidiaries, and/or affiliates that receive resources and services from them; (2) make publicly available or provide to any member of the public, on request, an annual report, which describes the charity's purposes, programs, activities, tax-exempt status, structure and responsibility of the governing body, and financial information; and (3) make publicly available or provide to any member of the public, on request, complete annual financial statements, including a summary of the results of the most recent audit, which present the overall financial condition of the organization and its financial activities in accordance with generally accepted accounting principles and reporting practices.

§3.7 COMMITTEE FOR PURCHASE PROPOSED BEST PRACTICES

The Committee for Purchase From People Who Are Blind or Severely Disabled proposed various criteria and tests that it believes are "widely considered as benchmarks of good nonprofit agency governance practices."[47] Pursuant to these proposed "best practices," (1) a nonprofit organization's board of directors should be composed of individuals who are "personally committed to the mission of the organization and possess the specific skills needed to accomplish the mission"; (2) where an employee of the organization is a voting member of the board, the "circumstances must [e]nsure that the employee will not be in a position to exercise 'undue influence'"; (3) the board should have at least five unrelated directors; (4) the chair of the board should not simultaneously be serving as the entity's chief executive officer/president; (5) there should be term limits for board members; (6) board membership should reflect the "diversity of the communities" served by the organization; (7) board members should serve without compensation; (8) the board or a designated committee of it should hire the executive director, establish the executive's compensation, and evaluate the director's performance at least annually; (9) the board should periodically review the "appropriateness of the overall compensation structure" of the organization; (10) the board should have at least one "financial expert" among its membership; (11) the board should approve the findings of the organization's annual audit and management letter; and (12) the board should approve a plan to implement the recommendations of the management letter.

According to these best practices, nonprofit organizations should (1) have a written conflict-of-interest policy that identifies the types of conflict or transactions that raise conflict-of-interest concerns, sets forth procedures for disclosure of actual or potential conflicts, and provides for review of individual transactions by the "uninvolved" members of the board of directors; (2) subject the accuracy of the organization's financial reports to audit by a certified public accountant; (3) periodically conduct an internal review of the organization's compliance with existing statutory, regulatory, and financial reporting requirements, and should provide a summary of the results of the review to the board; (4) prepare and make available annually to the public information about the organization's mission, program activities, and basic audit (if applicable) financial data; (5) require the board of directors to monitor compensation paid to the chief executive officer/president and "highly compensated individuals"; and (6) require the board to approve all compensation packages for the chief executive officer/president and all highly compensated employees through a "rebuttable presumption process"[48] to determine the reasonableness of the compensation.

---

47. *70 Fed. Reg.* (No. 241) 74722-74723 (Dec. 16, 2005).
48. See *Law of Tax-Exempt Organizations* § 21.9.

§3.8 PANEL ON NONPROFIT SECTOR RECOMMENDATIONS

The Panel on the Nonprofit Sector convened by Independent Sector (Panel) prepared a report to Congress and the nonprofit sector.[49] In this report, the Panel recommended that the federal tax regulations be amended to generally require that tax-exempt charitable organizations have a minimum of three members on their governing boards. Generally, at least one-third of the members of the board of a public charity[50] would have to be independent. *Independent* board members would be individuals (1) who have not been compensated as an employee or independent contractor by the organization within the past 12 months, except for reasonable compensation for board service; (2) whose compensation, except for board service, is not determined by individuals who are compensated by the organization; (3) who do not receive, directly or indirectly, material financial benefits from the organization, except as a member of the charitable class served by the organization; and (4) who are not related to any of the foregoing individuals.

Another recommendation of the Panel was to prohibit individuals who are barred from service on boards of publicly traded companies or convicted of crimes directly related to breaches of fiduciary duty in their service as an employee or board member of a charitable organization from serving on the board of a charitable organization for five years following their removal or conviction.

The Panel observed that experts in the realm of nonprofit organization board governance "are not of one mind as to the ideal maximum size of nonprofit boards." It was noted that board size "may depend upon such factors as the age of the organization, the nature and geographic scope of its mission and activities, and its funding needs." Some experts believe that a "larger board may be necessary to ensure the range of perspectives and expertise required for some organizations or to share in fundraising responsibilities." Others argue that "effective governance is best achieved by a smaller board, which then demands more active participation from each board member." The Panel concluded that "each charitable organization must determine the most appropriate size for its board and the appropriate number and responsibilities of board committees to ensure that the board is able to fulfill its fiduciary and other governance duties responsibly and effectively."

As to the recommendation concerning independent board members of public charities, the Panel wrote that "it is important that at least one-third of their board members be free of the conflicts of interest that can arise when they have a personal interest in the financial transactions of the charity." It concluded that the "effort to find independent members is important to the long-term success and accountability of the organization and should be a legal requirement for public charities that are eligible to receive tax-deductible contributions on the most favorable terms."

In its report, the Panel discourages board compensation by charitable organizations and strongly "encourages charitable organizations to support the long-standing tradition of asking boards of directors to serve on a voluntary basis." The Panel also states that "[a]ll boards should establish strong and effective mechanisms to ensure that the board carries out its oversight functions and that the board members are

---

49. Panel on the Nonprofit Sector, "Strengthening Transparency Governance Accountability of Charitable Organizations" (June 2005).
50. See *id*. § 12.3.

aware of their legal and ethical responsibilities in ensuring that the organization is governed properly."

§ 3.9 BOARDS OF EXEMPT CREDIT COUNSELING ORGANIZATIONS

The federal tax statutory law concerning tax-exempt organizations does not generally address the matter of board member compensation. The only instance where there is any reference to this aspect of board service is in connection with exempt credit counseling organizations.

Tax-exempt credit counseling organizations[51] must have a governing body (1) that is controlled by persons who represent the broad interests of the public, such as public officials acting in their capacities as such, persons having special knowledge or expertise in credit or financial education, and community leaders; (2) of which not more than 20% of the voting power is vested in individuals who are employed by the organization or who will benefit financially, directly or indirectly, from the organization's activities (other than through the receipt of reasonable directors' fees[52] or the repayment of consumer debt to creditors other than the credit counseling organization or its affiliates); and (3) of which not more than 49% of the voting power is vested in individuals who are employed by the organization or who will benefit financially, directly or indirectly, from the organization's activities (other than though the receipt of reasonable directors' fees).[53]

§ 3.10 DRAFT OF IRS GOOD GOVERNANCE PRINCIPLES

On February 7, 2007, the IRS posted on its Web site a preliminary discussion draft of the agency's "Good Governance Practices" for charitable organizations.[54] The IRS stressed that this draft document is "informal" and is "not an official IRS document," and that the "recommendations" in it "are not legal requirements for federal tax exemption."[55]

In this draft of good governance recommendations, the IRS expressed its view that governing boards of charitable organizations "should be composed of persons who are informed and active in overseeing a charity's operations and finances." If a governing board "tolerates a climate of secrecy or neglect, charitable assets are more likely to be used to advance an impermissible private interest." Successful governing boards "include individuals [who are] not only knowledgeable and passionate about the organization's programs, but also those with expertise in critical areas involving accounting, finance, compensation, and ethics."

---

51. See *id*. § 7.3(e).
52. See *id*. § 20.4(g).
53. IRC § 501(q)(1)(D).
54. "Good Governance Practices for 501(c)(3) Organizations." This posting was preceded by a presentation on February 2, 2007, by the Chief, EO Technical, IRS Office of Rulings and Agreements. See Bureau of Nat'l Affairs, *Daily Tax Report* (no. 33) TaxCore® (Feb. 2, 2007).
55. IRS Web site.

Organizations with "very small or very large governing boards may be problematic: Small boards generally do not represent a public interest[,] and large boards may be less attentive to oversight duties." If an organization's governing board is "very large, it may want to establish an executive committee with delegated responsibilities or establish advisory committees."

The IRS "strongly recommends" that charitable organizations review and consider the recommendations in this draft document "to help ensure that directors understand their roles and responsibilities and actively promote good governance practices." While adopting a particular practice is "not a requirement for tax exemption," the agency believes that an organization that "adopts some or all of these practices is more likely to be successful in pursuing its exempt purposes and earning public support." At the same time (even though these recommendations are not requirements for tax exemption), the IRS warned charitable organizations that "any decision by the Service to conduct a review of operations subsequent to [recognition of] exemption . . . will be influenced by whether an organization has voluntarily adopted good governance practices."[56]

(a) Mission Statement

The board of directors of a charitable organization should, according to these recommendations, adopt a "clearly articulated mission statement." This statement should "explain and popularize the charity's purpose and serve as a guide to the organization's work." A "well-written mission statement shows why the charity exists, what it hopes to accomplish, and what activities it will undertake, where, and for whom."

(b) Code of Ethics

The IRS stated that the "public expects a charity to abide by ethical standards that promote the public good." The board of directors of a charitable organization "bears the ultimate responsibility for setting ethical standards and ensuring [that] they permeate the organization and inform its practices." To that end, the board "should consider adopting and regularly evaluating a code of ethics that describes behavior it wants to encourage and behavior it wants to discourage." This code of ethics "should be a principal means of communicating to all personnel a strong culture of legal compliance and ethical integrity."

(c) Whistleblower Policy

The board of directors of a charitable organization "should adopt an effective policy for handling employee complaints and establish procedures for employees to report in confidence suspected financial impropriety or misuse of the charity's resources."

---

56. It is, to state the matter mildly, inconsistent for the IRS to state that good governance practices are not a requirement for federal tax exemption, and then state that an IRS examination may be triggered if such practices are not adopted.

(d) Due Diligence

The directors of a charitable organization "must exercise due diligence consistent with a duty of care that requires a director to act in good faith, with the care an ordinarily prudent person in a like position would exercise under similar circumstances, and in a manner the director reasonably believes to be in the charity's best interests." Directors "should see to it that policies and procedures are in place to help them meet their duty of care," such as by ensuring that each director is "familiar with the charity's activities and knows whether those activities promote the charity's mission and achieve its goals," is "fully informed about the charity's financial status," and has "full and accurate information to make informed decisions."

(e) Duty of Loyalty

The directors of a charity "owe it a duty of loyalty."[57] This duty requires a director to "act in the interest of the charity rather than in the personal interest of the director or some other person or organization." In particular, the duty of loyalty "requires a director to avoid conflicts of interest that are detrimental to the charity." The board of directors of a charitable organization "should adopt and regularly evaluate an effective conflict of interest policy" that "requires directors and staff to act solely in the interests of the charity without regard for personal interests," includes "written procedures for determining whether a relationship, financial interest, or business affiliation" results in a conflict of interest, and prescribes a "certain course of action in the event a conflict of interest is identified."

Directors and staff "should be required to disclose annually in writing any known financial interest that the individual, or a member of the individual's family, has in any business entity that transacts business with the charity."

(f) Transparency

By making "full and accurate information about its mission, activities, and finances publicly available, a charity demonstrates transparency." The board of directors of a charitable organization "should adopt and monitor procedures to ensure that the charity's Form 990, annual reports, and financial statements are complete and accurate, are posted on the organization's public [Web site], and are made available to the public upon request."

(g) Fundraising Policy

The IRS observed that "[c]haritable fundraising is an important source of financial support for many charities." "Success at fundraising," the agency said, "requires care and honesty." The board of directors of a charitable organization "should adopt and monitor policies to ensure that fundraising solicitations meet federal and state law requirements and [that] solicitation materials are accurate, truthful, and candid." Charities "should keep their fundraising costs reasonable." In selecting paid fundraisers, a charity "should use those that are registered with the state and that can

---

57. See § 1.5(b).

provide good references." Performance of professional fundraisers "should be continuously monitored."

(h) Financial Audits

Directors "must be good stewards of a charity's financial resources." A charitable organization "should operate in accordance with an annual budget approved by the board of directors." The board "should ensure that financial resources are used to further charitable purpose[s] by regularly receiving and reading up-to-date financial statements including Form 990, auditor's letters, and finance and audit committee reports."

If the charity has "substantial assets or annual revenue, its board of directors should ensure that an independent auditor conduct an annual audit." The board "can establish an independent audit committee to select and oversee the independent auditor." The auditing firm "should be changed periodically (e.g., every five years) to ensure a fresh look at the financial statements." For a charity with "lesser assets or annual revenue, the board should ensure that an independent certified public accountant conduct an annual audit."

The IRS observed that "[s]ubstitute practices for very small organizations would include volunteers who would review financial information and practices." The agency suggested that "[t]rading volunteers between similarly situated organizations who would perform these tasks would also help maintain financial integrity without being too costly."

(i) Compensation Practices

The IRS is of the view that a "successful charity pays no more than reasonable compensation for services rendered." Charitable organizations "should generally not compensate persons for service on the board of directors except to reimburse direct expenses of such service." Director compensation "should be allowed only when determined [to be] appropriate by a committee composed of persons who are not compensated by the charity and have no financial interest in the determination." Charities "may pay reasonable compensation for services provided by officers and staff."

(j) Document Retention Policy

An "effective charity" will, according to the IRS, "adopt a written policy establishing standards for document integrity, retention, and destruction." This document retention policy "should include guidelines for handling electronic files." The policy "should cover backup procedures, archiving of documents, and regular check-ups of the reliability of the system."

(k) IRS Draft of Practices Jettisoned

The IRS, in early 2008, quietly abandoned its draft of good governance practices for charitable organizations. The proffered reason for this development was said to be the issuance of the redesigned annual information return, in that, as the IRS stated, its positions on nonprofit governance "are best reflected in the reporting required by the revised Form 990."[58] The agency's views on governance principles for charitable organizations are also summarized in its LifeCycle educational tool.

§ 3.11 AMERICAN NATIONAL RED CROSS GOVERNANCE MODERNIZATION ACT PRINCIPLES

The American National Red Cross Governance Modernization Act of 2007 was signed into law on May 11, 2007.[59] This legislation amended the congressional charter of the Red Cross to modernize its structure and otherwise strengthen its governance. Changes include a substantial reduction in the size of the organization's board, delegation to management of the day-to-day operations of the organization, elimination of distinctions as to how board members are elected, and transition of some board members into an advisory council.

The essence of the legislation is unique to the National Red Cross entity. Yet, there are elements of the act with larger significance. For example, the legislation refers to the governing board as a "governance and strategic oversight board."[60] It outlines the board's responsibilities (a checklist for boards in general):

- Review and approve the organization's mission statement.
- Approve and oversee the organization's strategic plan and maintain strategic oversight of operational matters.
- Select, evaluate, and determine the level of compensation of the organization's chief executive officer.
- Evaluate the performance and establish the compensation of the senior leadership team and provide for management succession.
- Oversee the financial reporting and audit process, internal controls, and legal compliance.
- Ensure that the chapters of the organization are geographically and regionally diverse.
- Hold management accountable for performance.
- Provide oversight of the financial stability of the organization.
- Ensure the inclusiveness and diversity of the organization.
- Provide oversight of the protection of the brand of the organization.[61]
- Assist with fundraising on behalf of the organization.[62]

This legislation contains the following "sense of Congress" that (1) "charitable organizations are an indispensable part of American society, but these organizations can only fulfill their important roles by maintaining the trust of the American public," (2) "trust is fostered by effective governance and transparency," and (3) "Federal and

---

58. See § 3.13; Chapter 4.
59. Pub. L. No. 110-26, 110th Cong., 1st Sess. (2007); 36 U.S.C. § 300101.
60. *Id.* § 2(a)(5).
61. This is a category of board responsibility rarely found in a list of this nature.
62. Pub. L. No. 110-26, 110th Cong., 1st Sess. (2007).

State action play an important role in ensuring effective governance and transparency by setting standards, rooting out violations, and informing the public."[63]

§ 3.12 PANEL ON NONPROFIT SECTOR GOOD GOVERNANCE PRINCIPLES

The Panel on the Nonprofit Sector (Panel), convened by Independent Sector, issued, on October 18, 2007, its "Principles for Good Governance and Ethical Practice" for public and private charitable organizations.[64] The principles are predicated on the need for a "careful balance between the two essential forms of regulation—that is, between prudent legal mandates to ensure that organizations do not abuse the privilege of their exempt status, and, for all other aspects of sound operations, well-informed self-governance and mutual awareness among nonprofit organizations." These principles, organized under four categories, are as follows:

(a) Legal Compliance and Public Disclosure

The Panel's first principle is that an organization "must comply with all applicable federal laws and regulations, as well as applicable laws and regulations of the states and the local jurisdictions in which it is based or operates." If the organization conducts programs outside the United States, it must abide by applicable international laws and conventions that are legally binding on the United States. The Panel observed that an organization's governing board is "ultimately responsible for overseeing and ensuring that the organization complies with all its legal obligations and for detecting and remedying wrongdoing by management." The Panel added that, "[w]hile board members are not required to have specialized legal knowledge, they should be familiar with the basic rules and requirements with which their organization must comply and should secure the necessary legal advice and assistance to structure appropriate monitoring and oversight mechanisms."

The Panel stated that an organization should have a "formally adopted, written code of ethics with which all of its directors or trustees, staff and volunteers are familiar and to which they adhere." This principle is predicated on the thought that "[a]dherence to the law provides a minimum standard for an organization's behavior."[65] The adoption of a code of ethics "helps demonstrate the organization's commitment to carry out its responsibilities ethically and effectively." The code should be "built on the values that the organization embraces, and should highlight expectations of how those who work with the organization will conduct themselves in a number of areas, such as the confidentiality and respect that should be accorded to clients, consumers, donors, and fellow volunteers and board and staff members."[66]

---

63. *Id.* § 2(b). In general, Josephson, "American Red Cross Governance," 55 *Exempt Org. Tax Rev.* (No. 1) 71 (Jan. 2007).
64. These principles are available at www.nonprofitpanel.org/report/principles/Principles_Guide.pdf.
65. The Panel noted that adoption of this type of a code of ethics is not required by law.
66. The Panel observed that the process of adopting and implementing a code of ethics "can be just as important as the code itself," recommending that the board and staff be "engaged in developing, drafting, adopting, and implementing a code that fits the organization's characteristics."

An organization should "adopt and implement policies and procedures to ensure that all conflicts of interest, or the appearance thereof, within the organization and the board are appropriately managed though disclosure, recusal, or other means." A conflict-of-interest policy "must be consistent with the laws of the state in which the nonprofit is organized and should be tailored to specific organizational needs and characteristics." This policy "should require full disclosure of all potential conflicts of interest within the organization" and "should apply to every person who has the ability to influence decisions of the organization, including board and staff members and parties related to them."[67]

An organization "should establish and implement policies and procedures that enable individuals to come forward with information on illegal practices or violations of organizational policies." This whistleblower policy "should specify that the organization will not retaliate against, and will protect the confidentiality of, individuals who make good-faith reports." The Panel recommended that "[i]nformation on these policies . . . be widely distributed to staff, volunteers[,] and clients, and should be incorporated both in new employee orientations and ongoing training programs for employees and volunteers." These policies "can help boards and senior managers become aware of and address problems before serious harm is done to the organization" and "can also assist in complying with legal provisions that protect individuals working in charitable organizations from retaliation for engaging in certain whistle-blowing activities."

An organization should "establish and implement policies and procedures to protect and preserve the organization's important documents and business records." The Panel observed that a document-retention policy "is essential for protecting the organization's records of its governance and administration, as well as business records that are required to demonstrate legal compliance." This type of policy "also helps to protect against allegations of wrongdoing by the organization or its directors and managers."

An organization's board "should ensure that the organization has adequate plans to protect its assets—its property, financial and human resources, programmatic content and material, and its integrity and reputation—against damage or loss." The board "should review regularly the organization's need for general liability and directors' and officers' liability insurance, as well as take other actions necessary to mitigate risks." The Panel noted that the board is "responsible for understanding the major risks to which the organization is exposed, reviewing those risks on a periodic basis, and ensuring that systems have been established to manage them." It was observed that the "level of risk to which the organization is exposed and the extent of the review and risk management process will vary considerably based on the size, programmatic focus, geographic location, and complexity of the organization's operations."

The Panel wrote that an organization "should make information about its operations, including its governance, finances, programs[,] and activities, widely available to the public." Charitable organizations "also should consider making information available on the methods they use to evaluate the outcomes of their work and sharing

---

67. The Panel noted that some organizations have their conflict-of-interest policy encompass substantial contributors.

the results of those evaluations." The theme underlying this principle is that charities should "demonstrate their commitment to accountability and transparency" by offering additional information about their finances and operations to the public, such as by means of annual reports and Web sites, with the latter containing mission statements, codes of ethics, conflict-of-interest policies, whistleblower policies, and the like.

(b) Effective Governance

An organization must have a governing body that is "responsible for reviewing and approving the organization's mission and strategic direction, annual budget and key financial transactions, compensation practices, and fiscal and governance policies." The board "bears the primary responsibility for ensuring that a charitable organization fulfills its obligations to the law, its donors, its staff and volunteers, its clients, and the public at large." The board "must protect the assets of the organization and provide oversight to ensure that its financial, human[,] and material resources are used appropriately to further the organization's mission." The board "also sets the vision and mission for the organization and establishes the broad policies and strategic direction that enable the organization to fulfill its charitable purpose."

The board of an organization "should meet regularly enough to conduct its business and fulfill its duties." Regular board meetings provide the "chief venue for board members to review the organization's financial situation and program activities, establish and monitor compliance with key organizational policies and procedures, and address issues that affect the organization's ability to fulfill its charitable mission." The Panel observed: "While many charitable organizations find it prudent to meet at least three times a year to fulfill basic governance and oversight responsibilities, some with strong committee structures, including organizations with widely dispersed board membership, hold only one or two meetings of the full board each year."

The board of an organization "should establish its own size and structure and review these periodically." The board "should have enough members to allow for full deliberation and diversity of thinking on governance and other organizational matters." Except for very small organizations, "this generally means that the board should have at least five members." Nonetheless, the Panel noted that the "ideal size of a board depends on many factors, such as the age of the organization, the nature and geographic scope of its mission and activities, and its funding needs."

The board of an organization should include members with the "diverse background (including, but not limited to, ethnic, racial and gender perspectives), experience, and organizational and financial skills necessary to advance the organization's mission." Boards of charitable organizations "generally strive to include members with expertise in budget and financial management, investments, personnel, fundraising, public relations and marketing, governance, advocacy, and leadership, as well as some members who are knowledgeable about the charitable organization's area of expertise or programs, or who have a special connection to its constituency." Some organizations "seek to maintain a board that respects the culture of and reflects the community served by the organization." An organization should "make every effort" to ensure that at least one member of the board has "financial literacy."

A "substantial majority of the board of a public charity, usually meaning at least two-thirds of the members, should be independent." "Independent" members are those who are not compensated by the organization, do not have their compensation determined by individuals who are compensated by the organization, do not receive material financial benefits from the organization (except as a member of the charitable class served by the organization), or are not related to or residing with any of the foregoing persons. An individual who is not independent is, in the view of the Panel, potentially in violation of the directors' duty of loyalty,[68] which requires the directors to "put the interests of the organization above their personal interests and to make decisions they believe are in the best interest of the nonprofit." The Panel declared that it is "important to the long-term success and accountability of the organization that a sizeable majority of the individuals on the board be free of financial conflicts of interest."

The board should "hire, oversee, and annually evaluate the performance of the chief executive officer of the organization, and should conduct such an evaluation prior to any change in that officer's compensation," unless a multiyear contract is in force or the change consists solely of routine adjustments for inflation or the cost of living. The Panel stated that "[o]ne of the most important responsibilities of the board . . . is to select, supervise, and determine a compensation package that will attract and retain a qualified chief executive." The organization's governing documents should require the full board to evaluate the executive's performance and approve his or her compensation.

The board of an organization that has paid staff "should ensure that the positions of chief staff officer, board chair, and board treasurer are held by separate individuals."[69] Organizations without paid staff should ensure that the positions of board chair and treasurer are separately held.[70] The Panel was of the view that "[c]oncentrating authority for the organization's governance and management practices in one or two people removes valuable checks and balances that help ensure that conflicts of interest and other personal concerns do not take precedence over the best interests of the organization."

The board "should establish an effective, systematic process for educating and communicating with board members to ensure that they are aware of their legal and ethical responsibilities, are knowledgeable about the programs and [other] activities of the organization, and can carry out their oversight functions effectively." The Panel observed that all board members "should receive oral and written instruction regarding the organization's governing documents, finances, program activities, and governing policies and practices." Encompassed by this principle is the thought that board members should receive agendas and background materials well in advance of board meetings.

---

68. See § 1.5(b).

69. This is a curious "principle." First, the treasurer is the treasurer of the organization, not of the board. Second, while the term "chief staff officer" is unclear, it is common for an organization's board chair and president to be the same individual.

70. This, too, is an odd "principle." First, the positions of president (not board chair) and secretary are the ones that should be separate; this is usually required by state law. Second, this separation of positions should be maintained irrespective of "paid staff."

Board members "should evaluate their performance as a group and as individuals no less frequently than every three years, and should have clear procedures for removing board members who are unable to fulfill their responsibilities." The Panel noted that a "regular process of evaluating the board's performance can help to identify strengths and weaknesses of its processes and procedures and to provide insights for strengthening orientation and educational programs, the conduct of board and committee meetings, and interactions with board and staff leadership." The board "should establish clear guidelines for the duties and responsibilities of each member, including meeting attendance, preparation[,] and participation; committee assignments; and the kinds of expertise board members are expected to have or develop in order to provide effective governance."

The board "should establish clear policies and procedures setting the length of terms and the number of consecutive terms a board member may serve." The matter of term limits continues to be controversial. The Panel stated the view in favor of term limits as follows: "Some organizations have found that such limits help in bringing fresh energy, ideas[,] and expertise to the board through new members." The contrary view: "Others have concluded that term limits may deprive the organization of valuable experience, continuity[,] and, in some cases, needed support provided by board members."

The board should review the "organizational and governing instruments no less frequently than every five years." This process will "help boards ensure that the organization is abiding by the rules it has set for itself and determine whether changes need to be made to those instruments." The board may elect to delegate some of this deliberation to a committee; if so, the "full board should consider and act upon the committee's recommendations."

The board "should establish and review regularly the organization's mission and goals and should evaluate, no less frequently than every five years, the organization's programs, goals and [other] activities to be sure they advance its mission and make prudent use of its resources." Every board should "set strategic goals and review them annually." The Panel noted that, "[b]ecause organizations and their purposes differ, it is incumbent on each organization to develop its own process for evaluating effectiveness." At a minimum, "interim benchmarks can be identified to assess whether the work is moving in the right direction."

Board members are "generally expected to serve without compensation, other than reimbursement for expenses incurred to fulfill their board duties."[71] An organization that provides compensation to its board members should use "appropriate comparability data" to determine the amount to be paid,[72] document the decision, and provide full disclosure to anyone, on request, of the amount of and rationale for the compensation. Board members of charitable organizations are responsible for "ascertaining that any compensation they receive does not exceed to a significant degree the compensation provided for positions in comparable organizations with similar responsibilities and qualifications."[73] It is the view of the Panel that board members

---

71. Again (see *supra* note 31), expense reimbursement, however, generally is not *compensation*.
72. Compensation of board members of charitable organizations, however, is so uncommon (other than in unique circumstances such as private foundations) that *appropriate comparability data* is essentially nonexistent.
73. *Id.*

"of public charities often donate both time and funds to the organization, a practice that supports the sector's spirit of giving and volunteering."

(c) Strong Financial Oversight

An organization "must keep complete, current, and accurate financial records." Its board "should receive and review timely reports of the organization's financial activities and should have a qualified, independent financial expert audit or review these statements annually in a manner appropriate to the organization's size and scale of operations." Each organization "must ensure that it has its annual financial statements audited or reviewed as required by law in the states in which it operates or raises funds or as required by government or private funders." The Panel observed that a charitable organization "that has its financial statements independently audited, whether or not it is legally required to do so, should consider establishing an audit committee composed of independent board members with appropriate financial expertise."

The board of an organization "must institute policies and procedures to ensure that the organization (and, if applicable, its subsidiaries) manages and invests its funds responsibly, in accordance with all legal requirements." The full board "should review and approve the organization's annual budget and should monitor actual performance against the budget." The Panel observed that "[s]ound financial management is among the most important responsibilities of the board of directors," which "should establish clear policies to protect the organization's financial assets and ensure that no one person bears the sole responsibility for receiving, depositing, and spending its funds."

An organization "should not provide loans (or the equivalent, such as loan guarantees, purchasing or transferring ownership of a residence or office, or relieving a debt or lease obligation) to directors, officers, or trustees." These practices have "created both real and perceived problems for public charities." (The Panel noted that the federal tax law has prohibitions in this regard in the case of private foundations, supporting organizations, and donor-advised funds.[74])

An organization "should spend a significant percentage of its annual budget on programs that pursue its mission." The budget "should also provide sufficient resources for effective administration of the organization, and, if it solicits contributions, for appropriate fundraising activities." The Panel, noting that some watchdog groups assert that public charities should (or must) spend at least 65% of their funds on program activities,[75] found that standard to be "reasonable for most organizations," yet also noted that "there can be extenuating circumstances that require an organization to devote more resources to administrative and fundraising activities."

An organization "should establish clear, written policies for paying or reimbursing expenses incurred by anyone conducting business or traveling on behalf of the organization, including the types of expenses that can be paid for or reimbursed and the documentation required." These policies "should require that travel on behalf of the organization is to be undertaken in a cost-effective manner." The Panel advised

---

74. See, e.g., *Law of Tax-Exempt Organizations* §§ 12.1, 12.3(c), 11.8, respectively.
75. See § 5.13.

that decisions as to travel expenditures "should be based on how best to further the organization's charitable purposes, rather than on the title or position of the person traveling," noting that "lavish, extravagant or excessive" expenditures are to be avoided.

An organization "should neither pay for nor reimburse travel expenditures for spouses, dependents[,] or others who are accompanying someone conducting business for the organization unless they, too, are conducting such business." Nonetheless, the Panel added that, if an organization "deems it proper to cover expenses for a spouse, dependent, or other person accompanying someone on business travel, the payment generally must, by law, be treated as compensation to the individual traveling on behalf of the organization."

(d) Responsible Fundraising

Solicitation materials and other communications addressed to prospective donors and the public "must clearly identify the organization and be accurate and truthful." The Panel stated that a prospective donor "has the right to know the name of anyone soliciting contributions, the name and location of the organization that will receive the contribution, a clear description of its activities, the intended use of the funds to be raised, a contact for obtaining additional information, and whether the individual requesting the contribution is acting as a volunteer, employee of the organization, or hired solicitor."[76]

Contributions "must be used for purposes consistent with the donor's intent, whether as described in the relevant solicitation materials or as specifically directed by the donor." The Panel stated that solicitations should "indicate whether the funds they generate will be used to further the general programs and operations of the organization or to support specific programs or types of programs." The Panel advised charitable organizations to "carefully review the terms of any contract or grant agreement before accepting a donation."

An organization "must provide donors with specific acknowledgments of charitable contributions, in accordance with [federal tax law] requirements, as well as information to facilitate the donor's compliance with tax law requirements." The Panel noted that not only is this type of acknowledgment generally required by law, "it also helps in building donors' confidence in and support for the activities they help to fund."

An organization should adopt "clear policies, based on its specific exempt purpose, to determine whether accepting a gift would compromise its ethics, financial circumstances, program focus[,] or other interests." The Panel warned that "[s]ome charitable contributions have the potential to create significant problems for an organization or a donor," noting that funds may be disbursed for "illegal or unethical" purposes, may subject the donee organization to legal liability (e.g., under environmental protection laws), or result in unrelated business income.

An organization "should provide appropriate training and supervision of the people soliciting funds on its behalf to ensure that they understand their responsibilities and applicable federal, state[,] and local laws, and do not employ techniques that are coercive, intimidating, or intended to harass potential donors." The Panel

---

76. The source of this *right* is not identified.

amplified this principle by recommending that a charitable organization should ensure that its fundraisers "are respectful of a donor's concerns and do not use coercive or abusive language or strategies to secure contributions, misuse personal information about potential donors, pursue personal relationships that are subject to misinterpretation by potential donors, or mislead potential donors in other ways."

An organization "should not compensate internal or external fundraisers based on a commission or a percentage of the amount raised." Compensation on this basis "can encourage fundraisers to put their own interests ahead of those of the organization or the donor and may lead to inappropriate techniques that jeopardize the organization's values and reputation and the donor's trust in the organization," and can lead to or be perceived as "excessive compensation."

An organization "should respect the privacy of individual donors and, except where disclosure is required by law, should not sell or otherwise make available the names and contact information of its donors without providing them an opportunity at least once a year to opt out of the use of their names." The Panel observed that "[p]reserving the trust and support of donors requires that donor information be handled with respect and confidentiality to the maximum extent permitted by law."

§ 3.13 REDESIGNED IRS ANNUAL INFORMATION RETURN (FORM 990)

The IRS significantly revised the principal annual information return (Form 990) filed by tax-exempt organizations. This return, applicable beginning with the 2008 filing season, includes a series of questions that directly reflect the agency's views as to governance principles applicable to exempt organizations, principally public charities.[77] Indeed, this return, particularly in Part VI, is designed to influence and modify exempt organizations' behavior, by in essence forcing them to adopt certain policies and procedures[78] so they can check "yes" rather than "no" boxes. Almost none of these policies and procedures is required by the federal tax law.[79]

§ 3.14 IRS LIFECYCLE EDUCATIONAL TOOL PRINCIPLES

The most recent formal views of the IRS on the matter of governance principles for tax-exempt organizations are found in the components of the agency's LifeCycle educational tool, posted on the IRS Web site on February 14, 2008.[80] The IRS stated: "Good governance is important to increase the likelihood that organizations will comply with the tax law, protect their charitable assets and, thereby, best serve their charitable beneficiaries."

The contents of this document follow, albeit condensed in places, with the stated text essentially verbatim.

---

77. See Chapter 4.
78. See Chapter 6.
79. In general, Nilles and Meier, "IRS Places New Emphasis on Nonprofit Corporate Governance Policies: Are You Ready for the New Form 990?," 57 *Exempt Org. Tax Rev.* (no. 3) 283 (Sep. 2007).
80. IRS, "Governance and Related Topics—501(c)(3) Organizations," available on the IRS Web site at www.irs.gov/pub/irs-tege/governance practices.pdf.

(a)   Introduction

The IRS believes that a well-governed charity is more likely to obey the tax laws, safe-guard charitable assets, and serve charitable interests than one with poor or lax governance. A charity that has clearly articulated purposes that describe its mission, a knowledgeable and committed governing body and management team, and sound management practices is more likely to operate effectively and consistent with tax law requirements. Although the tax law generally does not mandate particular management structures, operational policies, or administrative practices, it is important that each charity be thoughtful about the management practices that are most appropriate for that charity in assuring sound operations and compliance with the tax law.

(b)   Mission

The IRS encourages every charity to establish and regularly review its mission. A clearly articulated mission, adopted by the board of directors, serves to explain and popularize the charity's purpose and guide its work. It also addresses why the charity exists, what it hopes to accomplish, and what activities it will undertake, where, and for whom.[81]

(c)   Organizational Documents

Regardless of whether a charity is a corporation, trust, unincorporated association, or other type of organization, it must have organizational documents that provide the framework for its governance and management. State law often prescribes the type of organizational document and its content. State law may require corporations to adopt bylaws. Organizational documents must be filed with applications for recognition of exemption.[82]

(d)   Governing Body

The IRS encourages an active and engaged board, believing that it is important to the success of a charity and to its compliance with applicable tax law requirements. Governing boards should be composed of persons who are informed and active in overseeing a charity's operations and finances. The IRS is concerned that if a governing board tolerates a climate of secrecy or neglect, charitable assets are more likely to be diverted to benefit the private interests of insiders at the expense of public and charitable interests. Successful governing boards include individuals who not only are knowledgeable and engaged but selected with the organization's needs in mind (e.g., accounting, finance, compensation, and ethics).

Attention should also be paid to the size of the board, ensuring that it is the appropriate size to effectively make sure that the organization obeys tax laws, safeguards its charitable assets, and furthers its charitable purposes. Small boards run the

---

81. Organizations required to file Form 990 may describe their mission in Part I, line 1, and are required to describe their mission (if board-approved) in Part III, line 1. See *New Form 990* §§ 1.5(a), 1.6(a), 2.2(a).
82. The Form 990, Part VI, Section A, line 4, requires organizations to report significant changes to their organizational documents since the previous Form 990 was filed. See *New Form 990* §§ 5.1(k), 5.2(a)(4).

risk of not representing a sufficiently broad public interest, and of lacking the required skills and other resources required to effectively govern the organization. On the other hand, very large boards may have a more difficult time getting down to business and making decisions.

A governing board should include independent members and not be dominated by employees or others who are not independent individuals because of family or business relationships. The IRS reviews the board composition of charities to determine whether the board represents a broad public interest; to identify the potential for insider transactions that could result in misuse of charitable assets; to determine whether an organization has independent members, stockholders, or other persons with the authority to elect members of the board or approve or reject board decisions; and to ascertain whether the organization has delegated control or key management authority to a management company or other persons.[83]

If an organization has local chapters, branches, or affiliates, the IRS encourages it to have procedures and policies in place to ensure that the activities and operations of these subordinates are consistent with those of the parent organization.[84]

(e) Governance and Management Policies

Although the federal tax law does not require charities to have governance and management policies, the IRS will nonetheless review an organization's application for recognition of exemption and annual information returns to determine whether it has implemented policies relating to executive compensation, conflicts of interest, investments, fundraising, documenting governance decisions, document retention and destruction, and whistleblower claims.

Persons who are knowledgeable in compensation matters and who have no financial interest in the determination should determine a charity's executive compensation. The federal tax law does not, however, require charities to follow a particular process in ascertaining the amount of this type of compensation. Organizations that file Form 990 will find that the return inquires as to whether the process used to determine the compensation of an organization's top management official and other officers and key employees included a review and approval by independent persons, comparability data, and contemporaneous substantiation of the deliberation and decision.[85] In addition, the return solicits compensation information for certain trustees, directors, officers, key employees, and highest compensated employees.[86]

The IRS encourages reliance on the *rebuttable presumption*, which is part of the intermediate sanctions rules. Under this test, payments of compensation are presumed to be reasonable if the compensation arrangement is approved in advance by an authorized body composed entirely of individuals who do not have a conflict of interest with respect to the arrangement, if the authorized body obtained and relied on appropriate data as to comparability prior to making its determination, and if the

---

83. The Form 990, Part VI, Section A, lines 1, 2, and 7, ask questions about the governing body. See *New Form 990* § 5.2(a)(1), (2), and (6).
84. The Form 990, Part VI, Section A, line 9, inquires about these types of procedures and policies. See *New Form 990* § 5.2(a)(8).
85. Form 990, Part VI, Section B, line 15. See *New Form 990* § 5.2(b)(3).
86. Form 990, Part VII; Schedule J. See *New Form 990*, Chapter 6.

authorized body adequately documented the basis for its determination concurrently with making the determination.[87]

The duty of loyalty, which requires a director to act in the interest of the charity,[88] requires a director to avoid conflicts of interest that are detrimental to the charity. The IRS encourages a charity's board of directors to adopt and regularly evaluate a written conflict-of-interest policy that requires directors and staff to act solely in the interests of the charity without regard for personal interests; includes written procedures for determining whether a relationship, financial interest, or business affiliation results in a conflict of interest; and prescribes a course of action in the event a conflict of interest is identified.[89]

Increasingly, charities are investing in joint ventures, for-profit entities, and complicated and sophisticated financial products or investments that require financial and investment expertise and, in some instances, the advice of outside investment advisors. The IRS encourages charities that make these types of investments to adopt written policies and procedures requiring the charity to evaluate its participation in these investments and to take steps to safeguard the organization's assets and tax-exempt status if they could be affected by the investment arrangement. The return asks whether an organization has adopted this type of policy.[90] Also, the return asks for detailed information about certain investments.[91]

The IRS encourages charities to adopt and monitor policies to ensure that fundraising solicitations meet federal and state law requirements, and that solicitation materials are accurate, truthful, and candid. Charities are encouraged to keep their fundraising costs reasonable, and to provide information about fundraising costs and practices to donors and the public. The return solicits information about fundraising activities, revenues, and expenses.[92]

The IRS encourages the governing bodies and subcommittees to take steps to ensure that minutes of their meetings, and actions taken by written action or outside of meetings, are contemporaneously documented. The return asks whether an organization contemporaneously documents meetings or written actions undertaken during the year by its governing body and committees with authority to act on behalf of the governing body.[93]

The IRS encourages charities to adopt a written policy establishing standards for document integrity, retention, and destruction. This type of policy should include guidelines for handling electronic files; it should also cover backup procedures, archiving of documents, and regular checkups of the reliability of the system. The return asks whether an organization has a written document retention and destruction policy.[94]

---

87. See *Law of Tax-Exempt Organizations* § 21.9.

88. See § 1.5(b).

89. Form 990, Part VI, Section B, line 12, asks whether an organization has a written conflict-of-interest policy, and whether it regularly and consistently monitors and enforces compliance with the policy. See *New Form 990* § 5.2(b)(1).

90. Form 990, Part VI, Section B, line 16. See *New Form 990* § 5.2(b)(4).

91. Form 990, Schedule D. See *New Form 990*, Chapter 11.

92. Form 990, Schedules G, M. See *New Form 990*, Chapters 14, 19.

93. Form 990, Part VI, Section A, line 8. See *New Form 990* § 5.2(a)(7).

94. Form 990, Part VI, Section B, line 14. See *New Form 990* § 5.2(b)(3).

The IRS also encourages a charity's board to consider adopting and regularly evaluating a code of ethics that describes behavior it wants to encourage and behavior it wants to discourage. A code of ethics will serve to communicate and further a strong culture of legal compliance and ethical integrity to all persons associated with the organization.[95]

The IRS further encourages the board to adopt an effective policy—a whistle-blower policy—for handling employee complaints and to establish procedures for employees to report in confidence any suspected financial impropriety or misuse of the charity's resources. The return asks whether the organization became aware during the year of a material diversion of its assets and whether an organization has a written whistleblower policy.[96]

(f) Financial Statements and Form 990 Reporting

The IRS is of the view that a charity with substantial assets or revenue should consider obtaining an audit of its finances by an independent auditor. The board may establish an independent audit committee to select and oversee an auditor. The return asks whether the organization's financial statements were compiled or reviewed by an independent accountant, audited by an independent accountant, and subject to oversight by a committee within the organization.[97] Also, the return asks whether, as the result of a federal award, the organization was required to undergo an audit.[98]

Practices differ widely as to who sees the Form 990, when they see it (before or after its filing), and the extent of the reviewers' input, review, or approval. Some organizations provide copies of the return to the members of the board and other governance or management officials. The return asks whether the organization provides a copy of the return to its governing body and requires the organization to explain any process of review by its directors or management.[99]

(g) Transparency and Accountability

By making full and accurate information about its mission, activities, finances, and governance publicly available, a charity encourages transparency and accountability to its constituents. The IRS encourages every charity to adopt and monitor procedures to ensure that its Form 1023, Form 990, Form 990-T, annual reports, and financial statements are complete and accurate, are posted on its public Web site, and are made available to the public on request.[100]

---

95. See § 6.3(t).
96. Form 990, Part VI, Section B, lines 5 and 13. See *New Form 990* §§ 5.2(a)(5), (b)(2).
97. Form 990, Part XI, line 2. See *New Form 990* § 7.2(b)(1).
98. Form 990, Part XI, line 3. See *New Form 990* § 7.2(b)(1).
99. Form 990, Part VI, Section A, line 10. See *New Form 990* § 5.2(a)(9).
100. The Form 990, Part VI, Section C, lines 18 and 19, ask whether and how an organization makes its returns, governing instruments, conflict-of-interest policy, and financial statements available to the public. See *New Form 990* § 5.2(c)(2).

§ 3.15 COMMENTARY

No one can be objective about the substance (content) of nonprofit organizations' governance principles (or best practices). Obviously, there can be disagreement over particular principles. But, each individual brings to the analysis his or her attitudes about regulation (as a liberal, conservative, moderate, libertarian, faith-based, whatever) in general. This viewpoint informs one's reaction to a particular set of standards or to a single standard. For example, an individual's stance in connection with term limits generally will inevitably be brought to bear on the individual's view toward term limits for members of the board of nonprofit organizations. (Are term limits a good idea because they continually introduce fresh thinking about the direction and programs of the organization or are they a bad idea because they are predicated on the notion that people ought not to be trusted to decide for whom they wish to vote?) As another example, someone who has a general antipathy toward regulation is likely to be repulsed by a proposal that the law should dictate the size of the board of a nonprofit organization (other than the general minimum standard of three).

Somewhat related to an individual's attitude about regulation is the view of some that, when it comes to programs, board functions, fundraising expense, and the like, one size does not fit all. Thus, the matter of the size of a nonprofit board is also enmeshed in this element. But this factor goes beyond board size, raising other questions. Does every nonprofit organization need 16 different policies? Need the full board review the annual information return? Are three board meetings a year sufficient, as opposed to, say, four? And, of course, the biggest bugaboo of all: Should a charitable organization be stigmatized because its fundraising expense ratio is above a certain percentage?

One aspect of nonprofit organization governance that is almost never addressed in these standards is the financial cost of "good governance" or "best practices." An organization with a board of individuals scattered throughout the nation is financially impacted if there are nine board members instead of five (airfare, lodging, meals, and the like). Detailed annual reports and a well-designed Web site are nice to have but can be expensive.

These standards for governance of nonprofit organizations all seem predicated on an unstated assumption that an organization has unlimited numbers of individuals waiting to serve on the board. Thus, the piling on of board member responsibilities, term limits, even the IRS's proposal that board members be traded, from time to time, to other nonprofit organizations (maybe replete with their picture on a card accompanied by a slab of bubble gum).

How about rating the raters? What criteria should be used in doing this (other than the above factors concerning personal predilections)? Are the standards complete? (Certainly, all of these standards together haven't missed much.) Are they rational? Are they reasonable? Why are they so contradictory? Do they amount to overreaching? Are some of the proposals bad ideas or nonsensical ones? Are some of the standards too wordy? Poorly written? Is poor grammar in there?

Your authors' take on this is that there is a tie: The best of the standards are those written by Independent Sector's Panel on the Nonprofit Sector and the Standards for Excellence Institute. The worst of the lot was the draft of good governance principles offered up by the IRS. Although there is disagreement from here as to some of the principles issued from these two sources, the standards promulgated by the Panel and the Institute generally pass the tests as to completeness, rationality, and reasonableness. (Yes, there is poor writing and bad grammar in them.) The IRS' principles raise questions, such as whether the agency has added anything to the realm of standards-setting (it hasn't) and whether the IRS came up with some nonsensical proposals (it did).

CHAPTER FOUR

Governance and the Redesigned Form 990

The Form 990 is the annual information return that most tax-exempt organizations file with the Internal Revenue Service (IRS). (Private foundations, however, file a Form 990-PF.) The IRS issued the return in dramatically redesigned form on December 19, 2007, to be filed for the 2008 tax year and thereafter.[1]

The IRS, by means of the new Form 990, has significantly increased the focus of the annual information return on the governance, practices, policies, and procedures of nonprofit, tax-exempt organizations. Not only is a significant part of the Form 990 devoted to governance—Part VI—but woven throughout the form are questions regarding the filing organization's policies and practices regarding matters such as executive compensation (Part VII and Schedule J),[2] grantmaking (Schedules F and I),[3] fundraising and gaming (Schedule G),[4] and gifts of noncash property (Schedule M).[5] In addition, the form requests a significant amount of information regarding relationships among an organization's officers and directors, relationships between interested persons and the organization, and an organization's relationship with other entities, both taxable and tax-exempt.

The bulk of the governance questions on the redesigned Form 990 is found in Part VI, where the IRS requests information about the tax-exempt organization's board composition and independence, its governance and management structure and policies, and whether (and, if so, how) the organization promotes transparency and accountability to its constituents and beneficiaries. By requesting the information, the IRS will likely conform the practices of many exempt entities to its own view of good governance principles. The process of completing the redesigned Form 990 will likely cause many organizations to, in effect, engage in a certain amount of self-reformation by changing their governance practices and adopting policies and procedures that will enable them to respond to the form's

---

1. Changes have also been made in the Form 990-EZ, filed by small tax-exempt organizations (see *Law of Tax-Exempt Organizations* § 27.2(a)(iv); *New Form 990 Book* § 1.9). The IRS has not yet made any alterations of the Form 990-PF (see *Private Foundations*, Chapter 12; Hopkins, *Private Foundation Law Made Easy* (Hoboken: Wiley 2008), Chapter 10).
2. See *New Form 990 Book*, Chapter 6.
3. *Id.*, Chapters 13, 16.
4. *Id.*, Chapter 14.
5. *Id.*, Chapter 19.

questions in the affirmative, thus hoping to look better in the eyes of the IRS, potential funding sources, and the public.[6]

In an indication of the importance the IRS is placing on matters of governance in this context, the Commissioner, Tax Exempt and Government Entities, characterized Part VI as the "crown jewel" of the Form 990.[7] The IRS states that, while many of the Part VI questions address policies and procedures that are not required by the Internal Revenue Code, the IRS considers such policies and procedures generally to improve tax compliance.[8] Further, the IRS states that the "absence of appropriate policies and procedures may lead to opportunities for excess benefit transactions, inurement, operation for non-exempt purposes, or other activities inconsistent with exempt status."[9] Many of the questions asked in Part VI do not reflect legal requirements to which exempt organizations are subject, but instead are designed to determine whether an exempt entity is engaging in practices that are closely aligned with principles of good corporate governance.

The IRS believes that the "existence of an independent governing body and well-defined governance and management policies and practices increases the likelihood that an organization is operating in compliance with federal tax law."[10] In addition, the agency has stated that a "well-governed charity is more likely to obey the tax laws, safeguard charitable assets, and serve charitable interests than one with poor or lax governance."[11]

The Form 990's questions on governance may be grouped into three categories: governing body and management, policies, and disclosure practices.

§4.1 GOVERNING BODY AND MANAGEMENT

Section A of Part VI of the redesigned Form 990 is formulated to solicit information regarding a tax-exempt organization's governing structure, composition of its governing body, and governing body procedures. Some of this information is also set forth in Part I of the Form 990, which is the summary portion of the information return. Exempt organizations that are organized as corporations are typically governed by either a board of directors or a board of trustees. If the exempt organization is a trust, it may have a board of trustees or be governed by a single, sometimes corporate, trustee. On the Form 990, a filing organization must disclose various information as to how its board operates.

(a) Board Size and Composition

On the Form 990, a filing organization must report the number of members of its governing body (that is, its board of directors or trustees) that are entitled to vote.[12]

---

6. Tax-exempt organizations must make available to the public their three most recently filed information returns. See § 4.3.
7. Remarks of Steven T. Miller, April 24, 2008, at the Representing & Managing Nonprofit Organizations conference, Georgetown University Law Center, Washington, D.C. See § 5.13(c).
8. Form 990 instructions, Part VI Governance, Management, and Disclosure.
9. *Id.*
10. Form 990 instructions, Highlights, Part VI Governance, Management, and Disclosure Rationale.
11. See § 3.14.
12. Form 990, Part I, lines 2 and 3, and Part VI, lines 1a and 1b.

Voting members of the governing body are members with the power to vote on all matters that may come before the governing body (other than when a conflict of interest disqualifies the member from voting). If the members of the governing body do not all have the same voting rights, the organization is instructed to explain any material differences in voting rights.

With respect to the required number of members of a tax-exempt organization's governing body, state law typically mandates that at least three individuals comprise the governing body of a nonprofit corporation, although a few states require only one. Some nonprofit corporations have very large boards of directors; state law typically does not set a maximum on the number of directors of nonprofit organizations. Some agencies and organizations suggest a minimum of three or five directors in their good governance guidelines, and at least one suggests a 15-person maximum.[13] The IRS, in its LifeCycle Educational Tool principles, states

> Very small or very large governing boards may not adequately serve the needs of the organization. Small boards may run the risk of not representing a sufficiently broad public interest and of lacking the required skills and other resources required to effectively govern the organization. On the other hand, very large boards may have a more difficult time getting down to business and making decisions.[14]

The document further cautions that if an organization's "governing board is large, the organization may want to establish an executive committee with delegated responsibilities or advisory committees." In this document, the IRS expressed its view that governing boards of charitable organizations "should be composed of persons who are informed and active in overseeing a charity's operations and finances."[15] If a governing board "tolerates a climate of secrecy or neglect, [the IRS is] concerned that charitable assets are more likely to be diverted to benefit the private interests of insiders at the expense of public and charitable interests."[16] According to the IRS, successful governing boards "include individuals who not only are knowledgeable and engaged, but selected with the organization's needs in mind (e.g., accounting, finance, compensation and ethics)."[17]

Generally, most organizations commenting on nonprofit board size agree that one size does not fit all governing bodies. The Panel on the Nonprofit Sector, in its "Principles for Good Governance and Ethical Practice A Guide for Charities and Foundations" (*33 Principles*),[18] states that a board of a charitable organization should establish its own size and structure and review its size periodically, and, further, that a board "should have enough members to allow for full deliberation and diversity of thinking on governance and other organization matters."[19] The Panel on the Nonprofit Sector, in its 2005 report to Congress, stated that "[i]n the end, each charitable

---

13. See, for example, the Standards for Excellence Institute standards, which state that a nonprofit organization's board should have no fewer than five unrelated directors, and that seven or more directors are preferable (see § 3.3(e)). See also the Evangelical Council for Financial Accountability standards, which state that each of its members "shall be governed by a responsible board of not less than five individuals" (see § 3.3(d)).
14. LifeCycle Educational Tool, § 3.
15. *Id.*
16. *Id.*
17. *Id.*
18. See § 3.12.
19. See 33 Principles § 10.

organization must determine the most appropriate size for its board and the appropriate number and responsibilities of board committees to ensure that the board is able to fulfill its fiduciary and other governance duties responsibly and effectively."[20]

The composition of a nonprofit organization's governing board is generally a matter of state law. There are four exceptions to this general rule embodied in the federal tax law: (1) tax-exempt healthcare organizations are required to satisfy a community benefit test, which includes having a board that is reflective of the community; (2) organizations qualifying as publicly supported charities by reason of the facts-and-circumstances test may need to have a governing board that is representative of the community, as a community board is one of the factors considered in meeting the test; (3) organizations that qualify as supporting organizations are subject to certain requirements as to their board composition and/or selection; and (4) entities qualifying as exempt credit counseling organizations are subject to board composition requirements regarding financial independence from the organization. [21]

(b) Independent Board Members

There is no general requirement that a nonprofit organization have a certain number of independent board members. The inclusion of independent directors on the board of a nonprofit entity, however, is considered a good governance practice. The 33 Principles suggests that two-thirds of a charity's board should be composed of independent members, that is, members who (1) are not compensated by the organization as employees or independent contractors, (2) do not have their compensation set by individuals who are compensated by the organization, (3) do not receive, directly or indirectly, material financial benefits from the organization except as a member of the charitable class served by the organization, or (4) are not related to anyone described in the foregoing three categories or residing with a person so described.[22]

This recommendation represents an increased proportion of independent board members over the Panel's earlier recommendation. In the Panel on the Nonprofit Sector's 2005 report to Congress, the Panel recommended that public charities be required by law to have independent board members, because public charities are not subject to the self-dealing rules with which private foundations are expected to comply and therefore have a heightened need for independence on their boards.[23] In the report, the Panel suggests a one-third minimum for independent board members.[24] IRS agents, when reviewing initial applications for recognition of exemption, often try to impose their own views on board compositions, such as requiring the addition of independent directors;[25] these views are not correct assertions of the law.[26]

Independent members of a governing body are generally those members with no financial or family connections with respect to the organization. The recommendation

---

20. Panel on the Nonprofit Sector, "Report to Congress and the Nonprofit Sector on Governance, Transparency, and Accountability," (2005), § 13.
21. See § 5.3(a).
22. See 33 Principles § 12.
23. Panel on the Nonprofit Sector, "Report to Congress and the Nonprofit Sector on Governance, Transparency, and Accountability," (2005) § 13.
24. *Id.*
25. See § 5.21(g).
26. See § 5.21(h).

of independent directors stems from the notion that directors will be less conflicted, and more mindful of the organization's mission, if they are independent from the other members of the governing body and the organization itself. Directors who are related through family and business relationships, or whose compensation is set by the other directors, may be less inclined to exercise independence in their decision-making. The TE/GE Commissioner stated that "outside of the very smallest organizations, or possibly family foundations," an active, independent, and engaged board of directors is the "gold standard" of board composition.[27]

A member of the governing body is considered *independent* for Form 990 reporting purposes only if all three of these circumstances applied at all times during the organization's tax year:

1. The member was not compensated as an officer or other employee of the organization or of a related organization, except for the religious exception discussed below.

2. The member did not receive total compensation or other payments exceeding $10,000 for the year from the organization or from related organizations as an independent contractor, other than reimbursement of expenses or reasonable compensation for services provided in the capacity as a member of the governing body. For example, a person who receives reasonable expense reimbursements and reasonable compensation as a director of the organization does not cease to be independent merely because he or she also receives payments of $7,500 from the organization for other arrangements.

3. Neither the member, nor any family member of the member, was involved in a transaction with the organization, directly or indirectly through affiliation with another organization, that is required to be reported on Form 990 Schedule L (Transactions with Interested Persons) for the organization's tax year or in a transaction with a related organization of a type and amount that would be reportable on Form 990, Schedule L if required to be filed by the related organization.[28]

A member of the governing body is not considered to lack independence merely because of any of the following circumstances:

1. The member is a major donor to the organization, regardless of the amount of the contribution.

2. The member has taken a bona fide vow of poverty and either (a) receives compensation as an agent of a religious order or of a religious and apostolic organization, but only under circumstances in which the individual does not receive taxable income or (b) belongs to a religious order that receives sponsorship or payments from the organization that do not constitute taxable income to the member.

---

27. Remarks of Steven T. Miller, Commissioner, Tax Exempt and Government Entities, Internal Revenue Service, Georgetown University Law Center, Seminar on Representing & Managing Tax-Exempt Organizations, Panel on Nonprofit Governance (April 23, 2008). See § 5.13(c).

28. Generally, these transactions are business transactions between a tax-exempt organization and its interested persons that exceed certain monetary thresholds.

3. The member receives financial benefits from the organization solely in the capacity of being a member of the charitable or other class served by the organization in the exercise of its exempt function, such as being a member of a trade association, so long as the financial benefits comply with the organization's terms of membership.[29]

The IRS states that an organization does not need to engage in more than a *reasonable effort* to obtain the necessary information to determine the independence of members of the governing body and may rely on information provided to the organization by its directors and trustees. As an example of this, the IRS states the organization may rely on information it obtains through an annual questionnaire sent to each member of the governing body that includes the name, title, date, and signature of each person reporting the information and gives pertinent instructions and definitions to determine whether the governing body member is independent.[30]

(c) Family and Business Relationships

On the Form 990, the IRS asks whether any officer, director, trustee, or key employee has a family relationship or a business relationship with any other officer, director, trustee, or key employee.[31] This question is designed to identify relationships (sometimes called horizontal relationships) that could create a bias in the decision-making process. For each family and business relationship, the reporting organization is required to identify the persons and describe their relationship; it is sufficient for the organization to state "family relationship" or "business relationship" without greater detail.[32]

The family of an individual includes his or her spouse, ancestors, brothers and sisters (whether whole or half blood), children (whether natural or adopted), grandchildren, and spouses of brothers, sisters, children, and grandchildren. Business relationships between two persons include the following:

1. One person is employed by the other in a sole proprietorship or by an organization with which the other is associated as a trustee, director, officer, key employee, or greater-than-35% owner.

2. One person is transacting business with the other (other than in the ordinary course of either party's business on the same terms as are generally offered to the public), directly or indirectly, in one or more contracts of sale, lease, license, loan, performance of services, or other transaction involving transfers of cash or property valued in excess of $10,000 in the aggregate during the tax year. Indirect transactions are transactions with an organization with which the one person is associated as a trustee, director, officer, key employee, or greater-than-35% owner.

3. The two persons are each a director, trustee, officer, or greater than 10% owner in the same business or investment entity.[33]

---

29. Form 990 instructions, Part VI, line 1b.
30. *Id.*
31. Form 990, Part VI, line 2.
32. Form 990 instructions, Part VI, line 2.
33. *Id.*

Ownership is measured by stock ownership (either voting power or value) of a corporation, profits or capital interest in a partnership or limited liability company, membership interest in a nonprofit organization, or beneficial interest in a trust.[34] Ownership includes indirect ownership (e.g., ownership in an entity that has ownership in the entity in question); there may be ownership through multiple tiers of entities.[35]

Because the relationships among the officers, directors, trustees, and key employees may not be known to the filing organization, tax-exempt organizations should distribute a questionnaire to these persons requesting information on family and business relationships for purposes of completing the Form 990. This questionnaire can be part of the annual disclosure statement used to determine actual or potential conflicts of interest under an organization's conflict-of interest-policy. The IRS states that an organization need not engage in more than a *reasonable effort* to obtain the information necessary to answer the questions regarding family and business relationships; the agency has provided, as an example of this type of a reasonable effort, the distribution of an annual questionnaire to each member of an organization's governing body that includes the name, title, date, and signature of each person reporting the information and containing the pertinent information to respond to the question.[36]

(d) Delegation to a Management Company

The IRS, in Part VI of Form 990, asks whether the tax-exempt organization delegated control over management duties customarily performed by or under the direct supervision of officers, directors or trustees, or key employees to a management company or other person.[37] The inquiry is designed to determine the extent to which an exempt organization has outsourced its management functions and may have ceded control of the organization to others, in search of instances of private inurement, private benefit, and/or excess benefit transactions.[38] Management duties include hiring, firing, and supervising personnel, planning or executing budgets or financial operations, or supervising exempt operations or unrelated trades or businesses of the organization.[39]

(e) Significant Changes to Organizational Documents

On the Form 990, the IRS asks whether the reporting tax-exempt organization made any significant changes to its organizational documents since the prior Form 990 was filed or that were not reported on a prior Form 990 and to describe its significant changes.[40] An exempt entity should report material changes in its character,

---

34. *Id.*
35. *Id.*
36. Form 990 instructions, Part VI, line 2. There are other parts of Form 990 for which a filing organization is deemed to have engaged in a reasonable effort to obtain requested information, including the independence of a director (Form 990, Part VI, Part A) and the existence of interested party grants and business transactions (Form 990, Schedule L).
37. Form 990, Part VI, line 3.
38. See, e.g., § 8.4(d)–(f).
39. Form 990 instructions, Part VI, line 3.
40. Form 990, Part VI, line 4.

purposes, or methods of operation to the IRS as soon as possible after the change is made or becomes effective. Other changes that are not material, but that are not insubstantial, should be reported to the IRS on the organization's Form 990.

While there is no automatic sanction for failure to report a material change, a tax-exempt organization may not rely on a determination letter or ruling recognizing its exempt status if there has been a material change in the organization's character, purposes, or methods of operation.[41] Likewise, it has been held that, if there have not been any such material changes, the IRS is bound by its determination letter and thus may not retroactively revoke exempt status.[42]

If an organization changes its form, the IRS generally regards this change as the creation of a new legal entity.[43] This includes the conversion of a trust to a corporation, the incorporation of an unincorporated association, and the reincorporation of a nonprofit corporation in another jurisdiction. In these instances, the organization must file a new application for recognition of exemption with the IRS if the organization needs or desires to have its tax-exempt status recognized by the IRS.

The IRS provides examples of significant changes to a tax-exempt organization's governing documents that are reportable to the IRS, such as changes in the:

- Number, composition, qualifications, authority, or duties of the governing body's voting members
- Number, composition, qualifications, authority, or duties of the organization's officers or key employees
- Role of the stockholders or membership in governance
- Distribution of assets upon dissolution
- Provisions to amend the organizing or enabling document or bylaws
- Quorum, voting rights, or voting approval requirements of the governing body members or the organization's stockholders or membership
- Organization's exempt purposes or mission
- Policies or procedures contained within the organizing document or bylaws regarding compensation of officers, directors, trustees, or key employees, conflicts of interest, whistleblowers, or document retention and destruction
- Composition or procedures contained within the organizing document or bylaws of an audit committee[44]

Insignificant changes made to organizing or enabling documents or bylaws, such as changes to the organization's registered agent with the state or the required or permitted number or frequency of governing body or member meetings, are not required to be reported.[45] Organizations are instructed not to report changes to policies described or established outside of the organizing or enabling document and bylaws, such as the adoption of, or change to, a policy adopted by resolution of the governing body that does not entail a change to the organizing document or bylaws. For

---

41. Reg. § 601.201(n)(6)(i).
42. Democratic Leadership Council, Inc. v. United States, 542 F. Supp. 2d 63 (D.D.C. 2008).
43. See *Law of Tax-Exempt Organizations* § 27.1(b).
44. Form 990 instructions, Part VI, line 4.
45. *Id.*

example, if an organization revises its written conflict-of-interest policy by board resolution and the policy is not within the organization's articles of incorporation or bylaws, then the change does not need to be reported.[46]

(f) Material Diversion of Assets

The IRS requests a filing organization to state whether it became aware during the year of a material diversion of the organization's assets and to explain the nature of the diversion, amounts or property involved, corrective actions taken to address the matter, and pertinent circumstances surrounding the diversion.[47] A *diversion of assets* includes any unauthorized conversion or use of the organization's assets other than for the organization's authorized purposes, including embezzlement or theft.[48] An organization should report diversions by the organization's officers, directors, trustees, employees, volunteers, independent contractors, grantees, or any other person, even if not associated with the organization other than by the diversion.[49] A diversion of assets does not include an authorized transfer of assets for fair market value consideration, such as to a joint venture or for-profit subsidiary in exchange for an interest in the joint venture or subsidiary.[50] For this purpose, a diversion is considered *material* if it exceeds the lesser of $250,000 or 5% of the organization's gross receipts for its tax year or total assets as of the end of its tax year.[51] This threshold may be sufficiently high, in most instances, to exclude more minor infringements, such as smaller misappropriations and expense account abuse.

(g) Members and Stockholders of a Tax-Exempt Organization

Nonprofit organizations can be formed as membership organizations, with the member having various rights, including the right to elect the organization's directors, or may be formed with a self-perpetuating governing body, whereby the directors or trustees elect their successors. A few states allow nonprofit corporations to be formed as stock corporations, with stockholders electing the directors of the corporation.[52]

On the Form 990, the IRS requests a filing organization to indicate whether or not it has members or stockholders,[53] and if so, whether the members had the right to elect the members of the organization's governing body.[54] An organization does not have to indicate which it has (members or stockholders), but merely that it has one or the other. An organization has members or stockholders for Form 990 reporting purposes if the organization is organized as a stock corporation, a joint-stock company, a partnership, a joint venture, or a limited liability company.[55] In addition, an organization is a membership entity if it is organized as a nonstock or nonprofit corporation or

---

46. *Id.*
47. Form 990, Part VI, line 5.
48. Form 990 instructions, part VI, line 5.
49. *Id.*
50. *Id.*
51. *Id.*
52. For example, the corporate laws of Delaware, Kansas, and Michigan allow nonprofit corporations to have shareholders.
53. Form 990, Part VI, line 6.
54. Form 990, Part VI, line 7a.
55. Form 990 instructions, Part VI, line 6.

association with members if (1) the right to participate in and benefit from the organization's activities is limited primarily to members (as with a cooperative or mutual benefit corporation), (2) the members elect the members of the governing body (but not if the persons on the governing body are the organization's only members), (3) the members approve decisions of the governing body, or (4) the members may receive a share of the organization's profits, excess dues, or net assets upon the organization's dissolution.[56] The IRS also requests information as to whether any decisions of the governing body are subject to approval by members, stockholders, or other person.[57]

(h) Documentation of Meetings

The IRS requests information as to a filing organization's practices with respect to minutes. Specifically, the agency asks whether an organization contemporaneously documented, by any means permitted by state law, every meeting held or written action undertaken during the year by the governing body and each committee with authority to act on behalf of the governing body.[58] *Documentation* may include minutes, strings of e-mails, or similar writings that explain the action taken, when it was taken, and who made the decision.[59] For this purpose, *contemporaneous* means by the later of (1) the next meeting of the governing body or committee, or (2) 60 days after the date of the meeting or written action.[60]

(i) Local Chapters, Branches, and Affiliates

Some tax-exempt organizations are national or regional organizations, with local chapters or affiliates. In some instances, the local affiliates are part of the national or regional organization; in other instances, the local organizations are separate legal entities. In the former case, the national or regional organization is liable for the acts of the local groups, in as much as they are part of the same legal entity. For this reason, exempt organizations often encourage chapters and affiliates to be organized as separate entities.

Certain organizations, such as a chapter or affiliate of a larger exempt organization, may be tax-exempt solely on the basis of affiliation with and being subject to the general supervision or control of a central organization (typically, a state, regional, or national organization). A central organization can file for a *group exemption* for all the affiliates or chapters (called *subordinate organizations*). With a group exemption, the subordinate organizations are recognized as exempt organizations without each of them having to file an application for recognition of exemption.

The IRS has set forth a procedure for a central, or parent, organization to seek a group exemption letter on behalf of its subordinates.[61] The central organization must first obtain its own recognition of exemption before filing for a group exemption for its subordinates. As part of the group exemption filing, the central organization must

---

56. *Id.*
57. Form 990, Part VI, line 7b.
58. Form 990, Part VI, line 8
59. Form 990 instructions, Part VI, line 8.
60. *Id.* See § 6.3(g) for further discussion of corporate minutes.
61. Rev. Proc. 80-27, 1980-1 C.B. 677. See also *Law of Tax-Exempt Organizations* § 25.6.

establish that all subordinates to be included in the group exemption are affiliated with the central organization and subject to its general supervision or control, exempt under the same paragraph of the general exemption rules (although not necessarily the section under which the central organization is tax-exempt), and not private foundations or foreign organizations. In addition, all subordinates must be on the same accounting period as the central organization if they are to be included in a group information return, and must be formed within requisite time period prior to the date of submission of the group exemption application; otherwise the exemption will not relate back to the formation date of the subordinates. Each subordinate must authorize, in writing, the central organization to include it in the group exemption application.

Once the group exemption letter is issued, the parent organization must make an annual filing with the IRS listing its qualifying tax-exempt subordinate organizations and providing certain information relating to them. Because the central organization is attesting to the qualification of the subordinate organizations, it is important that the central organization conduct an evaluation of its subordinates. The central organization can make additions to and deletions from the group from year to year.

On the Form 990, the IRS asks if the tax-exempt organization has local chapters, branches, or affiliates and, if so, whether the organization has written policies and procedures governing the activities of these chapters, branches, and affiliates to ensure that their operations are consistent with those of the reporting organization.[62] Regardless of whether the chapters or affiliates are organized as separate entities, an exempt entity with branches, chapters, or affiliates should have some standardization and consistency regarding the branches, chapters, and affiliates, given their common mission and goals, as well as the public perception that the organizations are all part of one entity, despite what may otherwise be the case as a matter of law. In addition, an exempt organization that is a central organization in a group exemption should ensure that its chapters and affiliates are generally subject to its control and do not engage in activities that jeopardize their exempt status of the organizations. For Form 990 reporting purposes, *written policies and procedures governing the activities of chapters, branches, and affiliates to ensure their consistency with activities of the organization* are documents used by the organization and its local units to address the policies, practices, and activities of the local unit.[63] These policies and procedures may include required provisions in the chapter's articles of organization or bylaws, a manual provided to chapters, a constitution, or similar documents. Organizations with affiliates may also wish to address standards of conduct, permissible activities, and approved use of the national or parent organization's name in the policy.

(j) Review of Final Form 990

On the Form 990, a filing tax-exempt organization is asked whether a copy of the organization's final Form 990 (including required schedules), as ultimately filed with the IRS, was provided to each voting member of the organization's governing body, whether in paper or electronic form, *prior to* its filing with the IRS.[64] This question does not ask whether the Form 990 was *reviewed* by the governing body prior to filing,

---

62. Form 990, Part VI, lines 9a and 9b.
63. Form 990 instructions, Part VI, line 9b.
64. Form 990, Part VI, line 10.

but whether it was *provided* to each voting member of the governing body prior to the filing of the return. An organization may answer "yes" to this question even if none of the board members undertook a review of the form, either before or after filing, as long as a copy was provided to each board member.[65]

In addition, organizations are required to describe the process, if any, they used to review the Form 990, whether before or after it was filed with the IRS, including specifics regarding who conducted the review, when they conducted it, and the extent of any such review. While there is no federal tax law requirement that the governing body receive or review the Form 990 before it is filed, an exempt organization would be wise to have a procedure for the review of its Form 990 prior to its filing, such as a review by its executive committee or its audit committee.[66]

§4.2 POLICIES

Section B of Part VI of the redesigned Form 990 is dedicated to inquiries regarding whether a filing tax-exempt organization has implemented various policies. There is no federal tax law requirement that exempt organizations adopt any of the policies referenced in Part VI of the Form 990; the form contains a statement to this effect.[67] Exempt organizations should, however, consider adoption of at least some of the policies inventoried in the new Form 990 as a matter of good practice and to demonstrate they are well-governed, in the event of an audit or investigation.[68]

(a) Conflict-of-Interest Policy

The Form 990 asks whether the organization has a conflict-of-interest policy.[69] If the organization has this type of policy, the organization is asked to indicate whether the officers, directors or trustees, and key employees are required to disclose, at least annually, interests that could give rise to conflicts.[70] The Form 990 instructions provide as an example of annual disclosure a requirement that members of the governing body provide a list of family members, substantial business or investment holdings, and other transactions or affiliations with businesses and other organizations.[71] This is typically accomplished through an annual disclosure statement signed by the individuals.[72]

A filing organization must also disclose whether it regularly and consistently monitors and enforces compliance with the policy.[73] If the answer is "yes," the organization is instructed to disclose the manner in which this is done with a significant level of detail, such as which persons are covered under the policy, the level at which determinations of whether a conflict exists are made, and the level at which actual conflicts are reviewed. A filing organization should also explain any restrictions

---

65. Form 990 instructions, Part VI, line 10.
66. See § 6.3(i).
67. Form 990, Part VI.
68. See § 6.2 for a listing of all policies and procedures referenced in the redesigned Form 990.
69. Form 990, Part VI, line 12a.
70. Form 990, Part VI, line 12b.
71. Form 990 instructions, Part VI, line 12b.
72. See § 6.3(b).
73. Form 990, Part VI, line 12c.

imposed on persons with a conflict, such as prohibiting them from participating in the governing body's deliberations and decision in the transaction.[74]

(b) Whistleblower and Document Retention and Destruction Policies

The Form 990 contains questions on whether a tax-exempt organization has a written whistleblower policy and a written document retention and destruction policy.[75] An organization should answer "yes" to these questions if the organization implemented these policies on or before the last day of the organization's tax year.[76]

(c) Process for Determining Compensation

Parts VI and VII of the redesigned Form 990 solicit information on the method a tax-exempt organization uses in establishing compensation. Questions on the Form 990 ask if the process for determining the compensation of certain persons includes a review and approval by independent persons, comparability data, and contemporaneous substantiation of the deliberation and decision-making; this rule pertains to the organization's chief executive officer, executive director, or top management officials, and other officers or key employees of the organization.[77] In addition, the form solicits information as to whether an exempt organization uses any of these methods to establish compensation for the organization's chief executive officer or executive director: compensation committee, independent compensation consultant, review of other organizations' information returns, written employment contract, compensation survey or study, or approval by the board or compensation committee.[78]

Tax-exempt organizations are instructed to describe the process used to set compensation, identify the offices or positions for which the process was used to establish compensation, and state the year in which this process was last undertaken. Through a series of questions, the IRS is effectively asking if the organization invokes the rebuttable presumption of reasonableness,[79] which is a procedure found in the intermediate sanctions law applicable to public charities and social welfare organizations. If the three elements of the procedure can be met, payments of compensation or other transactions between a public charity or social welfare organization and its insiders are presumed to be reasonable and the burden of proof is shifted to the IRS to prove that compensation is not reasonable. Accordingly, if at all possible, charitable organizations will want to invoke the rebuttable presumption of reasonableness.

The three requirements of the rebuttable presumption are as follows:

1. *Approval by an independent body.* The compensation must be approved by an independent, authorized body, which may include an independent committee. No one approving the compensation can have a conflict of interest with respect to the transaction.[80]

---

74. See § 6.3(c) (additional discussion of whistleblower policies).
75. Form 990, Part VI, lines 13 and 14.
76. See § 6.3(d) (additional discussion of document retention and destruction policies).
77. Form 990, Part VI, line 15 and Part VII.
78. Form 990, Schedule J, line 3.
79. Federal Tax Regulations (Reg.) § 53.4958-6(a). See *Law of Tax-Exempt Organizations* § 21.9.
80. Reg. § 53.4958-6(c)(1).

2. *Appropriate data as to comparability.* The approving board or committee, in determining the appropriateness of the compensation, takes into account appropriate data as to comparability. Relevant data includes, but is not limited to, compensation levels paid by similarly situated organizations, both taxable and tax-exempt, for functionally comparable positions; the availability of similar services in the geographic area of the applicable tax-exempt organization; current compensation surveys compiled by independent firms; and actual written offers from similar institutions competing for the services of the compensated individual. For transfers of property, relevant information includes current independent appraisals of the value of all property to be transferred and offers received as part of an open and competitive bidding process.[81]

3. *Documentation.* The decision by the board or compensation committee as to the amount of compensation paid to an individual should be documented adequately and contemporaneously in written form. The records of the committee or board should note (a) the terms of the transaction that was approved and the date it was approved, (b) the members of the authorized body present during debate on the transaction and those who voted on it, (c) the comparability data obtained and relied on by the authorized body and how that data was obtained, and (d) any actions taken with respect to consideration of the transaction by anyone who is otherwise a member of the authorized body but who had a conflict of interest with respect to the transaction. For a decision to be documented *contemporaneously*, records must be prepared before the later of the next meeting of the authorized body or 60 days after the final actions of the authorized body are taken. Records must be reviewed and approved by the authorized body as reasonable, accurate, and complete within a reasonable period thereafter.[82]

If an organization can meet the above three requirements with respect to a transaction, the IRS may rebut the presumption of reasonableness that arises only if it develops sufficient contrary evidence to rebut the probative value of the comparability data relied upon by the authorized body.[83] As stated by the director of the IRS Exempt Organizations Division at the time the intermediate sanctions regulations were issued, the rebuttable presumption "gives taxpayer's [sic] added protection if they faithfully find and use *contemporaneous* persuasive comparability data."[84] He referred to the rebuttable presumption as "a type of safe harbor," and stated that while organizations may find it impossible or impractical to fully implement each step of the rebuttable presumption process, they should try to implement as many steps as possible to substantiate the reasonableness of benefits.[85]

---

81. Reg. § 53.4958-6(c)(2).
82. Reg. § 53.4958-6(c)(3).
83. Reg. § 53.4958-6(b).
84. Miller, "Easier Compliance Is Goal of New Intermediate Sanction Regulations" (IRS 2001) (emphasis original).
85. *Id.* Implementation of as many steps of the rebuttable presumption as possible also weighs in favor of allowing an organization to maintain its tax-exempt status even though it violated the private inurement doctrine. See Reg. § 1.501(c)(3)-1(f)(2)(iv), Example 6.

(d) Participation in a Joint Venture

The Form 990, in Part VI, asks if the organization invested in, contributed assets to, or participated in a joint venture or similar arrangement with a taxable entity during the year, regardless of whether the venture or arrangement is taxed as a partnership or as an association taxable as a corporation.[86] An organization, in responding to this question, should include all such arrangements whether the purpose is to conduct an exempt activity, an investment activity, or an unrelated trade or business activity, and regardless of whether the organization controls the joint venture or arrangement. Joint ventures with only tax-exempt entities do not need to be disclosed.

On Form 990, the IRS inquires whether the organization, if it participates in a joint venture or similar arrangement with a taxable entity, has adopted a written policy or procedure that requires the organization to evaluate its participation in joint ventures under applicable federal tax law, and taken steps to safeguard the organization's exempt status with respect to the venture or arrangement.[87]

Typically, a joint venture with a nonprofit entity that has the same tax-exempt status does not pose a concern with an organization's own exempt status, as both parties will need to operate the joint venture in a manner that protects each member's exempt status. With a joint venture between a tax-exempt organization and a for-profit entity or an individual, both parties will not necessarily be concerned with operating the joint venture in furtherance of exempt purposes. If not structured carefully, these arrangements can jeopardize an organization's exempt status or, less severely, result in taxable unrelated business income to the nonprofit organization. Recent court decisions and IRS rulings in this area provide that a nonprofit organization can protect its exempt status by maintaining a controlling position in the joint venture and taking steps to ensure that the joint venture will be conducted solely in furtherance of the nonprofit organization's exempt purposes.[88]

(e) Other Policies and Procedures in Form 990

Not all policies and procedures for good governance are located in Part VI of Form 990 (although a majority are referenced there). For example, Parts I and III of Form 990 refer to a mission statement adopted by the governing body of the tax-exempt organization.[89] If a governing body has not adopted the mission statement, the organization will be unable to describe its mission on its Form 990.[90] Part X of Form 990 asks if an exempt organization has an audit committee that assumes responsibility for oversight of the audit, review, or compilation of its financial statements and selection of an independent accountant.[91] Form 990, Schedule H asks hospitals to disclose information on various policies and procedures, such as a charity care report, a debt collection policy, and the preparation of a community benefit report.[92] Schedule J of Form 990 requests information regarding the travel and reimbursement policies

---

86. Form 990, Part VI, Section B, line 16a.
87. *Id.*, line 16b.
88. For a summary of the federal tax law concerning joint ventures and revenue-sharing, see § 8.12. Also, see § 6.3(f) (further discussion of joint venture policies).
89. See § 5.13 (discussion of mission statements).
90. See § 6.3(a).
91. See § 6.3(t).
92. Form 990, Schedule H, lines 1a, 6a, and 9a.

and practices of an exempt entity and the procedures used to establish compensation.[93] Schedule M of Form 990 asks whether an organization has a gift acceptance policy for the review of nonstandard gifts.[94] Other parts and schedules of Form 990 ask still more questions on policies and practices of nonprofit entities.[95] Tax-exempt organizations are advised to carefully review the new Form 990 to determine which policies and procedures they will be asked to disclose and the level of information they must give regarding their governance practices.

§4.3 DISCLOSURE

The redesigned Form 990 has increased its requests for information as to a tax-exempt organization's disclosure practices. These questions, which are found in Part VI, Section C, involve questions about filing copies of an organization's Form 990 with state officials, making documents publicly available, and the location of an organization's books and records.[96] Not all questions in Part VI, Section C reflect legal requirements to which exempt organizations are subject; certain questions request information on disclosure practices that, if followed, would be voluntary.

(a) States with which a Copy of Form 990 Is Filed

An organization must provide a list of the states in which a copy of this Form 990 is required to be filed.[97] With the exception of private foundations, tax-exempt organizations are not required under federal income tax law to file a copy of the Form 990 with the states in which they conduct their activities. For other reasons, however, an exempt organization may be required to file a Form 990 with various states. For example, most states require a copy of the Form 990 as part of the charitable solicitation registration process.[98]

(b) Disclosure of Documents

Most good governance guidelines have, as one of their tenets, a principle that a nonprofit organization should make information regarding the entity widely known and available to the public, including information about its mission, activities, finances, board, and staff. Some of these matters are already part of the law applicable to tax-exempt organizations. Others represent opinions as to good governance and the level of transparency pursuant to which nonprofit organizations should operate, but are not requirements of law.

Generally, a tax-exempt organization must make its IRS application for recognition of exemption[99] (including documents submitted in support of the application and any letter or other document issued by the IRS regarding the application) and its three most recent annual information returns (Form 990) available for public

---

93. Form 990, Schedule J, lines 1 and 3.
94. Form 990, Schedule M, line 31.
95. These policies and procedures are listed in § 6.2.
96. Form 990, Part VI, Section C.
97. *Id.*, line 17.
98. See *Law of Fundraising* § 3.4.
99. Generally, Form 1023 or 1024.

inspection.[100] Exempt organizations other than private foundations and political entities are not required to disclose the names and addresses of their donors and may redact this information prior to providing copies or otherwise making information returns available.[101] Beginning with tax returns filed after August 17, 2006, charitable organizations are required to make their Forms 990-T available for public inspection.[102] The IRS also established a procedure for requesting copies of these documents and returns from the IRS using IRS Form 4506-A, Request for Public Inspection or Copy of Exempt or Political Organization IRS Form.[103]

Documents required to be disclosed must be made available for inspection at the organization's principal office and certain regional and/or district offices during regular business hours; organizations are required to provide copies of these documents to those who request them, either in person or in writing.[104] If the request is made in person, the organization must provide the copy immediately.[105] For requests made in writing, the organization has 30 days to provide a copy. Copies must be provided without charge, other than a reasonable fee for reproduction and mailing costs.[106]

A tax-exempt organization is not required to comply with the requests for copies of its application for recognition of exemption or annual information returns if the organization has made the document widely available.[107] For this purpose, making the documents *widely available* is satisfied if an organization posts the documents on a Web page that the organization establishes and maintains, or if the documents are posted as part of a database of similar documents by other exempt organizations on a Web page established or maintained by another entity, provided certain other criteria regarding the ability to access and download the document are met.[108] The rules for public inspection of the documents will continue to apply, even if the organization makes the documents widely available to satisfy the requirements regarding copies, meaning that the organization will still have to make these documents available for inspection at the required offices during regular business hours.[109]

If the IRS determines that a tax-exempt organization is the subject of a harassment campaign and that compliance with the requests would not be in the public interest, the tax-exempt organization does not have to fulfill a request for a copy that it reasonably believes is part of the campaign.[110] The document disclosure rules apply to the notice that must be filed by political organizations to establish their tax-exempt status and to the reports they must file.[111]

In its LifeCycle Educational Tool principles,[112] the IRS encourages all charities to adopt and monitor procedures to ensure that its Form 1023, Form 990, Form 990-T, annual reports, and financial statements are complete and accurate, and that these

---

100. IRC § 6104(d)(1). See *Law of Tax-Exempt Organizations* § 27.9.
101. IRC § 6104(d)(3).
102. IRC § 6104(d)(1)(A)(ii); *Law of Tax-Exempt Organizations* § 27.9.
103. See *Law of Tax-Exempt Organizations* § 27.8.
104. IRC § 6104(d)(1), (2).
105. IRC § 6104(d)(1).
106. IRC § 6104(d)(1)(B).
107. IRC § 6104(d)(4); Reg. § 301.6104(d)-2(a).
108. Reg. § 301.6104(d)-2(b).
109. Reg. § 301.6104(d)-2(a).
110. *Id.*
111. IRC § 6104(d)(1)(A)(iii).
112. See § 3.14.

documents are posted on their Web sites and made available to the public upon request.[113] In addition, the Panel on the Nonprofit Sector, in its 33 Principles, recommends that all charities publish an annual report, and post copies of the charity's annual report, Forms 990, and financial statements on the organization's Web site.[114] The Better Business Bureau Wise Giving Alliance's "Standards for Charity Accountability" include standards that an organization makes available to all, on request, complete annual financial statements and an annual report.[115] Even though the IRS and others make these comments, at this time there is no requirement in the law that a tax-exempt organization produce its annual report and audited financial statements to the public. Each nonprofit organization must determine its own disclosure practices and how much information it should, and is willing to, make available to the public.

---

113. LifeCycle Educational Tool, § 6.
114. 33 Principles, § 7.
115. See Standards for Charitable Accountability, §§ 11 and 17. See § 3.3(c).

CHAPTER FIVE

Nonprofit Governance Issues

The body of law (the little there is) concerning governance of nonprofit organizations is a disjointed and inconsistent clump of state and federal law, accompanied by a host of "voluntary" good governance standards and best practices (which, of course, are not "law"). As to the principal issues concerning nonprofit entity governance, there is little consensus as to the answers.[1] Barring some unusual (and unanticipated) legislative development, a considerable amount of time is going to pass before these issue areas are resolved, if they ever are. Before addressing these issues, however, three observations are in order.

§ 5.1 PERSPECTIVES ON NONPROFIT GOVERNANCE

First, the fact must be faced that much of the subject of governance of nonprofit organizations is, for most normal people (including lawyers), rather monotonous. One really has to be a governance geek to enjoy wallowing around in this morass of management issues (particularly when one realizes that what constitutes proper governance policy and structure is often unique to an organization). For example, what sane person can really get excited about the topic of the number of individuals who should sit on a nonprofit board? Who can honestly say that he or she likes to read (let alone write) bylaws? Who can long pontificate on the nature of the executive authority as between the chair of the board and the president of the organization? Should there be one vice president or two? Should there be an audit committee or a finance committee? What does it mean to say that fundraising practices must be in compliance with all federal, state, and local law? (As to the latter, there is not a charity in the land that is in compliance with every local ordinance.[2]) Some of these issues and documents are interesting, but a huge chunk of what has to be dealt with here is grossly tedious—and, as discussed next, perhaps somewhat pointless.

---

1. In remarks delivered on November 10, 2007, Steven T. Miller, Commissioner, Tax Exempt and Government Entities, said that the IRS "contributes to a compliant, healthy charitable sector by expecting the tax-exempt community to adhere to commonly accepted standards of good governance" (Bureau of Nat'l Affairs, *Daily Tax Report* (no. 222) G-11, TaxCore® (Nov. 19, 2007). See § 5.13(b). As Chapter 3 reflects, however, there are no such "commonly accepted" standards.
2. See § 5.12.

Second, in reality, how far can policies and procedures[3] take a nonprofit organization in assuring its good governance? At bottom, what counts are the personalities, morals, and leadership capabilities (or lack thereof) of the individuals at the organization's helm. If someone is intent on manipulating a nonprofit organization so as to cause mischief (or, worse, some form of evil), articles of organization, bylaws, policies, and procedures are not likely to throw up sufficient boundaries and barriers to thwart the wrongdoing. Independent Sector's Panel on the Nonprofit Sector noted that it has served up, in 2005 and 2006, "more than 100 recommendations for improving government oversight, including new rules to prevent unscrupulous individuals from abusing charitable organizations for personal gain."[4] It is unlikely that "rules" will hinder, let alone deter, those who are unscrupulous from the pursuit of abuse.

Policies and the like may slow the evildoer down and force more cleverness on the part of the bad-intentioned than would otherwise be the case, but the bad stuff is still going to happen (if malevolence is the intent). An analogy may be made to political science (which is not a science): one can study political institutions without end, but in the long run, the political outcomes (elections, policy determinations, and the like) are not going to be dictated by documents and structures but by the individuals involved, undoubtedly augmented by good fortune, good timing, and similar factors.[5] The political institutions are obviously necessary (even in some instances critical) but it is what individuals do with (and within) them that ultimately counts. The same is true with the management of a nonprofit organization: policies and procedures galore will make the entity look attractive,[6] but if the governance of it is indeed *good*, the directors, officers, and employees at the controls should be thanked, not a pile of documents. There should be, these days, greater emphasis on shaping effective programs and the funding of them, and less emphasis on the crafting of a pretty infrastructure.

Third, some of this good governance business should be—yet rarely is—evaluated in the far larger and more significant context of political philosophy. Government in America is touted as a democracy. It is a fundamental principle of the meaning of a democratic state that there be a strong nonprofit sector.[7] Another obvious corollary of democratic government is that the people live—within bounds necessary to forge a civil society—in freedom. When these two precepts are combined, it becomes perfectly clear that, in the United States, if a group of individuals wants to start a charity it should be free—indeed, encouraged—to do so.[8] There should be minimal (if any) fretting about laws that dictate governing board size, composition, independence, and the like. The Nonprofit Panel observed that "[a]ny approach to preserving the soundness and integrity of the nonprofit community

---

3. See Chapter 7.

4. See § 3.8.

5. It is asserted that the formation of the United States came about that way (Ellis, *American Creation: Triumphs and Tragedies in the Founding of the Republic* (New York: Alfred A. Knopf, 2007).

6. They will also help in producing an attractive annual information return (see Chapter 4).

7. See *Law of Tax-Exempt Organizations* §§ 1.3, 1.4.

8. A popular contemporary argument has it that tax exemptions and charitable deductions available to and for the benefit of charitable organizations are government-provided subsidies that entitle the government to dictate the operations of these organizations. This is a dangerous fallacy and is inaccurate (see *Law of Tax-Exempt Organizations* § 1.4). Simply put, it's not the government's money to begin with.

must strike a careful balance between the two essential forms of regulation—that is, between prudent legal mandates to ensure that organizations do not abuse the privilege of their exempt status, and, for all other aspects of sound operations, well-informed self-governance and mutual awareness among nonprofit organizations." For the most part, this statement is true, but the balance today is out of whack; the former is more dominant than it should be in relation to the latter. The nonprofit sector is currently overwhelmed with demands for many policies and procedures and assertions as to which governance principles to apply.

For the most part, nonprofit governance practices will take care of themselves; there is plenty of law to apply should matters go amiss. Examples are the operational test,[9] the primary purpose test,[10] the commensurate test,[11] the private inurement doctrine,[12] the private benefit doctrine,[13] and the intermediate sanctions rules.[14] Revocation of tax-exempt status is a sanction; the Internal Revenue Service (IRS) routinely revokes the exemption of organizations when they fail to operate primarily for an exempt purpose,[15] become inactive,[16] do not file annual information returns,[17] do not keep adequate records,[18] and/or do not respond to requests from the IRS for information.[19]

It is submitted that the many issues surrounding the matter of governance of nonprofit organizations should be evaluated from the foregoing perspectives. A discussion of these issues follows.

§5.2 GOVERNING BOARD SIZE

As noted, some are exercised about the size of the governing board of a nonprofit organization. There is no federal law on the subject. Most state nonprofit corporation acts mandate a minimum of three directors; a few jurisdictions permit one director. For decades, it was understood that this is a setting where one size does not fit all, and certainly not a topic that required heavy thinking, let alone more law.

(a) Summary of Standards

This placid view of board member size changed suddenly in 2004 when the staff of the Senate Finance Committee published a discussion draft of a paper asserting in part that the board of directors of a tax-exempt, charitable organization should be comprised of at least three members and have no more than 15 members.[20] That proposal immediately stimulated (at least) two questions: (1) although the idea of three board members is, as noted, solidly embodied in the law, what is the magic inherent

---

9. See *The Law of Tax-Exempt Organizations* § 4.5.
10. *Id.* § 4.4.
11. *Id.* § 4.7.
12. *Id.*, Chapter 20.
13. *Id.* § 20.11.
14. *Id.*, Chapter 21.
15. E.g., Priv. Ltr. Rul. 200837043.
16. E.g., Priv. Ltr. Rul. 200844027.
17. E.g., Priv. Ltr. Rul. 200840051.
18. E.g., Priv. Ltr. Rul. 200844031.
19. E.g., Priv. Ltr. Rul. 200817063.
20. See § 3.5(b).

in the number 15? And (2) is it properly the province of the federal government to, as a condition of tax exemption, dictate nonprofit organizations' board size?

This matter of the size of a nonprofit organization's board has long been a focus of watchdog agency standards. Thus, the Philanthropic Advisory Service (PAS) standards proclaimed that a nonprofit organization (evaluated by these standards) had to have an "adequate governing structure"; a governing structure was considered inadequate if "fewer than three persons," functioning as the governing body or executive committee, made any policymaking decisions on behalf of the organization.[21] Yet, when the PAS standards morphed into the Better Business Bureau (BBB) Wise Giving Alliance standards, the acceptable principle became a "minimum of five voting members."[22] The Evangelical Council for Financial Accountability (ECFA) standards mandate at least five directors, although they also provide that the board should "[d]etermine and adjust the optimal board size by assessing organizational needs."[23] A minimum of five directors is also required by the Standards for Excellence Institute, although seven or more directors are "preferable."[24] The criteria of the American Institute of Philanthropy[25] are silent on the point.

The Committee for Purchase's proposed best practices calls for at least five directors;[26] the good governance principles proposed by the Panel on the Independent Sector does likewise,[27] although its prior recommendation was a minimum of three directors.[28] The Treasury Department's voluntary best practices[29] do not, and the IRS draft of good governance principles[30] did not provide for a specific number of directors of tax-exempt organizations. Indeed, the IRS danced all around the subject: organizations with "very small" or "very large" boards "may be problematic." Small boards, the IRS continued, "generally do not represent a public interest,"[31] and large boards "may be less attractive to oversight duties."[32]

As it happened, in the aftermath of issuance of the Senate Finance Committee staff paper and the Committee's investigation into the operations of the American National Red Cross,[33] Congress updated the Red Cross's federal charter. At the time, this organization had a 50-member board of directors.[34] Declaring that "[i]t is in the

---

21. See § 3.3(b)(v).
22. See § 3.3(c)(i).
23. See § 3.3(d)(ii).
24. See § 3.3(e)(iii).
25. See § 3.3(f).
26. See § 3.7.
27. See § 3.12(b).
28. See § 3.8.
29. See § 3.6.
30. See § 3.10.
31. This statement reflects a fallacy that flows in and around this debate; there is no requirement, in the general law of charity, that a charitable organization, by means of its board or otherwise, represent a "public interest."
32. Even these extremes were hedged; note the use of "generally" and "may."
33. See § 7.1.
34. The American National Red Cross Governance Modernization Act of 2007, Pub. L. 110-26, 110th Cong., 1st Sess. (2007) § 2(a)(6)(B). It has been noted that, as to 11 of the nonprofit corporations that are federally chartered, "Congress has specified the number of governing body members—generally from 9 to 15, although 1 corporation may have 10 to 23" (Josephson, "American Red Cross Governance," 55 *Exempt Org. Tax Rev.* (no. 1) 71, 73 (Jan. 2007)).

national interest to create a more efficient governance structure" of the Red Cross,[35] Congress legislated that, as of March 31, 2009, and thereafter, there shall be no fewer than 12 and no more than 25 members of the Red Cross board, and that, as of March 31, 2012, and thereafter, there shall be no fewer than 12 and no more than 20 members of this board.[36]

The Panel on the Nonprofit Sector nicely summed up this state of affairs when it observed that experts in the realm of nonprofit organization board governance "are not of one mind as to the ideal maximum size of nonprofit boards." It was noted that board size "may depend upon such factors as the age of the organization, the nature and geographic scope of its mission and activities, and its funding needs."[37] Some experts believe that a "larger board may be necessary to ensure the range of perspectives and expertise required for some organizations or to share in fundraising responsibilities." Others argue that "effective governance is best achieved by a smaller board, which then demands more active participation from each board member." The Panel concluded that "each charitable organization must determine the most appropriate size for its board and the appropriate number and responsibilities of board committees to ensure that the board is able to fulfill its fiduciary and other governance duties responsibly and effectively."[38]

The Panel, after first recommending a minimum of three board members,[39] subsequently stated that generally there should be at least five members of a nonprofit organization's board, yet it also observed that the "board of an organization should establish its own size and structure, and review these periodically." The Panel added that the board "should have enough members to allow for full deliberation and diversity of thinking on governance and other organizational matters."[40]

(b) Form 990 Reporting

As part of the filing of the annual information return (Form 990), an organization must report the number of members of its governing body that are entitled to vote.[41]

(c) Conclusion

It is clear that this matter of the number of board members of a nonprofit organization cannot be properly quantified except in generalizations. This is certainly an area where one size does not fit all. The Panel on the Nonprofit Sector pointed out the advantages of small and large boards; the IRS noted the disadvantages. What number of board members works for one organization will not work for others. Indeed, even as to the same organization, the suitable number of board members may change from

---

35. The American National Red Cross Governance Modernization Act of 2007, Pub. L. 110-26, 110th Cong., 1st Sess. (2007) § 2(a)(4). See § 3.11.
36. *Id*. § 6, amending 36 U.S.C § 300104(a)(2).
37. See § 3.8. These factors were noted by the Panel in its discussion about the "ideal size of a board" (see § 3.12(b)).
38. See § 3.8.
39. *Id*. Indeed, the Panel called for amendment of the federal tax regulations to generally require that charitable organizations have a minimum of three members on their governing boards (*id*.).
40. See § 3.12(b).
41. See § 4.1(a).

time to time. The Panel's judgment that "each charitable [and other type of nonprofit] organization must determine the most appropriate size for its board" is sound.

The Panel's understatement that experts in the realm of nonprofit organization board governance "are not of one mind as to the ideal maximum size of nonprofit boards" is notably accurate. There is no consensus on this point because there cannot be consensus; there are too many variables in play. This is a topic that should be left to organizations' judgment; the law should not dictate the size of nonprofit organizations' boards (although there is no need to disturb the general state law rule as to the minimum three-person standard). The Panel's recommendation is the best of the lot: the board of a nonprofit organization "should establish its own size and structure and review these periodically."[42] Certainly the size of a nonprofit organization's board should not be a factor in determining the organization's eligibility for recognition of tax exemption.[43]

§5.3 GOVERNING BOARD COMPOSITION

One of the more contentious issues surrounding the matter of nonprofit organizations' governing boards is the *composition* of them (a topic of more momentous concern than the *number* of them[44]). The mantra of the day in many quarters (including, often, the IRS) is that board members, or at least a majority of them, must be *independent*. State law is silent on the point. Some good governance standards place limitations, in the form of numbers or percentages, on certain types of individuals who may be on the board. Occasionally, the rule as to independence also applies to an executive or comparable committee.

In the absence of much law, the concept of *independence* in this context is vague. The principal aspect of it concerns board members who, directly or indirectly, have family, business, and/or financial ties to each other and/or the nonprofit organization involved. This element of the analysis looks, for example, to individuals with conflicts of interest, who are employees of the organization, or who are otherwise compensated by the organization (or an affiliated entity). Another dimension of independence in this setting pertains to some external (usually ephemeral) grouping of individuals that a board member ostensibly represents (such as the public, the community, a charitable class, and the like). The third, and most recent, variation on this theme is that a nonprofit board must be *diverse*.

A different take on this matter of board composition looks at the expertise and talents of the individual board members, to determine if certain professions and fields of interest are reflected in the makeup of the board of directors. Or, shifting this type of focus slightly, there are those who deem it appropriate to ascertain whether board members are *qualified*. Rotating this analysis a bit more, some rules have it that some categories of individuals are *precluded* from serving on a nonprofit organization's board.

---

42. *Id.*
43. Nonetheless, the redesigned Form 990 includes a question, ominously requesting the number of voting members of an applicant organization's governing body (see *New Form 990* § 1.7).
44. See § 5.2.

(a)   Federal Tax Law

The federal tax law, in four instances, addresses the matter of the composition of the governing boards of tax-exempt organizations:

1. The most detailed rule of the federal tax law pertaining to the membership of nonprofit boards is the one applicable to tax-exempt credit counseling organizations. These entities must have a governing body (a) that is controlled by individuals who represent the "broad interests of the public," such as public officials acting in their capacities as such, individuals having "special knowledge or expertise" in credit or financial education, and "community leaders"; (b) of which not more than 20% of the voting power is vested in individuals who are employed by the organization or who will benefit financially, directly or indirectly, from the organization's activities (other than through the receipt of reasonable directors' fees) or the repayment of consumer debt to creditors other than the credit counseling organization or its affiliates; and (c) of which not more than 49% of the voting power is vested in individuals who are employed by the organization or who will benefit financially, directly or indirectly, from the organization's activities (other than through the receipt of reasonable directors' fees).[45]

2. Supporting organizations may not be controlled, directly or indirectly, by one or more disqualified persons[46] (other than its managers and supported organizations).[47]

3. One way for an organization to qualify as a donative-type publicly supported charity[48] is to satisfy a *facts-and-circumstances test.*[49] One of the elements of this test is that the organization have a *representative* governing body (that is, a board that represents the broad interests of the public, rather than the personal or private interests of a limited number of individuals).[50] An organization can meet this component of the test if its board is comprised of (1) public officials acting in their capacities as such; (2) individuals selected by public officials acting in their capacities as such; (3) individuals having special knowledge or expertise in the field of discipline in which the organization is operating; (4) community leaders, such as elected or appointed officials, members of the clergy, educators, civic leaders, or other individuals representing a broad cross-section of the views and interests of the community; or (5), in the case of a membership organization, individuals elected pursuant to the organization's governing instruments by a broadly based membership.

---

45. See § 3.9.
46. For this purpose, disqualified persons are those persons described in IRC § 4946.
47. IRC § 509(a)(3)(C). See *Law of Tax-Exempt Organizations* § 12.3(c).
48. That is, an organization described in IRC § 170(b)(1)(A)(vi). See *Law of Tax-Exempt Organizations* § 12.3 (b)(i) (general rules).
49. Reg. § 1.170A-9(e)(3). See *Law of Tax-Exempt Organizations* § 12.3(b)(ii).
50. Reg. § 1.170A-9(e)(3)(v).

4. Tax-exempt healthcare institutions must meet a community benefit standard. This includes a requirement that these institutions have governing boards that are representative of their communities.[51]

(b) Summary of Standards

The notion of an independent board of a nonprofit, particularly charitable, organization has been in good governance standards from the outset. (From time to time, the IRS, either when reviewing an application for recognition of exemption or auditing a tax-exempt organization, will take the position that the organization's board must be independent, in the absence of any law or informal guidance on the subject.[52]) Thus, the standards promulgated by the Philanthropic Advisory Service, as part of a requirement that there be an "adequate governing structure," required that there be an "independent governing body." Organizations failed to meet this standard if "directly and/or indirectly compensated board members constitute more than one-fifth (20%) of the total voting membership of the board or of the executive committee." An organization also did not meet this standard if its board members had material conflicting interests resulting from any relationship or business affiliation.[53]

The BBB Wise Giving Alliance standards perpetuate this requirement, by calling for a board that is "independent." These standards provide that no more than one or 10% (whichever is greater) "directly or indirectly compensated person(s) [may] serv[e] as voting members of the board." Additionally, "[c]ompensated members shall not serve as the board's chair or treasurer." Further, these standards forbid "transaction(s) in which any board or staff members have material conflicting interests with the charity resulting from any relationship or business affiliation."[54]

The ECFA standards require that a majority of an organization's board be independent. That term is not defined in the standards; the ECFA best practices, however, state that "independent-minded" board members are "those with the ability to place the organization's interests first, apart from the interests of the staff and other board members." These practices add that the board should "[s]tructure board membership and the board's voting with *more* than a *mere* majority of independent board members" and the board meetings should be conducted "with *more* than a *mere* majority of independent board members in attendance" (emphasis in original).[55]

The standards of the Standards for Excellence Institute provide that an organization's board should consist of at least five unrelated directors; seven or more directors are preferable. If an employee of an organization is a voting member of the board, there must be assurance that that individual will "not be in a position to exercise undue influence." Also, these standards stipulate that board membership should reflect the "diversity of the communities" served by the organization.[56] The Senate Finance Committee staff paper states that no more than one board member should be directly

---

51. See Hyatt and Hopkins, *The Law of Tax-Exempt Healthcare Organizations, Third Edition* (Hoboken: John Wiley & Sons, 2008), Chapter 6; § 26.3.
52. See § 5.21(g).
53. See § 3.3(b)(v).
54. See § 3.3(c)(i).
55. See § 3.3(d)(ii).
56. See § 3.3(e)(iii).

or indirectly compensated by the organization; a compensated board member could not serve as the chair of the board or treasurer of the organization. In the case of public charities, according to this paper, at least one board member or one-fifth of the board would have to be independent; a "higher number of independent board members might be required in limited cases." For this purpose, an independent board member would be defined as an individual who is "free of any relationship with the corporation or its management that may impair or appear to impair the director's ability to make independent judgments."[57] The Committee staff also proposed that an individual who is not permitted to serve on the board of a publicly traded company because of a law violation be barred from serving on the board of a tax-exempt organization.[58]

The Treasury Department's voluntary best practices provide that the organization should define, in its governing instruments, its structure, including the composition of the board. The organization should establish procedures to be followed if a board member or employee has a conflict, or a perceived conflict, of interest. Organizations should maintain and make publicly available a current list of their board members and the salaries they are paid, and maintain records (albeit respecting individual privacy rights) identifying information about the board members of any subsidiaries or affiliates receiving funds from them.[59] According to the Committee for Purchase's proposed best practices, the board of an organization should have at least five unrelated directors; the chair of the board should not simultaneously serve as the entity's chief executive officer or president. Also, the board membership should reflect the "diversity of the communities" served by the organization and should include at least one "financial expert."[60]

The Panel on the Nonprofit Sector has gone the furthest in ruminating about the composition of the nonprofit board.[61] According to the Panel, a board of an organization should include members with the "diverse background (including, but not limited to, ethnic, racial and gender perspectives), experience, and organizational and financial skills necessary to advance the organization's mission." Boards of charitable organizations "generally strive to include members with expertise in budget and financial management, investments, personnel, fundraising, public relations and marketing, governance, advocacy, and leadership, as well as some members who are knowledgeable about the charitable organization's area of expertise or programs, or who have a special connection to its constituency." Some organizations "seek to maintain a board that respects the culture of and reflects the community served by the organization." An organization should "make every effort" to ensure that at least one member of the board has "financial literacy."[62]

The Panel is of the view that a "substantial majority of the board of a public charity, usually meaning at least two-thirds of the members, should be independent." "Independent" members are those who are not compensated by the organization, do

---

57. See § 3.5(b).

58. See § 3.5(c).

59. See § 3.6.

60. See § 3.7.

61. See § 3.12(b).

62. Oddly missing from all of this is any reference to having a lawyer on the nonprofit board, particularly in light of the fact that a common theme running throughout nonprofit organizations' governance practices is that they comply with all applicable federal, state, and local laws (see § 5.12).

not have their compensation determined by individuals who are compensated by the organization, do not receive material financial benefits from the organization (except as a member of the charitable class served by the organization), or are not related to or residing with any of the foregoing persons. An individual who is not independent is, in the view of the Panel, potentially in violation of the directors' duty of loyalty,[63] which requires the directors to "put the interests of the organization above their personal interests and to make decisions they believe are in the best interest of the non-profit." The Panel declared that it is "important to the long-term success and accountability of the organization that a sizeable majority of the individuals on the board be free of financial conflicts of interest."[64]

Previously, however, the Panel recommended that, in general, at least one-third of the members of the board of a public charity be independent. Independent board members were defined as individuals (1) who have not been compensated as an employee or independent contractor by the organization within the previous 12 months (other than reasonable compensation for board service); (2) whose compensation (except for board service) is not determined by individuals who are compensated by the organization; (3) who do not receive, directly or indirectly, material financial benefits from the organization, except as a member of the charitable class served by the organization; and (4) who are not related to any of the foregoing individuals.[65]

(c) Form 990 Reporting

On the redesigned annual information return, the IRS inquires as to the number of board members of the filing organization that are independent.[66]

(d) Conclusion

Once again, this is an aspect of good governance principles for nonprofit organizations as to which there is no consensus. Many nonprofit organizations today are finding it difficult to attract and retain qualified board members.[67] Others make the fundraising potential the prime criterion for board membership. Objectives such as diversity and representation of a community interest can be ephemeral. Rare is the nonprofit board that includes individuals who have professional experience in relation to the organization's programs and fundraising, and/or have formal expertise in budgeting, financial management, investments, personnel, public relations and marketing, governance, law, and advocacy.[68] In most instances, about the most that can be realistically hoped for is what the IRS originally advocated: a governing board "composed of persons who are informed and active in overseeing [the organization's] operations and finances."[69]

---

63. See § 1.5(b).
64. See § 3.12(b).
65. See § 3.8. The greatest detail in this regard is found in the rules for tax-exempt credit counseling organizations (see § 3.9).
66. See § 4.1(b).
67. Part of the reason for this is the increasing level of responsibility and exposure to legal liability (see §§ 2.6, 2.7).
68. It may be recalled that the IRS also wanted an ethicist to be among the nonprofit board mix (see § 3.10).
69. See § 3.10.

From a policy viewpoint, the notion that a majority of the governing board of a public charity (or any other type of nonprofit organization) must be independent (however defined) is plainly a bad idea. This is a free country; related persons should not be precluded from forming and managing charitable and other types of tax-exempt organizations. An independent board may be an ideal; a board that cannot meet that standard should not be absolutely prohibited. A board that is not independent may—properly—be subject to a higher degree of scrutiny.

From a law standpoint, the effort by the IRS to bootstrap its questionable position as to this "good governance" practice by invocation of the private benefit doctrine[70] is based on an erroneous application of the law and should be discontinued (voluntarily by the agency or involuntarily as the result of a court order). The private benefit doctrine (like the private inurement doctrine and the excess benefit transactions rules) is to be applied as a sanction should there be a violation of the law. Application of the doctrine is not to be triggered merely because an IRS agent thinks private benefit "might" occur or "may" take place. Speculation by the IRS is insufficient to cause invocation of the doctrine.

§ 5.4 ROLE OF GOVERNING BOARD

Traditionally, the role of the nonprofit board was oversight of operations and establishment of the organization's policy. Much of governance and management was seen as the province of the officers and key employees. Attitudes about this line-drawing are shifting, with the trend being to ascribe more duties and responsibilities to board members. This is perfectly illustrated by the reference in the Red Cross legislation to the nonprofit board as a "governance and strategic oversight board" and its reference to the 11 responsibilities of these boards.[71]

(a) Summary of Standards

The BBB Wise Giving Alliance Standards state, in reflection of the traditional view, that the governing board "has the ultimate oversight authority for any charitable organization." The board must provide "adequate oversight of the charity's operations and staff." This type of oversight is indicated by factors such as "regularly scheduled appraisals of the CEO's performance, evidence of disbursement controls such as board approval of the budget, fund raising practices, establishment of a conflict of interest policy, and establishment of accounting procedures sufficient to safeguard charity finances."[72]

The ECFA standards call for a nonprofit board to establish policy and spend its time on "governance, not on management issues." This is also the traditional view; today, some assert that effective governance entails at least some aspects of organization management. The board should "approve the annual budget and key financial transactions, such as major asset acquisitions, that can be realistically financed with existing or attainable resources." The board should "[a]pprove and document annually and in advance the compensation and fringe benefits of the CEO, Executive

---

70. See §§ 1.6(b), 5.21(g), 8.3(e).
71. See § 3.11.
72. See § 3.3(c)(i).

Director, or President (or similar position) unless there is a multi-year contract in force and there is no change in the compensation and fringe benefits except for an inflation or cost-of-living adjustment." Further, the board should (1) "[a]nnually and formally evaluate the CEO, Executive Director, or President (or similar position);" (2) "[r]outinely compare board actions and corporate bylaws;" (3) "[p]eriodically review organizational and governing documents;" (4) (if it "handles the financial statement review responsibilities") review the organization's annual information return (or have a board committee do it); (5) develop an "effective process to plan ahead for recruiting new board members, and (6) "understand clearly if they are expected to participate in stewardship activities and individual giving."[73]

The Standards for Excellence Institute standards state that the board of a nonprofit organization (or, in some instances, a board committee) should (1) determine the organization's mission; (2) define the entity's "specific goals and objectives"; (3) establish policies for the "effective management" of the organization (including financial and personnel policies); (3) annually "approve the organization's budget and periodically should assess the organization's financial performance in relation to the budget"; (4) "review the percentages of the organization's resources spent on program, administration, and fundraising"; (5) "approve the findings of the organization's annual audit and management letter and plan to implement the recommendations" of that letter;[74] (6) "hire the executive director, see the executive's compensation, and evaluate the director's performance at least annually"; (7) "periodically review the appropriateness of the overall compensation structure" of the organization; and (8) meet "as frequently as needed to fully and adequately conduct the business" of the organization.[75]

The Senate Finance Committee staff paper stipulated that a charitable organization must be "managed" by its board of directors. In performing their duties, board members must act "in good faith, with the care an ordinarily prudent person in a like position would exercise under similar circumstances; and in a manner the director[s] reasonably [believe] to be in the best interests of the mission, goals, and purposes of the organization."[76] Compensation for all management positions should be annually approved by the board (other than inflation adjustments); compensation consultants must be hired by and report to the board.

This Committee staff paper added that the board of a charitable organization must (1) "establish, review, and approve program objectives and performance measures"; (2) "review and approve significant transactions": (3) "review and approve the auditing and accounting principles and practices used in preparing the organization's financial statements"[77] and "retain and replace the organization's independent

---

73. See § 3.3(d)(ii).
74. Organizations need to proceed cautiously in this regard; the existence of "recommendations" in a management letter does not automatically mean that an organization should adopt them. For one thing, the motive underlying inclusion of the recommendations needs to be considered.
75. See § 3.3(e)(ii).
76. This paper added that an individual board member who has "special skills or expertise has a duty to use such skills or expertise" in his or her board service.
77. Boards will find, however, that these principles and practices are firmly set by the accounting profession and are not subject to much negotiation.

auditor"; (4) review and approve the organization's budget and financial objectives as well as significant investments, joint ventures, and business transactions"; and (5) oversee the conduct of the corporation's business and evaluate whether the business is being properly managed."[78]

The Treasury Department guidelines provide that the board of directors of a charitable organization should be an "active governing body" and should (1) oversee implementation of the governance practices to be followed by the organization, (2) exercise "effective and independent" oversight of the charity's operations, (3) approve and oversee the annual budget, (4) appoint a financial/accounting officer who is responsible for the day-to-day management of the charity's assets, and (5) see to an independent audit of the finances of the organization (where annual gross income is in excess of $250,000).[79]

The Committee for Purchase proposal states that the board of directors of a nonprofit organization (or perhaps a board committee) should (1) hire the executive director, establish the executive's compensation, and evaluate the director's performance; (2) periodically review the "appropriateness of the overall compensation structure" of the organization; (3) approve the findings of the organization's annual audit and management letter; and (4) approve a plan to implement the recommendations of the management letter.[80]

The IRS's draft of good governance principles did not have much to say about the role of the governing board. There was a recommendation that the board of a charitable organization adopt a "clearly articulated mission statement." This statement should "explain and popularize the charity's purpose and serve as a guide to the organization's work." A "well-written" mission statement, said the IRS, "shows why the charity exists, what it hopes to accomplish, and what activities it will undertake, where, and for whom."[81]

The good governance principles articulated by the Panel on the Nonprofit Sector state that a governing board must be "responsible for reviewing and approving the organization's mission and strategic direction, annual budget and key financial transactions, compensation practices, and fiscal and governance policies." The board "must protect the assets of the organization and provide oversight to ensure that its financial, human and material resources are used appropriately to further the organization's mission." The board should (1) set the "vision and mission for the organization and establish[] the broad policies and strategic direction that enable the organization to fulfill its charitable purpose"; (2) "hire, oversee, and annually evaluate the performance [and compensation[82]] of the chief executive officer of the organization"; (3) "ensure that the positions of chief staff officer, board chair, and board treasurer are held by separate individuals"; and (4) review the "organizational and governing instruments no less frequently than every five years."[83]

---

78. See § 3.5(a).

79. See § 3.6.

80. See § 3.7.

81. See § 3.10(a).

82. The Panel observed that "[o]ne of the most important responsibilities of the board . . . is to select, supervise, and determine a compensation package that will attract and retain a qualified chief executive."

83. See § 3.12(b).

The Panel's principles add that the board should (1) "receive and review timely reports of the organization's financial activities and . . . have a qualified, independent financial expert audit or review these statements annually in a manner appropriate to the organizations' size and scale of operations;" (2) institute "policies and procedures to ensure that the organization (and, if applicable, its subsidiaries) manages and invests its funds responsibly, in accordance with all legal requirements"; and (3) "review and approve the organization's annual budget and . . . monitor actual performance against the budget."[84]

As noted, the American National Red Cross Governance Modernization Act set forth 11 responsibilities of a "governance and strategic oversight board."[85] The IRS's LifeCycle Educational Tool principles encourage an engaged board, composed of individuals who are active and informed in overseeing a charity's operations and finances.[86] The American Institute of Philanthropy's standards are silent on the point.[87]

(b) Conclusion

It is clear that this matter of the duties and responsibilities of members of nonprofit governing boards is undergoing a dramatic evolution in thinking on the point. The role of the nonprofit board has shifted from a somewhat passive one of oversight and policymaking to much more involvement in management and governance (plus the oversight and policymaking functions). Again, the Red Cross legislation nicely summarizes the principles underlying the contemporaneous nonprofit board's duties and responsibilities.[88]

As, however, the duties and responsibilities of the nonprofit board accumulate, so too does the exposure (for commissions or omissions) to personal liability for board members increase. This phenomenon is causing existing and prospective board members to (1) think about whether they will serve or continue to serve on the board and (2) request or at least consider requesting reasonable compensation for their services.[89] Thus, just as the role of the nonprofit board is changing, likewise is the thinking by individual board members as to the legal and financial ramifications of board service.

§ 5.5 ORGANIZATION EFFECTIVENESS AND EVALUATION

Increasing emphasis is being placed on the effectiveness of nonprofit organizations and on ways for organizations to evaluate their performance. The BBB Wise Giving Alliance standards provide that an organization "should regularly assess its effectiveness in achieving its mission." An organization should have, according to these standards, "defined, measurable goals and objectives in place and a defined process in

---

84. See § 3.12(c).
85. See § 3.11.
86. See § 3.14(d).
87. See § 3.3(f).
88. See § 3.11.
89. See § 5.9.

place to evaluate the success and impact of its program(s) in fulfilling the goals and objectives of the organization" and a process that "identifies ways to address any deficiencies." The board should have a policy of "assessing, no less than every two years, the organization's performance and effectiveness and of determining future actions required to achieve the mission." There should be a submission to the board, "for its approval, a written report that outlines the results of the aforementioned performance and effectiveness assessment and recommendations for future actions."[90]

The Standards for Excellence Institute standards recommend that an organization "periodically revisit its mission" and evaluate whether the mission "needs to be modified to reflect societal changes, its current programs should be revised or discontinued, or new programs need to be developed." The Institute adds that a nonprofit organization should have "defined, cost-effective procedures for evaluating, both qualitatively and quantitatively, its programs and projects in relation to its mission."[91] The Panel on the Nonprofit Sector added that the board "should establish and review regularly the organization's mission and goals and . . . evaluate, no less frequently than every five years, the organization's programs, goals, and [other] activities to be sure they advance its mission and make prudent use of its resources." Every board should set "strategic goals and review them annually." At a minimum, "interim benchmarks can be identified to assess whether the work is moving in the right direction."[92]

The standards of the Evangelical Council for Financial Accountability[93] and the American Institute of Philanthropy,[94] and the IRS's LifeCycle Educational Tool,[95] do not address this subject.

§ 5.6   BOARD EFFECTIVENESS AND EVALUATION

More recently, emphasis is being placed on the effectiveness of the boards of nonprofit organizations and on ways for boards to evaluate their performance. The standards of the Evangelical Council for Financial Accountability state that board members should "annually pledge to carry out in a trustworthy and diligent manner their duties and obligations as a board member." There should be an annual monitoring of "individual board performance against the board members' service commitments." Board member participation should be evaluated "before extending terms"; board member evaluation and/or term limits should be used to "ensure that the organization is only served by effective members." There should be a process for "[p]roperly orient[ing] new board members for their board service and provid[ing] ongoing education to ensure that the board carries out its oversight functions and that individual members are aware of their legal and ethical responsibilities." The board should use "routine and periodic board self-evaluations to improve meetings, restructure committees, and address individual board member performance."[96]

---

90. See § 3.3(c)(ii).
91. See § 3.3(e)(i).
92. See § 3.12(b).
93. See § 3.3(d).
94. See § 3.3(f).
95. See § 3.14.
96. See § 3.3(d)(ii).

The Standards for Excellence Institute standards state that the nonprofit board is responsible for its operations, including the education, training, and development of its members, and recommends periodic evaluation of the board's performance.[97] The Panel on the Nonprofit Sector's principles expand on these points, stating that board members "should evaluate their performance as a group and as individuals no less frequently than every three years." The Panel noted that a "regular process of evaluating the board's performance can help to identify strengths and weaknesses of its processes and procedures and to provide insights for strengthening orientation and educational programs, the conduct of board and committee meetings, and interactions with board and staff leadership."[98]

The standards of the American Institute of Philanthropy[99] and the IRS's LifeCycle Educational Tool[100] do not address this subject.

§ 5.7 FREQUENCY OF BOARD MEETINGS

Just as there is dissension in these ranks about board size[101] and board composition,[102] so are there differences in view as to the frequency of board meetings.

(a) Summary of Standards

The Philanthropic Advisory Service standards started this debate when, as part of the requirement that there be an "active governing body," the rule was laid down that the board had to meet formally "at least three times annually, with meetings evenly spaced over the course of the year, and with a majority of the members in attendance (in person or by proxy) on average."[103] However, this dictate was tempered by this standard: the full board could meet only once annually if there were at least two other occasions where there were evenly spaced executive committee meetings during the year.[104] When the BBB Wise Giving Alliance standards were developed, the rule became a mandate of a "minimum of three evenly spaced meetings per year of the full governing body with a majority in attendance, with face-to-face participation," although this rule was softened by the rule that a "conference call of the full board can substitute for one of the[se] three meetings."[105]

Pursuant to the Evangelical Council for Financial Accountability standards, the board must meet at least semiannually.[106] The Standards for Excellence Institute standards state that the board "should meet as frequently as is needed to fully and adequately conduct the business of the organization," then assert that the board should meet, at a minimum, four times a year.[107] The Panel on the Nonprofit Sector's standards provide that the board "should meet regularly enough to conduct its business

---

97. See § 3.3(e)(ii).
98. See § 3.12(b).
99. See § 3.3(f).
100. See § 3.14.
101. See § 5.2.
102. See § 5.3.
103. State law generally, however, does not permit nonprofit board voting by proxies.
104. See § 3.3(b)(v).
105. See § 3.3(c)(i).
106. See § 3.3(d)(ii).
107. See § 3.3(e)(ii).

and fulfill its duties." The Panel observed that regular board meetings provide the "chief venue for board members to review the organization's financial situation and program activities, establish and monitor compliance with key organizational policies and procedures, and address issues that affect the organization's ability to fulfill its charitable purpose." The Panel noted that "[w]hile many charitable organizations find it prudent to meet at least three times a year to fulfill basic governance and oversight responsibilities, some with strong committee structures, including organizations with widely dispersed board membership, hold only one or two meetings of the full board each year."[108]

The Senate Finance Committee staff paper,[109] the Treasury Department's voluntary guidelines,[110] the Committee for Purchase proposed best practices,[111] the IRS's draft of good governance principles,[112] and the American Institute of Philanthropy standards[113] are silent on this point.

(b)   Conclusion

The topic of the frequency of board meetings is not appropriate for embodiment in the law. Too many variables in this equation preclude a general statutory rule. The best standard in this area is that formulated by the Panel on the Nonprofit Sector: The board "should meet regularly enough to conduct its business and fulfill its duties."[114]

There is, moreover, an undiscussed element (or a consequence) of this type of rule: The resulting expense. The various good governance principles that opine on this subject are silent on the matter of related expenses. This should be obvious, but here is an unavoidable fact—the more the number of board members, the greater the underlying administrative expense. This is particularly a problem for national boards that tend to meet frequently. Thus, board members generate costs for travel, lodging, meals, board packet (or notebook) preparation, other staff preparation functions, and the like. Every dollar spent for this element of management is a dollar not spent for tax-exempt purposes.

§ 5.8   TERM LIMITS

Term limits are inherently controversial rules. Term limits, for example, are imposed on the U.S. presidency[115] and many governorships; term limits are not imposed in connection with the terms of members of the House of Representatives and Senate. Term limits can lead to machinations, such as those unfolding in Russia (where the presidency has a two-term limit), in that Vladimir V. Putin allegedly installed Dmitri A. Medvedev as (interim) president so that Mr. Medvedev would resign and allow Mr. Putin to run for a third (and longer) term. A recent rule change allows the mayor of New York City, Michael R. Bloomberg, to run for a third term, after the voters had

---

108. See § 3.12(b).
109. See § 3.5.
110. See § 3.6.
111. See § 3.7.
112. See § 3.10.
113. See § 3.3(f).
114. See § 3.12(b).
115. U.S. Constitution, Am. XXII.

approved a two-term limit, and the ensuing public controversy illustrates the emotions that surround this issue.

The theory underlying term limits is to avoid concentration of power over a multiyear period in any one individual and to regularly infuse elective positions with "new blood" (and perhaps new energy). Opponents of term limits assert that the voters should be allowed to select whom they want in a political position; the corollary is that government should not arbitrarily circumscribe the voters' right to choose.

The Panel on the Nonprofit Sector, avoiding a definitive stance on this issue, addressed the dichotomy of positions on the point. The view in favor of term limits: "Some organizations have found that such limits help in bringing fresh energy, ideas and expertise to the board through new members." The opposite view: "Others have concluded that term limits may deprive the organization of valuable experience, continuity and, in some cases, needed support provided by board members."[116]

The issue in this context is whether the members of nonprofit boards should be subject to term limits. There is no federal or state law on the point; the matter is left to each organization to decide, and reflect the decision in its governing instruments.

(a) Summary of Standards

The standards of the Evangelical Council for Financial Accountability state that an organization should establish "clear policies and procedures on the length of terms and the removal of board members," then add that board member evaluation and/or term limits should be used to "ensure that the organization is only served by effective members."[117] The Standards for Excellence Institute and the Committee for Purchase state that there should be term limits for the service of board members.[118] The Panel on the Nonprofit Sector sidestepped the issue, echoing the first of the ECFA admonitions, stating that the board of a nonprofit organization "should establish clear policies and procedures setting the length of terms and the number of consecutive terms a board member may serve."[119]

The standards of the Philanthropic Advisory Service,[120] the BBB Wise Giving Alliance,[121] and the American Institute on Philanthropy,[122] as well as the Senate Finance Committee staff paper,[123] the Treasury Department's voluntary best practices,[124] and the draft of the IRS's good governance principles,[125] do not address this topic.

(b) Conclusion

On balance, the better view is to not mandate, by law, term limits on nonprofit board members. This is a matter best left to the discretion of a nonprofit board. The type,

---

116. See § 3.12(b).
117. See § 3.3(d)(ii).
118. See §§ 3.3(e)(iii), 3.7.
119. See § 3.12(b).
120. See § 3.3(b).
121. See § 3.3(c).
122. See § 3.3(f).
123. See § 3.5.
124. See § 3.6.
125. See § 3.10.

size, and culture of an organization is likely to dictate the best practice. Also, for organizations that have difficulty finding and retaining board members, term limits only exacerbate the problem.

§ 5.9 BOARD MEMBER COMPENSATION

Traditionally, compensation of individuals for service on the governing boards of nonprofit organizations, particularly public charities, has been soundly rejected as being a "bad" governance practice. This line of thinking is reflected in today's best practices standards. Yet, as the duties and responsibilities of nonprofit board members multiply and intensify, and the potential for personal liability increases, a growing minority view is that members of nonprofit boards deserve compensation for their services, particularly where the individuals are *executive* board members.[126]

(a) Summary of Standards

The BBB Wise Giving Alliance standards obliquely address the matter of the compensated nonprofit board by referencing a "volunteer" board. Some organizations have board members who are compensated but for service other than as board members. Thus, the Alliance standards provide that no more than one or 10% (whichever is greater) "directly or indirectly compensated person(s) may serv[e] as voting members of the board." Further, "[c]ompensated members shall not serve as the board's chair or treasurer."[127]

The Evangelical Council for Financial Accountability standards state that board members "should generally serve without compensation for board service." If compensation is paid to board members, however, "information on the compensation should be provided by the charity, upon request, to allow an evaluation of the reasonableness of the compensation."[128] The Standards for Excellence Institute and the Committee for Purchase standards also prohibit compensation for board member service.[129]

The Senate Finance Committee staff paper states that no more than one board member can be directly or indirectly compensated by the organization. A compensated board member could not serve as the chair of the board or treasurer of the organization.[130] Apparently, these rules would apply regardless of whether a board member is compensated for service as a board member or in some other capacity with the organization.

The Panel on the Nonprofit Sector opined that board members are "generally expected to serve without compensation." Then a big hole is opened in connection

---

126. The term *executive* board member is used to describe the board member of a nonprofit organization who serves, in terms of time and intensity, more in the nature of an officer or full-time employer, rather than a typical director (or trustee).
127. See § 3.3(c)(i).
128. See § 3.3(d)(ii).
129. See §§ 3.3(e)(iii), 3.7.
130. See § 3.5(b).

with the word *generally*, with the Panel stating that an organization that provides compensation to its board members should use "appropriate comparability data" in determining the amount to be paid, document the decision,[131] and provide full disclosure of the amount of and rationale for compensation. Indeed, board members of charitable organizations are responsible for "ascertaining that any compensation they receive does not exceed to a significant degree the compensation provided for positions in comparable organizations with similar responsibilities and qualifications."[132]

The Treasury Department's voluntary best practices, the IRS's LifeCycle Educational Tool principles, and the standards of the American Institute of Philanthropy are silent on this topic. The only body of law or standards that affirmatively references directors' compensation are the two references to "reasonable directors' fees" in the rules concerning the boards of tax-exempt credit counseling organizations.[133] The IRS draft of good governance principles went both ways on this topic, first by prohibiting board member compensation and second by allowing it "when determined [to be] appropriate by a committee composed of persons who are not compensated by the charity and have no financial interest in the determination."[134]

(b) Conclusion

The sensitive topic of board member compensation has been discussed.[135] The ideal remains, particularly in the charitable organization context, that directors should serve only as volunteers. However, as the duties and responsibilities of nonprofit board members increase, and the potential for personal liability correspondingly rises, the pressure for board member compensation (reasonable in scope) should not be surprising.

§ 5.10 AUDIT COMMITTEES

The good governance standards generally say little about committee structure. The type of committee that is receiving the most attention today is the finance, or modernly termed *audit*, committee. The concept of the audit committee was reinforced (if not conceived) by enactment of the Sarbanes-Oxley Act.[136]

---

131. This standard reflects two of the three prongs of the intermediate sanctions' rebuttable presumption of reasonableness. See *Law of Tax-Exempt Organizations* § 21.9. Compensation of board members of charitable organizations, however, is so uncommon (other than in unique circumstances such as private foundations) that *appropriate comparability data* is essentially nonexistent.
132. See § 3.12(b). This is a recitation of the general private inurement and excess benefit transactions rules, with exception for the reference to *to a significant degree*; the law rules do not permit that element of excess.
133. See § 3.9.
134. See § 3.10(i).
135. See Chapter 3, where the general principle is stated that board members should not be compensated. See, however, § 3.9.
136. See § 3.2.

(a) Summary of Standards and Law

The Evangelical Council for Financial Accountability standards were the first to foresee this trend. They call for the utilization, by nonprofit boards, of a committee of members with "financial expertise" to "annually review the financial statements." This committee should "[c]onduct at least a portion of the committee meeting to review the financial statements with the accounting firm in the absence of staff." These standards also called for a board committee to annually review the organization's annual information return.[137]

California's Nonprofit Integrity Act, the only state law mandating an audit committee for nonprofit organizations, provides that charitable corporations that have gross revenues of at least $2 million and are required to register and file reports with the state's attorney general must establish and maintain an audit committee. This audit committee, which must be appointed by the organization's governing board, may include individuals who are not board members. The committee, however, cannot include members of the organization's staff or the organization's president, chief executive officer, treasurer, or chief financial officer. If the organization has a finance committee, members of that committee may serve on the audit committee, although those individuals cannot comprise more than one-half of the members of the audit committee.

According to the California law, the audit committee, under the supervision of the organization's board, is responsible for making recommendations to the board as to the hiring and dismissal of independent certified public accountants. The audit committee can negotiate the CPA firm's compensation, on behalf of the board. This committee must confer with the auditor to satisfy committee members that the financial affairs of the charitable organization are in order, review the audit and decide whether to accept it, approve nonaudit services by the CPA firm, and ensure that the nonaudit services conform to the standards issued by the U.S. Comptroller General.[138]

The Panel on the Nonprofit Sector observed that a charitable organization "that has its financial statements independently audited, whether or not it is legally required to do so, should consider establishing an audit committee composed of independent board members with appropriate financial expertise."[139] By contrast, the standards of the BBB Wise Giving Alliance,[140] the Standards of Excellence Institute,[141] the Committee for Purchase,[142] and the American Institute of Philanthropy,[143] as well as the Senate Finance Committee staff paper,[144] the Treasury Department's voluntary best practices,[145] and the IRS's LifeCycle Educational Tool principles,[146] are silent on the point.

---

137. See § 3.3(d)(ii).
138. See § 3.4(b).
139. See § 3.12(c).
140. See § 3.3(c).
141. See § 3.3(e).
142. See § 3.7.
143. See § 3.3(f).
144. See § 3.5.
145. See § 3.6.
146. See § 3.14.

(b) Form 990 Reporting

There is a question on the redesigned annual information return, inquiring as to whether a tax-exempt organization has an audit committee that assumes responsibility for oversight of the audit, review, or compilation of its financial statements and selection of an independent accountant.[147]

(c) Conclusion

Organizations of any appreciable size should consider establishment of an audit committee, and follow the general precepts of the California statute and the Panel on the Nonprofit Sector standards.

§ 5.11 OTHER COMMITTEES

As noted,[148] the good governance principles (and, for that matter, the law) say little about committee structure; occasional references are made to executive committees. For example, the IRS's draft of good governance principles stated that, if an organization's governing board is "very large, it may want to establish an executive committee with delegated responsibilities."[149]

Aside from executive and audit committees, there is potential for a nominating, long-range planning, and/or development committee.[150] This is not a matter for the law to address; this is a matter for each organization to determine, based principally on its size and the nature of its governing board.

§ 5.12 COMPLIANCE WITH LAW

Some of the good governance or best practices principles insist that an organization comply with applicable law. This is somewhat ironic, inasmuch as these principles are often seen as being more stringent than the mandates of law[151] and frequently are inconsistent with what the law requires. Also, this principle is overly simplistic (notwithstanding the adage that "ignorance of the law is no excuse").

(a) Summary of Standards

According to the standards of the Standards for Excellence Institute, organizations must be "aware of and comply with all applicable Federal, state, and local laws." These laws include those pertaining to fundraising, licensing, financial accountability,

---

147. See §§ 4.2(e), 6.3(t).
148. See § 5.10.
149. See § 3.10.
150. The authors are aware of an organization that has an actively functioning Savories and Sweets Committee.
151. For example, the Standards for Excellence Institute standards are said to be higher "than the minimal requirements imposed by local, state and federal laws and regulations." See § 3.3(e). Given the vast array of regulation, it is difficult to understand why the requirements of these three levels of law are *minimal.*

document retention and destruction, human resources, lobbying and political advocacy, and taxation.[152] Likewise, the Treasury Department's voluntary best practices
state that the board of a charitable organization is responsible for the organization's
compliance with relevant laws.[153] The Senate Finance Committee staff paper advised
that the board of a charitable organization should "establish and oversee a compliance program to address regulatory and liability concerns."[154]

The Committee for Purchase proposal provides that nonprofit organizations
should periodically conduct an internal review of the organization's compliance with
existing statutory, regulatory, and financial reporting requirements, and prepare a
summary of the results of this review to the board.[155] The Treasury Department's
voluntary guidelines state that a charity must comply with all applicable federal,
state, and local law.[156] The IRS believes that an active and engaged board is important
to a charity's compliance with applicable tax law requirements.[157]

The Panel on the Nonprofit Sector's first principle is that an organization "must
comply with all applicable federal laws and regulations, as well as applicable laws
and regulations of the states and the local jurisdictions in which it is based or operates." If the organization conducts programs outside the United States, it must abide
by applicable international laws and conventions that are legally binding on the
United States. The Panel observed that an organization's governing board is "ultimately responsible for overseeing and ensuring that the organization complies with all
its legal obligations and for detecting and remedying wrongdoing by management."
The Panel added that "[w]hile board members are not required to have specialized
legal knowledge, they should be familiar with the basic rules and requirements with
which their organization must comply and should secure the necessary legal advice
and assistance to structure appropriate monitoring and oversight mechanisms."[158]

The BBB Wise Giving Alliance,[159] the Evangelical Council for Financial Accountability,[160] and the American Institute on Philanthropy[161] do not address this point,
nor does the IRS's draft of good governance principles.[162]

(b) Conclusion

Certainly, a nonprofit organization, like any person, should be in compliance with all
applicable law. It is possible, of course, for a board of directors of a nonprofit organization (and its officers and staff), acting in good faith, to be unaware of an applicable
law. That may turn out to be not much of a defense (inasmuch as ignorance of the
law is no excuse).

---

152. See § 3.3(e)(vi). These eight bodies of law apparently contribute to minimal levels of regulation (see
supra note 151).
153. See § 3.6.
154. See § 3.5(a).
155. See § 3.9.
156. See § 3.6.
157. See § 3.14(d).
158. See § 3.12(a).
159. See § 3.3(c).
160. See § 3.3(d).
161. See § 3.3(f).
162. See § 3.10.

Still, adherence to this standard is not as easy as it may first appear. As an illustration, nearly all of the states have a charitable solicitation act that regulates fundraising for charitable purposes; there are thousands of similar county, city, town, and like ordinances.[163] Suppose a charity posts a gift solicitation on its Web site. Is that solicitation a form of fundraising in every state and other jurisdiction (including internationally)? The answer to this question, technically, is yes.[164] Yet no state regulator has yet come forward to assert that Web site fundraising triggers registration and reporting in every state, in accordance with every charitable solicitation act; that would, as a practical matter, be a wholly untenuous position, with disastrous ramifications for charities. Still, a charity engaging in this form of fundraising can be said to not be in compliance with all applicable state and local law.

§ 5.13 CATEGORIES OF EXPENDITURES

From the beginning, good governance principles have fretted about appropriate relationships among an organization's spending for program, management, and fundraising. This has gotten to the point where some of these guidelines deteriorate into specific percentages—an approach that has repeatedly been found unconstitutional when undertaken by state law.[165]

(a) Summary of Standards

The Philanthropic Advisory Service started all of this when it stipulated that a charitable organization spend a "reasonable percentage" of its total income on programs, as well as a "reasonable percentage" of contributions on activities that are in accordance with donor expectations. In this context, PAS defined a "reasonable percentage" to mean "at least" 50%. Charities were also expected to ensure that their fundraising costs are "reasonable." In this context, fundraising costs are reasonable if those costs do "not exceed" 35% of related contributions. In the area of total fundraising and administrative costs, PAS standards also provided that these costs be "reasonable." In this latter context, these costs are reasonable if they do "not exceed" 50% of total income. A charity was expected to establish and exercise "adequate controls" over its disbursements.[166] This concept was carried over to the BBB Wise Giving Alliance standards, which require that an organization "[s]pend at least 65% of its total expenses on program activities" and "[s]pend no more than 35% of related contributions on fund raising."[167]

The Evangelical Council for Financial Accountability's best practices sidestep percentages and state that an organization should spend a "reasonable percentage" of its annual expenditures "on programs in pursuance of the organization's mission." An organization should "[p]rovide sufficient resources for effective administration

---

163. See *Law of Fundraising*, Chapter 3.
164. See *id.* § 3.2(c) (discussion of meaning of the term *solicitation*).
165. See *id.*§§ 4.1(b), 4.3(b).
166. See § 3.3(b)(ii).
167. See § 3.3(c)(iii).

and, if the organization solicits contributions, for appropriate fundraising activities."[168] The Standards for Excellence Institute standards state that a board should annually "review the percentages of the organization's resources spent on program, administration, and fundraising."[169] These standards inch back to a percentage approach but not quite, providing that an organization's fundraising costs "should be reasonable over time." That is, on average, over a five-year period, a charity should realize revenue from development activities that is "at least three times the amount spent on conducting them." Organizations with a fundraising ratio of less than 3:1 "should demonstrate that they are making steady progress toward achieving this goal, or should be able to justify why a 3:1 ratio is not appropriate for the individual organization."[170]

The American Institute of Philanthropy standards are rabid on the subject of fundraising costs. Like all of the watchdog agencies, AIP believes fundraising costs should be reasonable. In this organization's view, this means that a charity should expend at least 60% of its outlays for charitable purposes. The balance, of course, is to be allocated to fundraising and administration. Fundraising expenses should not exceed 35%. These percentages are based on related contributions, not total income (thereby usually making the fundraising cost ratio higher). AIP sometimes takes it on itself to adjust an organization's fundraising expense ratio (by making it higher), such as where the organization is in accordance with generally accepted accounting principles, allocating a portion of expenses to program in the context of direct mail fundraising. A charity that violates these standards will be assigned, by the AIP, an overall "F."[171]

The Panel on the Nonprofit Sector asserts that an organization "should spend a significant percentage of its annual budget on programs that pursue its mission." The budget "should also provide sufficient resources for effective administration of the organization, and, if it solicits contributions, for appropriate fundraising activities." The Panel, noting that some watchdog groups assert that public charities should (or must) spend at least 65% of their funds on program activities,[172] found that standard to be "reasonable for most organizations," yet also noted that "there can be extenuating circumstances that require an organization to devote more resources to administrative and fundraising activities."[173]

This issue is not discussed in the Senate Finance Committee staff paper,[174] the Treasury Department's voluntary guidelines,[175] the Committee for Purchase proposed best practices,[176] or the IRS's draft of good governance principles[177] or the agency's LifeCycle Educational Tool principles.[178]

---

168. See § 3.3(d)(viii).
169. See § 3.3(e)(ii).
170. See § 3.3(e)(ix).
171. See § 3.3(f)(i).
172. See, e.g., § 3.3(b).
173. See § 3.12(c)
174. See § 3.5.
175. See § 3.6.
176. See § 3.7.
177. See § 3.10.
178. See § 3.14.

(b) Conclusion

As a matter of law, government regulation of fundraising by charitable organizations, on the basis of the percentage of revenue devoted to the gift solicitation process, is illegal because it is blatantly unconstitutional.[179] The reason for this is that the rationale for this type of discrimination against charities is arbitrary, capricious, irrational, and unfair. It is, thus, imperious and irrational to have this percentage approach, in the fundraising setting, embedded in "good governance" standards.[180]

These standards need to get past the puerile insistence on application of percentages in the fundraising context. To be eliminated are these tiresome requirements that at least a certain percentage (such as 65%) of expenditures be for program and no more than another percentage (such as 35%) of related contributions be expended for fundraising. Amounts expended for program, fundraising, and management will vary (and vary year-to-year), depending on the organization's purpose, size, period of existence, nature of its donor base, and type(s) of fundraising.[181]

§5.14 DISCLOSURES TO PUBLIC

Good governance principles have always stressed dissemination of information about the organization to the public. The federal tax law requires disclosure of certain information;[182] these principles usually go beyond the requirements of law.

(a) Summary of Standards

The Philanthropic Advisory Service cast the topic of disclosure of information to the public as a matter of *public accountability*. The PAS required that a charity provide, on request, an annual report that includes various items of information about the charity's purposes, current activities, governance, and finances. A charity also was required to provide on request a complete annual financial statement, including an accounting of all income and fundraising costs of controlled or affiliated entities. Additionally, a charity was required to "present adequate information [in financial statements] to serve as a basis for informed decisions." According to the PAS, information needed as a basis for informed decisions included items such as significant categories of contributions or other income, expenses reported in categories corresponding to major programs and activities, a detailed description of expenses by "natural classification" (e.g., salaries, employee benefits, and postage), accurate presentation of fundraising and administrative costs, the total cost of multipurpose activities, and the method used for allocating costs among the activities. Organizations that receive a substantial portion of their income as the result of fundraising activities of controlled or affiliated entities were required to provide, on request, an accounting of all income received by and fundraising costs incurred by these entities.[183]

---

179. See *Law of Fundraising* §§ 4.1, 4.3, 8.1.
180. Much irony may be found in the fact that the standards-setters insist that covered entities be in full compliance with the law (e.g., § 5.12), yet they ignore the law when it is inconsistent with their objectives.
181. See *Law of Fundraising* § 4.1.
182. See § 8.9.
183. See § 3.3(b)(i).

The BBB Wise Giving Alliance requires that an organization prepare an annual report that is available to the public and that it post its annual information returns on its Web site.[184] Every member of the Evangelical Council for Financial Accountability is required to provide a copy of its current financial statements (including audited financial statements if required) on written request and provide other disclosures "as the law may require."[185] An ECFA member "must provide a report, on written request, including financial information, on any specific project for which it is soliciting gifts." One of the ECFA best practices recommendations is that the member organization post its most recent annual financial statement and annual information return (Form 990) (if the organization files such a return) on its Web site.[186]

The Standards for Excellence Institute's standards require an organization to "prepare, and make available annually to the public, information about the organization's mission, program activities, and basic audited (if applicable) financial data." This report should also "identify the names of the organization's board of directors and management staff." An organization "should provide members of the public who express an interest in the affairs of the organization with a meaningful opportunity to communicate with an appropriate representative of the organization." An organization "should have at least one staff member who is responsible to assure that the organization is complying with both the letter and the spirit of Federal and state laws that require disclosure of information to members of the public."[187] The Committee for Purchase's proposed best practices require an organization to prepare and make available annually to the public information about the organization's mission, program activities, and basic audit (if applicable) financial data.[188]

The Treasury Department's voluntary best practices call on organizations to set forth their requirements as to financial reporting and accountability, and make their audited financial statements available for public inspection. Moreover, pursuant to these guidelines, charitable organizations should (1) maintain and make publicly available a current list of any branches, subsidiaries, and/or affiliates that receive resources and services from them; (2) make publicly available or provide to any member of the public, on request, an annual report that describes the charity's purposes, programs, activities, tax-exempt status, structure and responsibility of the governing body, and financial information; and (3) make publicly available or provide to any member of the public, on request, complete annual financial statements, including a summary of the results of the most recent audit, which present the overall financial condition of the organization and its financial activities in accordance with generally accepted accounting principles and reporting practices.[189]

---

184. See § 3.3(c)(iv).
185. See § 3.3(d)(iv).
186. Id.
187. See § 3.3(e)(vii).
188. See § 3.7.
189. See § 3.6.

The IRS, in its draft of good governance principles, stated that by making "full and accurate information about its mission, activities, and finances publicly available, a charity demonstrates transparency." The board of directors of a charitable organization "should adopt and monitor procedures to ensure that the charity's Form 990, annual reports, and financial statements are complete and accurate, are posted on the organization's public website, and are made available to the public upon request."[190] The agency stated, in its LifeCycle Educational Tool principles, that by making full and accurate information about its mission, activities, finances, and governance publicly available, a charity encourages transparency and accountability to its constituents. The IRS encourages every charity to adopt and monitor procedures to ensure that its Form 1023, Form 990, Form 990-T, annual reports, and financial statements are complete and accurate, are posted on its public Web site, and are made available to the public on request.[191]

The Panel on the Nonprofit Sector wrote that an organization "should make information about its operations, including its governance, finances, programs and activities, widely available to the public." Charitable organizations "also should consider making information available on the methods they use to evaluate the outcomes of their work and sharing the results of those evaluations." The theme underlying this principle is that charities should "demonstrate their commitment to accountability and transparency" by offering additional information about their finances and operations to the public, such as by means of annual reports and Web sites, with the latter containing mission statements, codes of ethics, conflict-of-interest policies, whistleblower policies, and the like.[192]

The Senate Finance Committee staff paper[193] and the standards of the American Institute of Philanthropy[194] do not address this subject.

(b) Form 990 Reporting

The redesigned annual information return includes a question as to whether the filing organization makes certain documents available to the public, including documents that are not required, as a matter of law, to be disclosed (such as audited financial statements).[195]

(c) Conclusion

Thus, there are certain documents that a tax-exempt organization must, by requirement of the federal tax law, disclose to the public. There are other documents that the good governance standards suggest or require be made available to the public. Boards of nonprofit organizations must decide which (if any) of the latter category of documents will be disclosed. Of greatest controversy is disclosure of financial statements.

---

190. See § 3.10(f).
191. See § 3.14(g).
192. See § 3.12(a).
193. See § 3.5.
194. See § 3.3(f).
195. See § 4.3.

§ 5.15 MISSION STATEMENTS

As a matter of law, as part of its formation, an organization has a statement of its purposes, as part of compliance with the organizational test.[196] Some organizations, however, have developed a separate mission statement. This matter has increased in importance because of the emphasis placed by the IRS on mission statements as part of the redesign of the annual information return.[197]

(a) Summary of Standards

The standards of the Evangelical Council for Financial Accountability started things out in this area by providing that its members should develop a mission statement, "putting into words why the organization exists and what it hopes to accomplish." This statement should be "[r]egularly reference[d]" to assure that it is being "faithfully followed." The organization should "[h]ave the courage to refocus the mission statement, if appropriate."[198]

The Standards for Excellence Institute's standards provide that an organization's "purpose, as defined and approved by the board of directors, should be formally and specifically stated." A nonprofit organization "should periodically revisit its mission (e.g., every 3 to 5 years) to determine if the need for its programs continues to exist." An organization "should evaluate whether the mission needs to be modified to reflect societal changes, its current programs should be revised or discontinued, or new programs need to be developed."[199] The Treasury Department's voluntary best practices state simply that a charitable organization's governing instruments should delineate the organization's basic goal(s) and purpose(s).[200]

The IRS, in its draft of good governance principles, stated that the board of directors of a charitable organization should adopt a "clearly articulated mission statement." This statement should "explain and popularize the charity's purpose and serve as a guide to the organization's work." A "well-written mission statement shows why the charity exists, what it hopes to accomplish, and what activities it will undertake, where, and for whom."[201]

The Panel on the Nonprofit Sector wrote that the board "should establish and review regularly the organization's mission and goals and should evaluate, no less frequently than every five years, the organization's programs, goals and [other] activities to be sure they advance its mission and make prudent use of its resources."[202] The IRS encourages every charity to establish and regularly review its mission. A clearly articulated mission, adopted by the board of directors, serves to explain and popularize the charity's purpose and guide its work. It also addresses why the charity exists, what it hopes to accomplish, and what activities it will undertake, where, and for whom.[203]

---

196. See *Law of Tax-Exempt Organizations* § 4.3.
197. See Chapter 4.
198. See § 3.3(d)(vi).
199. See § 3.3(e)(i).
200. See § 3.7.
201. See § 3.10(a).
202. See § 3.12(b).
203. See § 3.14(b).

The standards of the BBB Wise Giving Alliance (and those of the Philanthropic Advisory Service) and the American Institute of Philanthropy standards, as well as the Senate Finance Committee staff paper and the Committee for Purchase's proposed best practices, do not address the matter of mission statements.

(b) Form 990 Reporting

The redesigned annual information return, in two instances, makes reference to recitation of a filing organization's mission statement.[204]

(c) Conclusion

A nonprofit organization, preferably at the board level, needs to decide whether it will have a mission statement. It may want one as a matter of good governance and/ or to use in connection with preparation of the Form 990. As noted, if the reason for the statement is to repeat it on the Form 990, the board must approve the mission statement. Mission statements are not required by law and should be consistent with the organization's statement of purposes.

§ 5.16 CODES OF ETHICS

Initiated by the Sarbanes-Oxley Act[205] and championed by the IRS,[206] the matter of organizations' codes of ethics is now at the forefront of policies and the like to be considered by charitable and other nonprofit organizations.

The IRS stated, in its draft of good governance principles, that the "public expects a charity to abide by ethical standards that promote the public good." The board of directors of a charitable organization "bears the ultimate responsibility for setting ethical standards and ensuring [that] they permeate the organization and inform its practices." To that end, the board "should consider adopting and regularly evaluating a code of ethics that describes behavior it wants to encourage and behavior it wants to discourage." This code of ethics "should be a principal means of communicating to all personnel a strong culture of legal compliance and ethical integrity."[207] The agency returned to this theme in its LifeCycle Educational Tool principles, when it stated that a charity's board should consider adopting and regularly evaluating a code of ethics that describes behavior it wants to encourage and behavior it wants to discourage. A code of ethics will, wrote the IRS, serve to communicate and further a strong culture of legal compliance and ethical integrity to all persons associated with the organization.[208]

The Panel on the Nonprofit Sector stated that an organization should have a "formally adopted, written code of ethics with which all of its directors or trustees, staff and volunteers are familiar and to which they adhere." This principle is predicated on the thought that "[a]dherence to the law provides a minimum standard for an organization's behavior." The adoption of a code of ethics "helps demonstrate the

---

204. See § 4.2(e).
205. See § 3.2.
206. See § 3.10(b).
207. See § 3.10(b).
208. See § 3.14(e).

organization's commitment to carry out its responsibilities ethically and effectively." The code should be "built on the values that the organization embraces, and should highlight expectations of how those who work with the organization will conduct themselves in a number of areas, such as the confidentiality and respect that should be accorded to clients, consumers, donors, and fellow volunteers and board and staff members."[209]

The standards of the BBB Wise Giving Alliance,[210] the Philanthropic Advisory Service,[211] the Evangelical Council for Financial Accountability,[212] the Standards for Excellence Institute,[213] the American Institute of Philanthropy,[214] as well as the Senate Finance Committee staff paper,[215] the Treasury Department's voluntary best practices,[216] and the Committee for Purchase proposed best practices,[217] do not speak to the matter of an organization's code of ethics.

§ 5.17 CONFLICT-OF-INTEREST POLICIES

Although a conflict-of-interest policy is not generally required, as a matter of law, of nonprofit organizations, it is the policy that the IRS has been pushing the hardest. Indeed, today, it is difficult for an entity to achieve status as a tax-exempt charity without having adopted a conflict-of-interest policy[218] and this type of policy is prominently referenced in the redesigned annual information return.[219]

(a) Summary of Standards

The Philanthropic Advisory Service, while not advocating the adoption of a policy, observed that the governing body of an organization could not be considered *independent* if board members had material conflicting interests resulting from any relationship or business affiliation.[220] The BBB Wise Giving Alliance standards forbid "transaction(s) in which any board or staff members have material conflicting interests with the charity resulting from any relationship or business affiliation." Factors that are considered in determining whether a transaction entails a *conflict of interest* and if so whether the conflict is *material* include "any arm's length procedures established by the charity; the size of the transaction relative to like expenses of the charity; whether the interested party participated in the board vote on the transaction; if competitive bids were sought[;] and whether the transaction is one-time, recurring[,] or ongoing."[221]

---

209. See § 3.12(a).
210. See § 3.3(c).
211. See § 3.3(b).
212. See § 3.3(d).
213. See § 3.3(e).
214. See § 3.3(f).
215. See § 3.5.
216. See § 3.6.
217. See § 3.7.
218. See § 5.21(g).
219. See § 5.17(b).
220. See § 3.3(b)(v).
221. See § 3.3(c).

Evangelical Council for Financial Accountability member organizations are to "avoid conflicts of interest." Nonetheless, members may engage in transactions with related parties if (1) a material transaction is fully disclosed in the audited financial statements of the organization, (2) the related party is excluded from the discussion and approval of the transaction, (3) a competitive bid or comparable valuation exists, and (4) the organization's board has demonstrated that the transaction is in the best interest of the entity. The ECFA best practices include the following: (1) a conflict-of-interest policy "relating to the governing board and key executives should be adopted," (2) the "governing board and key executives should document annually any potential related-party transactions," and (3) "[a]ll significant related-party transactions should be initially approved and, if continuing, reapproved annually by the governing board."[222]

The Standards for Excellence Institute's standards state that a nonprofit organization should have a written conflict-of-interest policy. This policy "should be applicable to all board members and staff, and to volunteers who have significant independent decision[-]making authority regarding the resources of the organization." The policy "should identify the types of conduct or transactions that raise conflict of interest concerns, should set forth procedures for disclosure of actual or potential conflicts, and should provide for review of individual transactions by the uninvolved members of the board of directors." A nonprofit organization "should provide board members, staff, and volunteers with a conflict of interest statement that summarizes the key elements of the organization's conflict of interest policy." This statement "should provide space for the board member, employee or volunteer to disclose any known interest that the individual, or a member of the individual's immediate family, has in any business entity [that] transacts business with the organization." The statement should be provided to and signed by board members, staff, and volunteers, "both at the time of the individual's initial affiliation with the organization and at least annually thereafter."[223]

The Senate Finance Committee staff paper states that the governing board of a charitable organization should "establish a conflicts of interest policy which would be required to be disclosed with the [Form] 990, and require a summary of conflicts determinations made during the 990 reporting year."[224] The Treasury Department's voluntary best practices provide that the board of directors of a charitable organization should establish a conflict-of-interest policy for board members and employees and establish procedures to be followed if a board member or employee has a conflict, or a perceived conflict, of interest.[225] According to the best practices proposed by the Committee for Purchase, nonprofit organizations should have a written conflict-of-interest policy that identifies the types of conflict or transactions that raise conflict-of-interest concerns, sets forth procedures for disclosure of actual or potential conflicts, and provides for review of individual transactions by the "uninvolved" members of the board of directors.[226]

---

222. See § 3.3(d)(v), (vi).
223. See § 3.3(e)(iv).
224. See § 3.5(a).
225. See § 3.6.
226. See § 3.7.

The draft IRS good governance principles, observing that directors of a charity "owe it a duty of loyalty,"[227] stated that this duty requires a director to "act in the interest of the charity rather than in the personal interest of the director or some other person or organization." In particular, the duty of loyalty "requires a director to avoid conflicts of interest that are detrimental to the charity." The board of directors of a charitable organization "should adopt and regularly evaluate an effective conflict of interest policy" that "requires directors and staff to act solely in the interests of the charity without regard for personal interests," includes "written procedures for determining whether a relationship, financial interest, or business affiliation" results in a conflict of interest, and prescribes a "certain course of action in the event a conflict of interest is identified." Directors and staff "should be required to disclose annually in writing any known financial interest that the individual, or a member of the individual's family, has in any business entity that transacts business with the charity."[228]

The Panel on the Nonprofit Sector stated that an organization should "adopt and implement policies and procedures to ensure that all conflicts of interest, or the appearance thereof, within the organization and the board are appropriately managed though disclosure, recusal, or other means." A conflict-of-interest policy "must be consistent with the laws of the state in which the nonprofit is organized and should be tailored to specific organizational needs and characteristics." This policy "should require full disclosure of all potential conflicts of interest within the organization" and "should apply to every person who has the ability to influence decisions of the organization, including board and staff members and parties related to them."[229]

The IRS, in its LifeCycle Educational Tool principles, returned to the matter of the duty of loyalty, which requires a director to avoid conflicts of interest that are detrimental to the charity. The IRS encourages a charity's board of directors to adopt and regularly evaluate a written conflict-of-interest policy that requires directors and staff to act solely in the interests of the charity without regard for personal interests; includes written procedures for determining whether a relationship, financial interest, or business affiliation results in a conflict of interest; and prescribes a course of action in the event a conflict of interest is identified.[230]

The standards of the American Institute of Philanthropy[231] are silent on the matter of a conflict-of-interest policy.

(b) Form 990 Reporting

The redesigned annual information return poses several questions concerning any conflict-of-interest policy adopted by the filing organization.[232]

---

227. See § 1.5(b).
228. See § 3.10(e).
229. See § 3.12(a)
230. See § 3.14(f).
231. See § 3.3(f).
232. See § 4.2(a).

(c) Conclusion

A conflict-of-interest policy has become a staple of good governance policies. Rarely required as a matter of law, the IRS has generally succeeded in making this type of policy mandatory, particularly for charitable organizations. A nonprofit organization may resist adoption of a conflict-of-interest policy as a matter of principle, but this has come down to the matter of picking battles—and avoidance of adoption of a conflict-of-interest policy is, today, probably a waste of time and effort. The way the IRS has gone about this process is not the correct approach, but what's done is done.

§ 5.18 WHISTLEBLOWER POLICIES

Again, largely because of enactment of the Sarbanes-Oxley Act, whistleblower policies for nonprofit organizations have become prevalent. The IRS is encouraging (although not with the vehemence it is insisting on conflict-of-interest policies) organizations, particularly charitable ones, to adopt and enforce these policies.

(a) Summary of Standards

The standards of the Evangelical Council for Financial Accountability state that an organization should adopt a whistleblower policy.[233] The Senate Finance Committee staff paper provides that an organization should establish "procedures to address complaints and prevent retaliation against whistleblowers."[234] The draft of the IRS good governance principles stated that the board of directors of a charitable organization "should adopt an effective policy for handling employee complaints and establish procedures for employees to report in confidence suspected financial impropriety or misuse of the charity's resources."[235] The Standards for Excellence Institute standards provide that organizations "should provide employees a confidential means to report suspected financial impropriety or misuse of organization resources and should have in place a policy prohibiting retaliation against persons reporting improprieties."[236]

The Panel on the Nonprofit Sector stated that an organization "should establish and implement policies and procedures that enable individuals to come forward with information on illegal practices or violations of organizational policies." This whistleblower policy "should specify that the organization will not retaliate against, and will protect the confidentiality of, individuals who make good-faith reports." The Panel recommended that "[i]nformation on these policies . . . be widely distributed to staff, volunteers and clients, and should be incorporated both in new employee orientations and ongoing training programs for employees and volunteers." These policies "can help boards and senior managers become aware of and address problems before serious harm is done to the organization" and "can also assist in complying with legal provisions that protect individuals working in charitable organizations from retaliation for engaging in certain whistle-blowing activities."[237]

---

233. See § 3.3((d)(vi).
234. See § 3.5(a).
235. See § 3.10(c).
236. See § 3.3(e)(v).
237. See § 3.12(a).

The IRS, in its LifeCycle Educational Tool principles, encourages boards to adopt an effective whistleblower policy for handling employee complaints and to establish procedures for employees to report in confidence any suspected financial impropriety or misuse of the charity's resources.[238] The resigned annual information return asks whether the organization became aware during the year of a material diversion of its assets and whether an organization has a written whistleblower policy.[239]

The standards of the BBB Wise Giving Alliance[240] and the American Institute of Philanthropy,[241] as well as the voluntary best practices of the Treasury Department[242] and the Committee for Purchase proposed best practices,[243] do not address the matter of a whistleblower policy.

(b)   Form 990 Reporting

The redesigned annual information includes a question as to whether the filing organization has a whistleblower policy.[244]

(c)   Conclusion

Management of a nonprofit organization should decide whether to have a whistleblower policy. Again, while the law does not mandate this type of policy, adoption of one is a matter of good governance and, for most organizations, an appropriate step administratively, if only to facilitate preparation of the Form 990.

§5.19   DOCUMENT RETENTION AND DESTRUCTION POLICIES

Likewise, largely because of enactment of the Sarbanes-Oxley Act, policies of nonprofit organizations concerning document retention and destruction practices have become prevalent. The IRS is encouraging (again, not to the extent it is insisting on conflict-of-interest policies) organizations, particularly charitable ones, to adopt and enforce these policies.

(a)   Summary of Standards

The standards of the Evangelical Council for Financial Accountability state that an organization should adopt a policy with respect to retention of records.[245] The IRS, in its draft of good governance principles, provided that an "effective charity" will "adopt a written policy establishing standards for document integrity, retention, and destruction." This document retention policy should include "guidelines for handling electronic files" and "cover backup procedures, archiving of documents, and regular check-ups of the reliability of the system."[246]

---

238. See § 3.14(e).
239. See §§ 4.1(f), 4.2(b).
240. See § 3.3(c).
241. See § 3.3(f).
242. See § 3.6.
243. See § 3.7.
244. See § 4.2(b).
245. See § 3.3(d)(vi).
246. See § 3.10(j).

The Panel on the Nonprofit Sector stipulated that an organization should "establish and implement policies and procedures to protect and preserve the organization's important documents and business records." The Panel observed that a document-retention policy "is essential for protecting the organization's records of its governance and administration, as well as business records that are required to demonstrate legal compliance." This type of policy "also helps to protect against allegations of wrongdoing by the organization or its directors and managers."[247]

The IRS, in its LifeCycle Educational Tool principles, encourages charities to adopt a written policy establishing standards for document integrity, retention, and destruction. This type of policy should include guidelines for handling electronic files; it should also cover backup procedures, archiving of documents, and regular checkups of the reliability of the system.[248]

The standards of the BBB Wise Giving Alliance,[249] the Standards for Excellence Institute,[250] and the American Institute of Philanthropy,[251] as well as the Senate Finance Committee staff paper,[252] the voluntary best practices of the Treasury Department,[253] and the Committee for Purchase proposed best practices,[254] do not address the matter of a document retention and destruction policy.

(b) Form 990 Reporting

The redesigned annual information return inquires as to whether the filing organization has a document retention and destruction policy.[255]

(c) Conclusion

The conclusion provided in connection with whistleblower policies[256] is equally applicable in connection with document retention and destruction policies.

§ 5.20 FUNDRAISING PRACTICES

Fundraising practices by charitable organizations have been at the forefront of watchdog agencies' and other entities' best practices standards from the beginning. Thus, the Philanthropic Advisory Service standards addressed the topic of the contents of solicitation and informational materials,[257] as well as a variety of fundraising practices, including controls over fundraising activities, confidentiality of information,

---

247. See § 3.12(a).
248. See § 3.14(e).
249. See § 3.3(c).
250. See § 3.3(e).
251. See § 3.3(f).
252. See § 3.5.
253. See § 3.6.
254. See § 3.7.
255. See § 4.2(b).
256. See § 5.18.
257. See § 3.3(b)(iii).

and avoidance of undue pressure.[258] Some of these aspects of the standards are reflected in the BBB Wise Giving Alliance standards.[259]

Other issues that may be addressed in these standards include the nature of compensation of outside fundraising consultants and of development personnel on a percentage basis, and adherence to donor intent. This is the case, for example, with the Evangelical Council for Financial Accountability standards[260] and those of the Standards for Excellence Institute.[261] The focus of the IRS in this area is more on fundraising policies,[262] which tend to focus on the content of gift solicitation materials; the reasonableness of fundraisers' compensation; and compliance with applicable federal, state, and local law.

The elements of law that tend to arise in this context are nicely summarized in the principles of the Panel on the Nonprofit Sector. There, it is stated that solicitation materials and other communications addressed to prospective donors and the public "must clearly identify the organization and be accurate and truthful." The Panel stated that a prospective donor "has the right to know the name of anyone soliciting contributions, the name and location of the organization that will receive the contribution, a clear description of its activities, the intended use of the funds to be raised, a contact for obtaining additional information, and whether the individual requesting the contribution is acting as a volunteer, employee of the organization, or hired solicitor."

Contributions "must be used for purposes consistent with the donor's intent, whether as described in the relevant solicitation materials or as specifically directed by the donor." The Panel stated that solicitations should "indicate whether the funds they generate will be used to further the general programs and operations of the organization or to support specific programs or types of programs." The Panel advised charitable organizations to "carefully review the terms of any contract or grant agreement before accepting a donation."

An organization "must provide donors with specific acknowledgments of charitable contributions, in accordance with [federal tax law] requirements, as well as information to facilitate the donor's compliance with tax law requirements." The Panel noted that not only is this type of acknowledgment generally required by law, "it also helps in building donors' confidence in and support for the activities they help to fund."

An organization should adopt "clear policies, based on its specific exempt purpose, to determine whether accepting a gift would compromise its ethics, financial circumstances, program focus or other interests." The Panel warned that "[s]ome charitable contributions have the potential to create significant problems for an organization or a donor," noting that funds may be disbursed for "illegal or unethical" purposes, may subject the donee organization to legal liability (e.g., under environmental protection laws), or result in unrelated business income.

An organization "should provide appropriate training and supervision of the people soliciting funds on its behalf to ensure that they understand their responsibilities and applicable federal, state and local laws, and do not employ techniques that

---

258. See § 3.3(b)(iv).
259. See § 3.3(c)(iv).
260. See § 3.3(d)(vii).
261. See § 3.3(e)(ix).
262. See, e.g., §§ 3.10(g), 3.14(e).

are coercive, intimidating, or intended to harass potential donors." The Panel amplified this principle by recommending that a charitable organization should ensure that its fundraisers "are respectful of a donor's concerns and do not use coercive or abusive language or strategies to secure contributions, misuse personal information about potential donors, pursue personal relationships that are subject to misinterpretation by potential donors, or mislead potential donors in other ways."

An organization "should not compensate internal or external fundraisers based on a commission or a percentage of the amount raised." Compensation on this basis "can encourage fundraisers to put their own interests ahead of those of the organization or the donor and may lead to inappropriate techniques that jeopardize the organization's values and reputation and the donor's trust in the organization," and can lead to or be perceived as "excessive compensation."

An organization "should respect the privacy of individual donors and, except where disclosure is required by law, should not sell or otherwise make available the names and contact information of its donors without providing them an opportunity at least once a year to opt out of the use of their names." The Panel observed that "[p]reserving the trust and support of donors requires that donor information be handled with respect and confidentiality to the maximum extent permitted by law."[263]

The standards of the American Institute of Philanthropy,[264] the principles embodied in the Senate Finance Committee staff paper,[265] the voluntary best practices of the Treasury Department,[266] and the Committee for Purchase proposed best practices,[267] do not address the matter of fundraising practices.

§5.21 ROLE OF IRS IN GOVERNANCE

The IRS is taking an increasing interest in the matter of governance of tax-exempt organizations, particularly charitable entities. This interest is being manifested in a variety of forms, ranging from promulgation (then abandonment) of a draft of good governance principles[268] to making governance a centerpiece of the redesigned Form 990[269] to issuance of private letter rulings about board composition based on application of the private benefit doctrine.[270] The best indicators of the evolution of IRS thinking and policymaking in this area, including the IRS's role in promoting good governance practices by charitable organizations, are reflected in three speeches presented by Steven T. Miller, Commissioner, Tax Exempt and Government Entities.

(a) TE/GE Commissioner Georgetown University 2007 Speech

Commissioner Miller, on April 26, 2007, opened the Georgetown University Law Center's annual conference on representing and managing tax-exempt organizations

---

263. See § 3.12(d).
264. See § 3.3(f).
265. See § 3.5.
266. See § 3.6.
267. See § 3.7.
268. See § 3.10.
269. See Chapter 4.
270. See §§ 1.6, 8.3(e), 5.21(g).

with an intriguing speech focusing on various "powerful and persistent forces" that are shaping today's nonprofit sector and could potentially cause the IRS to "significantly change or modify" the agency's approach to the sector.[271] Commissioner Miller identified five of these forces.

One force is the rise of the Internet. He spoke of Web-based fundraising and the "possibility of virtual stateless charities." He said that the Internet "blurs what now seems like the quaint concept of state and national borders, with all that means for local jurisdiction over the charity."

Another force is the "continued concentration of wealth and the forthcoming transfer of that wealth to the next generation." Large parts of this wealth will be contributed to charity, driving the "creation and marketing of a variety of new giving techniques, both good and bad." This phenomenon caused the Commissioner to muse whether there should be concern with the level of annual charitable expenditures by charitable organizations, whether organizations created by single donors should exist in perpetuity, and the nature of the efficiency and effectiveness of exempt organizations.

The third force is the rise of the large nonprofit organization—what the Commissioner termed the "nation-sized nonprofits that are global in scope and scale." The "vast wealth" of these organizations is changing the nature of public policy debates, "especially to the degree these organizations may be able to implement programs with significant social impact on their own say-so, without meaningful public input or debate."

The fourth force is the "increasingly blurred line between the tax-exempt and the commercial sectors." This is raising the specter of an increase in the tax expenditure for exempt organizations, the matter of unfair competition, and the potential for undermining the "precious good will" possessed by most charitable entities. There are issues, the Commissioner said, as to whether "there has been drift in the nonprofit sector toward the commercial sector, and if so, how much."

The final (and most relevant) force is the "presence of abuse in the charitable sector." In this context, the Commissioner spoke of the "three main pillars" of the IRS's compliance program for the tax-exempt sector: customer education and outreach, determinations, and examinations. The third of these pillars, he lamented, "still leaves much to chance." Some of the problems in the sector are "insufficient transparency, lax management and a lack of meaningful ways to measure the effectiveness of an organization."

The Commissioner suggested two new pillars for the IRS's exempt organizations division program. One is use of the resources of the agency to gather "significant and reliable information about the sector, and to make it broadly available to the public, in a timely[,] user-friendly fashion." Two obvious elements of this are the wholesale revamping of the Form 990[272] and electronic filing.[273]

The second of these new pillars is promotion of "standards of good governance, management[,] and accountability." The Commissioner observed that "[w]hat

---

271. The formal text of this speech is available at Bureau of Nat'l Affairs, *Daily Tax Report* (no. 81) TaxCore® (April 27, 2007).
272. See § 3.13, Chapter 4.
273. See *Tax-Exempt Organizations* § 27.6.

precisely the Service should do with governance practice is an intriguing concept, in part because it's neither self-evident that we should get involved, nor obviously something we should avoid." He made probably the best case that can be asserted for the intertwining of the matter of governance and tax-exempt organizations' compliance with the law: a "well-governed organization is more likely to be compliant, while poor governance can easily lead an exempt organization into trouble." He spoke, for example, of an "engaged, informed, and independent board of directors accountable to the community [the exempt organization] serves."

The Commissioner revealed that he was pondering this question: "whether it would benefit the public and the tax-exempt sector to require organizations to adopt and follow recognized principles of good governance." He was, of course, thinking about whether the IRS can make a "meaningful contribution" in this area by "going beyond its traditional spheres of activity" by asking the exempt community to meet "accepted standards of good governance." The Commissioner concluded these remarks by asserting that there is a "vacuum" that needs to be filled in the realm of education on "basic standards and practices of good governance and accountability." Said the Commissioner: "Someone needs to lead the sector on this issue. If not the IRS, then who?"

(b) TE/GE Commissioner Philanthropy Roundtable 2007 Speech

Commissioner Miller, on November 10, 2007, spoke at the Philanthropy Roundtable, revisiting many of the themes evoked at the Georgetown presentation earlier in that year.[274] On this occasion, however, he referenced a trend not addressed in the Georgetown University presentation: the "constant increase in the number of tax-exempt organizations." Seventy thousand or more (gross, not net) exempt organizations are added to the sector annually, raising the question "whether we now have, or will get to the point where we will have, too many exempt organizations?" He noted this entails the addition of over 175 new exempt entities every day (Saturdays, Sundays, and holidays included)—one exempt organization for every 228 Americans. The Commissioner stated that the presence of a "very large number of tax-exempt organizations" presents the question as to whether "Americans are spending too much on duplicative infrastructure."

Returning to the matter of governance, the Commissioner expressed his view that the IRS "contributes to a compliant, healthy charitable sector by expecting the tax-exempt community to adhere to commonly accepted standards of good governance." He said that IRS involvement in this area is "not new"; the agency has been "quietly but steadily promoting good governance for a long time." He noted that "[o]ur determination agents ask governance-related questions" and "our agents assess an organization's internal controls as the agents decide how to pursue an examination." He continued: "We are comfortable that we are well within our authority to act in these areas." And: "To more clearly put our weight behind good governance may represent a small step beyond our traditional sphere of influence, but we believe the subject is well within our core responsibilities."

---

274. The formal text of this speech is available at Bureau of Nat'l Affairs, *Daily Tax Report* (no. 222) TaxCore® (Nov. 19, 2007).

(c)   TE/GE Commissioner Georgetown University 2008 Speeches

On April 23 and 24, 2008, Commissioner Miller spoke at the Georgetown University Law Center annual conference on tax-exempt organizations.[275] His remarks were a continuation of his thinking on governance issues and charitable organizations reflected in his speech at the conference the previous year and at the Philanthropy Roundtable 2007 meeting.

Mr. Miller, in his remarks on April 23, 2008, made three points clear: (1) the IRS is of the view that it has a "robust role" to play in the realm of charitable governance, (2) the IRS does not even entertain the thought that involvement in governance matters is beyond the sphere of the agency's jurisdiction, and (3) he cannot be convinced that, "outside of very very small organizations and perhaps family foundations, the gold standard should not be to have an active, independent and engaged board of directors overseeing the organization." Thus, the "question is no longer whether the IRS has a role to play in this area, but rather, what that role will be." That role will be primarily dictated by the governance section of the new Form 990, what he termed the "crown jewel" of the return.

One of the areas of discussion in the April 24, 2008, speech was the application process, which obviously forces the IRS to struggle with "competing goals": "good customer service," which requires the agency to be "expeditious in processing and approving an application for [recognition of] tax exemption" and "take sufficient care to identify those who are trying to game the system, so that we can properly deny their applications."

As Mr. Miller noted, "organizations come to us inchoate." These entities are "just getting started, and we are asked to grant them [recognition of] exemption based on suppositions, intentions and guesstimates." This process, he said, "is not really built to ferret out all questionable organizations; it is built to get applicants to a favorable result within a reasonable period of time."

(d)   Commissioner of Internal Revenue Speech

The Commissioner of Internal Revenue, Douglas Shulman, spoke at the annual meeting of Independent Sector on November 10, 2008, with much to say about nonprofit governance.[276] He said that he "admires" the tax-exempt sector: "its diversity, its creativity and its risk-taking." This diversity "means many points of view are expressed, many problems are attacked in many ways, many solutions are found, and many benefits are created for the nation." He continued: I firmly believe that the IRS must recognize and allow for this diversity—and not become a barrier to it." He added: "We shouldn't supplant the business judgment of organizational leaders, and certainly shouldn't determine how a nonprofit fulfills its individual mission. That's not our role."

But then, he noted, the sector "has had its encounters with abuse and misuse." He stated that the IRS "will continue to insist that the sector be squeaky clean, and that the high ideal of public benefit that underlies tax exemption is honored." He said

---

275. The formal text of these speeches is available at Bureau of Nat'l Affairs, *Daily Tax Report* (no. 83) TaxCore® (April 30, 2008).
276. The formal text of this speech is available at Bureau of Nat'l Affairs, *Daily Tax Report* (no. 218) TaxCore® (Nov. 12, 2008).

that he "clearly see[s] our role as working with you and others to promote good governance, beginning with the proposition that an active, engaged and independent board of directors helps assure that an organization is carrying out a tax-exempt purpose and acts as its best defense against abuse." He said that "all of us must follow best practices in organizational leadership and management." There must be, he added, "clearly articulated values, mission, goals and accountability."

The Commissioner concluded his remarks with this: "We want to arm you with information and guidance you need to help you comply. We want to pay especially close attention to the largest segments of the exempt sector. And lastly, we want to protect the tax-exempt sector and the public by identifying and stopping those bad actors who misuse tax-exempt organizations or the privilege of tax-exempt status."

(e) IRS Fiscal Year 2009 Annual Report

The IRS, late in 2008, issued an Exempt Organizations annual report, which included the agency's exempt organization's work plan for the government's fiscal year 2009. This report revealed that the IRS's Exempt Organizations Division is developing a checklist to be used by agents in examinations of tax-exempt organizations to determine whether an organization's governance practices "impacted the tax compliance issues identified in the examination" and to educate organizations "about possible governance considerations." The Division will commence a training program to educate employees about "nonprofit governance implications" in the determinations, rulings and agreements, and education and outreach areas. The IRS is to begin identifying Form 990 governance questions that could be used in conjunction with other Form 990 information in possible compliance initiatives, such as those involving executive compensation, transactions with interested persons, solicitation of noncash contributions, or diversion or misuse of exempt assets.

(f) Perspective

There is, thus, this question: Should the IRS be as deeply involved as it is in the matter of nonprofit governance, particularly in the absence of any law in support of the agency's involvement? This is, in some respects, a moot question, inasmuch as the IRS is quite active in nonprofit governance and can be expected to intensify its efforts as the redesigned Form 990 is filed, data collected, and audits commence. Still, it is a legitimate question, one that may be eventually resolved in court.

(i) Answer: Yes. A well-governed organization, that is, one that is adhering to good governance principles, is likely to be one that is compliant with the law. That rationale is being seen as sufficient justification for IRS regulation of nonprofit, particularly charitable, governance. As Commissioner Miller sees the point, the IRS's role in nonprofit good governance may be a "small step beyond our traditional sphere of influence, but we believe the subject is well within our core responsibilities."

(ii) Answer: No. Throughout the course of the Charles Dickens novel, *A Tale of Two Cities*, Madame De Farge knits; she indefatigably knits. It can be said with confidence that she sticks to her knitting. According to the *Dictionary of American Slang*, the phrase *stick to one's knitting* means to "attend strictly to one's own affairs; not interfere with others; be singleminded." The mission of the IRS is to "provide America's taxpayers with top quality service by helping them understand and meet their *tax*

responsibilities and by applying the *tax law* with integrity and fairness to all."[277] The mission of the Tax Exempt and Government Entities Division is the "uniform interpretation and application of the *Federal tax laws* on matters pertaining to the Division's customer base."[278] The mission of the IRS and this Division is not to make pronouncements on good governance principles applicable (ostensibly or otherwise) to nonprofit organizations. The agency should attend strictly to its own affairs and not interfere with others. The IRS should stick to its knitting.

Here is a government agency that is way behind in the processing of applications for recognition of exemption, lacks the resources to respond in a timely fashion to ruling requests, is overwhelmed by the need to issue guidance in connection with recently enacted statutory law, and is lagging in the provision of other needed guidance. So, what does it do? Rather than devote time and energy to these important tasks, it wanders off into an area over which it has little or no jurisdiction or expertise.

According to the TE/GE Commissioner, the IRS expects the tax-exempt community to adhere to "commonly accepted standards of good governance." The difficulty with this is that such standards do not exist. There are at least 14 of these standards, some in draft form.[279] Many of these standards are inconsistent. The standard-setters cannot even agree on what size a nonprofit board should be, let alone how it should comport itself.

The IRS is sending the nonprofit community a mixed message on the topic of nonprofit governance. The TE/GE Commissioner is now quite adamant that the IRS is going to be playing a "robust role" in nonprofit governance and that the "gold standard" is an "active, independent and engaged board of directors." The Commissioner of Internal Revenue echoed these words, yet also said that the IRS should not "supplant the business judgment of [nonprofit] organizational leaders"; he added that the IRS wants to "arm" the charitable sector "with information and guidance you need to help you comply," suggesting an emphasis on education rather than dictation of governance modes and practices. The IRS fiscal year 2009 annual report recognizes the huge gap between its agents' rulings and examinations practices and applicable law,[280] announcing a training program to educate its employees about "nonprofit governance implications."[281]

---

277. IRS Web site and each issue of the weekly *Internal Revenue Bulletin* (emphasis added).
278. IRS Web site (emphasis added).
279. See Chapter 3.
280. See § 5.21(g).
281. In a speech on June 19, 2008, the Director of the Exempt Organizations Division acknowledged that, in connection with the processing of applications for recognition of exemption, "not all IRS agents have gotten the message" that the IRS focus, as to governance, should be on education. On January 9, 2009, she said that her view of the governance issue is not being followed by IRS agents; she added: "By that, I mean I go out and give a speech and I say 'I'm not going to tell you how to govern your organization; I'm not going to tell you that you need a conflicts-of-interest policy; I'm not going to tell you [that] you need this type of structure to oversee your dealings with insiders—you have to look at the issue and see what works for your organization'." On this later occasion, she continued, speaking about the need for agents' training on governance: "That's a legitimate concern," so these individuals will receive instruction to ensure that they understand that, if an organization does not have a conflict-of-interest policy, "that in and of itself does not mean anything."

In a nation that prides itself on government based on "rules of law," it is arbitrary and unfair for the IRS to be promoting good governance for nonprofit organizations in the absence of any law or even articulated informal standards that the agency may be using. The most we have are IRS-prepared forms and instructions. This hide-the-ball approach is a strange way for an administrative agency to be functioning, particularly one that is trumpeting "transparency."[282]

(g) Application of Private Benefit Doctrine

IRS agents (at least some of them) are blindly adhering to the IRS's views as to what constitutes good governance, with particular emphasis on adoption of a conflict-of-interest policy and structuring of a charitable organization's board so that a majority of it is independent. These agents are refusing to grant recognition of exemption to an organization that refuses to capitulate on these points. The fact statement in a court opinion[283] reflects the IRS's adamance in this regard, resting its positions on the doctrine of private benefit.

Private letter rulings are also surfacing, reflecting the IRS's stance. In the first of these rulings, the IRS held that, on the grounds of lack of serving a public interest and of the presence of private benefit, an organization could not qualify as a tax-exempt charitable organization inasmuch as it has only two directors, who are related.[284] Thereafter, the agency ruled that an organization cannot qualify as an exempt charitable entity, in part because it was not "operated by a community-based board of directors" (or because the board "lacks members who are representative of the community").[285] Subsequently, the agency ruled that an entity was not an exempt charity inasmuch as it did not adopt a conflict-of-interest policy and lacks an independent board.[286] In this third instance, the agency wrote that the control by a family over the organization "could be used" for private ends and that the "structure of your organization indicates that it can be used to benefit private individuals."[287] The IRS also ruled that a religious organization does not qualify for exemption in part because its pastor exercises "excessive control" over the entity.[288] Indeed, the IRS has taken this application of the private benefit doctrine so far that it ruled that an organization could not be an exempt charitable entity in part because its three (unrelated) directors have "unfettered control" over the organization and its assets.[289]

---

282. In general, Owens, "Charities and Governance: Is the IRS Subject to Challenge?," 60 *Exempt Org. Tax Rev.* (no. 3) 287 (June 2008); Silk, "Good Governance Practices for 501(c)(3) Organizations: Should the IRS Become Further Involved?," 57 *Exempt Org. Tax Rev.* (no. 2) 183 (Aug. 2007).

283. Exploratory Research, Inc. v. Commissioner, 95 T.C.M. 1347 (2008).

284. Priv. Ltr. Rul. 200736037, reissued as Priv. Ltr. Rul. 200737044.

285. Priv. Ltr. Rul. 200828029.

286. Priv. Ltr. Rul. 200830028. A commentary on this ruling observed that, in issuing it, the IRS took an "unusual step" (Kelderman, "IRS Denies Organization's Application as a Church," XXI *Chron. of Phil.* (no. 2) 69 (Oct. 30, 2008)).

287. Where private inurement recurred and the organization did not implement safeguards to eliminate the practices, the IRS revoked the entity's tax-exempt status (Priv. Ltr. Rul. 200844021); this is how the doctrine is supposed to be applied; as a sanction when wrongdoing has actually occurred, not when there is merely some possibility that it *might* occur.

288. Priv. Ltr. Rul. 200843032.

289. Priv. Ltr. Rul. 200845053. If this control is not to be with an organization's governing board, where is it to vest? (see Chapter 2).

(h)   Commentary

These private letter rulings are, from the standpoint of tax law analysis, inherently unfair. No other agency of the federal government can get away with this sort of behavior—application of nonexistent rules and decisions based on pure speculation. The IRS is supposed to be bound by rules of law.

The organizations that are the subject of these rulings were denied recognition of exempt status, in part because they are engaging in two practices that are not required by the federal tax law as a condition for tax exemption: failure to adopt a conflict-of-interest policy and lack of an independent board. How can a government agency action be lawfully based on an insinuation of requirements that are not mandated by the law's criteria?

This attempt to invoke the private benefit doctrine is plain error. That doctrine is to be applied when there is actual private benefit—it is a sanction.[290] It is not to be invoked on the basis of wild speculation, such as the possibility that the organization's assets "could" be used to benefit one or more board members. Were that the standard, there would be few tax-exempt charitable organizations.

---

290. See § 1.6(c); *supra* note 287.

CHAPTER SIX

Policies and Procedures for Good Governance

One of the products of the emergence and evolution of nonprofit governance princi-ples is the increase in the importance of a multitude of written policies, processes, and procedures. Certain of the recommended policies are traceable to enactment of the Sarbanes-Oxley Act in 2002.[1] The recommendation for policies can be found at the core of most of the "best practices" guidelines published by the various agencies focusing on the matter.[2] The redesigned Form 990 repeatedly inquires as to which of the various recommended policies and procedures the filing organization has implemented.[3]

Nonprofit organizations need to assess which of the various policies they should implement as a matter of good governance and organizational effective-ness, in addition to evaluating the adoption of policies for purposes of Form 990 reporting. Development of policies alone will not cause an organization to be well-governed; however, adherence to policies may help a nonprofit organization maintain standards of good governance and deter certain forms of undesired or inappropriate behavior.

§6.1 SOURCES OF POLICIES AND PROCEDURES

Many of the recommended policies have been developed, in one form or another, by various entities that are in the business, in whole or in part, of formulating govern-ance principles, largely for public charities. These entities fall into three categories. The first category consists of components of the federal government, namely, the investigatory staff of the Senate Finance Committee, the Department of the Treasury, the U.S. Congress, and the Internal Revenue Service (IRS). The Finance Committee

---

1. Only two of the provisions of the Sarbanes-Oxley Act apply to nonprofit organizations: the provisions regarding protection of whistleblowers and the criminal law concerning the destruction of documents with the intent to impede, obstruct, or influence a federal investigation or matter. See 18 U.S.C. §§ 1513(e) and 1519. Other than these two noted exceptions, Sarbanes-Oxley does not apply to exempt organizations. Even so, many nonprofit organizations are choosing to voluntarily adopt some of the act's provisions, even if not specifically applicable to tax-exempt organizations, such as rotating audit-ing firms, separating auditing and accounting functions, and establishing audit and compensation committees. See § 3.2.
2. See Chapter 3.
3. See Chapter 4.

staff in 2004 developed a paper that referenced some nonprofit governance policies.[4] The Treasury Department in 2005 promulgated voluntary best practices in the form of antiterrorist financing guidelines.[5] Congress legislated (in addition to the Sarbanes-Oxley Act) the American National Red Cross Governance Modernization Act (in 2007)[6] and criteria for tax-exempt credit counseling agencies (in 2006).[7] The IRS published a draft of good governance principles (early 2007),[8] the redesigned annual information return (late 2007),[9] and then jettisoned its good governance principles and substituted an educational document predicated on the redesigned Form 990 (early 2008).[10] Only California (so far), with its Nonprofit Integrity Act, has enacted this type of governance legislation at the state level.[11]

The second category of these entities consists of nonprofit organizations, or appendages of them, formed to study and promulgate nonprofit governance principles. The principal organization in this category is the Independent Sector, which convened a Panel on the Nonprofit Sector that formulated a package of good governance principles for nonprofit entities (on balance, the best of the lot), termed its "Principles for Good Governance and Ethical Practices: A Guide for Charities and Foundations" (33 Principles).[12] In addition, the Panel on the Nonprofit Sector submitted a report to Congress entitled "Strengthening Transparency, Governance, Accountability of Charitable Organizations," which was filled with recommendations for improving the governance of charitable organizations. The Standards for Excellence Institute also published useful good governance principles, entitled Standards for Excellence: An Ethics and Accountability Code for the Nonprofit Sector (the Standards for Excellence).[13]

The third category of these organizations consists of the watchdog agencies, where adoption and enforcement of governance principles is one of their mainstays. These entities include the Better Business Bureau (by means of the Wise Giving Alliance),[14] the Evangelical Council for Financial Accountability (ECFA),[15] Charity Navigator, Ministry Watch, the Philanthropy Group, the Standards for Excellence Institute, and the American Institute of Philanthropy.[16]

Each of these organizations published a version of standards and best practices for tax-exempt organizations, filled with recommendations for policies and procedures to be implemented by exempt organizations. Not surprisingly, the advice given by these organizations is not always uniform and is sometimes contradictory. Exempt organizations are left to decide for themselves which of the many recommendations they should incorporate into their own practices. This chapter discusses the various

---

4. See § 3.5.
5. See § 3.6
6. See § 3.11.
7. See § 3.9.
8. See § 3.10.
9. See Chapter 4.
10. See § 3.14.
11. See § 3.4.
12. See § 3.12.
13. See § 3.3(e).
14. See § 3.3(c).
15. See § 3.3(d).
16. See § 3.3(f).

recommended practices, providing comments by the various agencies and organizations as to the importance and recommended content of the policy or procedure.

§ 6.2 IRS FOCUS ON POLICIES AND PROCEDURES

Whether the nonprofit world likes it or not, the IRS is becoming extremely active in pushing public charities and other tax-exempt organizations to enactment of good governance policies. This attention to nonprofit governance will, unless checked by the judicial system, continue unabated, quickly move beyond the education and outreach approach, and become rooted in IRS demands as conditions of tax exemption.[17]

In an effort to move tax-exempt organizations toward the agency's view of good governance, the IRS has redesigned the Form 990 to solicit information on an exempt organization's policies and procedures, particularly in what the TE/GE Commissioner has labeled the "crown jewel" of the return, which is its section on governance (Part VI).[18] One of the principal features of the new return is the structuring of the form so that pointed questions are answered by checking a "yes" box or a "no" box, with a check in a "no" box often plummeting the nonprofit organization into a morass of difficult and uncomfortable questions. Consequently, the organization is not-so-subtlely encouraged to look good in the eyes of the IRS, the watchdog groups, the media, and the public by having checked only "yes" boxes. This phenomenon is termed *shaming* by psychologists.

The Form 990, however, is signed under penalties of perjury, so an organization preparing it is well-advised to be truthful when checking a box "yes." What does it take to check all these "yes" boxes? The answer: adoption of a battery of policies, processes, and procedures, all picked up by the IRS from the efforts of the many undertakings, referenced above, to formulate good governance principles. Here is a listing of the many policies and procedures mentioned in the redesigned Form 990:

- A mission statement, adopted by the board of directors[19]
- A conflict-of-interest policy[20]
- A whistleblower policy[21]
- A document retention and destruction policy[22]
- A process for determining executive compensation, including use of the rebuttable presumption of reasonableness[23]
- A policy or procedure concerning participation in a joint venture arrangement[24]

---

17. Currently, only a conflict-of-interest policy is requested as part of the application for recognition of exemption (Form 1023). Even so, agents reviewing exemption applications often request other governance procedures be implemented, such as a resolution that the organization will have an independent governing body.
18. See Chapter 4.
19. Form 990, Parts I and III.
20. Part VI, line 12.
21. *Id.,* line 13.
22. *Id.,* line 14.
23. *Id.,* line 15.
24. *Id.,* line 16.

- A policy regarding documentation of meetings[25]
- A policy or procedure concerning activities of chapters, affiliates, and branches[26]
- A process used to review the Form 990[27]
- A copy of the Form 990 sent to the members of the governing body prior to filing[28]
- An audit committee[29]
- A compensation committee[30]
- A travel and reimbursement policy[31]
- A gift acceptance policy[32]
- A policy concerning the acceptance and maintenance of conservation easements[33]
- Procedures regarding international grantmaking[34]
- Procedures regarding domestic grantmaking[35]
- A Policy regarding tax-exempt bond compliance[36]
- If a hospital, a policy as to charity care[37]
- If a hospital, a community benefit report[38]
- If a hospital, a policy on debt collections[39]

Although not reflected in the Form 990, the IRS also encourages an investment policy and a fundraising policy.[40] Many of the good governance principles advocate adoption of a code of ethics, which is also referenced in the IRS's LifeCycle Educational Tool principles.[41]

§ 6.3 DISCUSSION OF SPECIFIC POLICIES AND PROCEDURES

What follows is a discussion of the various policies that a tax-exempt entity may wish to consider adopting. Organizations will need to evaluate their structures and

---

25. *Id.*, line 8.
26. *Id.*, line 9.
27. *Id.*, line 10.
28. *Id.*
29. Form 990, Part XI, line 2c.
30. Form 990, Schedule J, Part I, line 3.
31. Form 990, Schedule J, line 1b.
32. Form 990, Schedule M, line 31.
33. Form 990, Schedule D, Part II, line 5.
34. Form 990, Schedule F, Part I, line 2.
35. Form 990, Schedule I, Part I, line 2.
36. Form 990, Schedule K, Part III, line 7.
37. Form 990, Schedule H, Part I, line 1a.
38. *Id.*, line 6a.
39. *Id.*, Part III, line 9a.
40. LifeCycle Educational Tool principles, § 4.
41. *Id.*, § 4.G. For a listing of 30 policies nonprofit organizations can consider adopting, see § 2.1(f).

activities to determine which of the many recommended policies are desirable for their own governance. Once adopted, organizations should routinely monitor and implement procedures for compliance with the policies.

(a) Mission Statement

Many aspects of a nonprofit organization's operations can be the subject of a policy (or a procedure or process). Take, for example, the matter of an entity's mission statement. In the summary portion of the annual information return, which is Part I of the return, an organization can describe either its mission or its most significant activity for the year. An organization is requested to describe its mission in Part III of the return but can do this only if it has a mission statement that has been adopted by its governing body.[42] Thus, an organization may consider it important to adopt a policy or other formal procedure for having a mission statement that has been approved and periodically reviewed by its board, such as at its annual meeting.[43]

Regarding mission statements generally, the Standards for Excellence advise that a "nonprofit should have a well-defined mission, and its program should effectively and efficiently work toward achieving that mission."[44] The ECFA Standards and Best Practices published by the Evangelical Council for Financial Accountability direct nonprofits to develop a mission statement, "putting into words why the organization exists and what it hopes to accomplish." The standards further advise that the organization should regularly reference the mission statement "to assure that it is being faithfully followed" and that organizations should "[h]ave the courage to refocus the mission statement, if appropriate."[45] The Panel on the Nonprofit Sector's 33 Principles state that the board "should establish and review regularly the organization's mission and goals, and should evaluate, no less frequently than every five years, the organization's programs, goals and activities to be sure they advance its mission and make prudent use of its resources."[46]

The IRS's draft of good governance principles suggest that a charitable organization should have a "clearly articulated mission statement that is adopted by its board of directors."[47] The IRS continues this theme in its LifeCycle Educational Tool principles, in which it encourages charities "to establish and review regularly the organization's mission," which "serves to explain and popularize the charity's purpose and guide its work." The IRS goes on to state that the mission statement addresses why the charity exists, what it hopes to accomplish, and what activities it will undertake, where, and for whom."[48]

(b) Conflict-of-Interest Policy

The most venerable of the policies in the bundle of emerging good governance practices involving nonprofit organizations (and the one most heartily insisted on by the

---

42. See Form 990 instructions, Part III, line 1 ("If the organization does not have a mission that has been adopted by its governing body, state 'None.'").
43. For more information on mission statements, see § 5.15.
44. Standards for Excellence, p. 6
45. Evangelical Council for Financial Accountability, "ECFA Standards and Best Practices" (2008), p. 10.
46. 33 Principles, § 19.
47. IRS Draft of Good Governance Practices for 501(c)(3) Organizations, § 1.
48. LifeCycle Tool Document, § 1.

IRS) is the *conflict-of-interest policy*. There has long been inherent tension in this area, between the view that conflicts of interest should be prohibited (a wholly unrealistic notion) and the approach that calls for disclosure (and, if necessary, resolution) of one or more conflicts of interest. The conflict-of-interest policy is a manifestation of the latter view.

The Better Business Bureau (BBB) Wise Giving Alliance Standards for Charity Accountability (BBB Standards) reflect the first of these views, in that they forbid "transaction(s) in which any board or staff members have material conflicting interests with the charity resulting from any relationship or business affiliation."[49] Factors that are considered in determining whether a transaction entails a *conflict of interest* and if so whether the conflict is *material* include "any arm's length procedures established by the charity; the size of the transaction relative to like expenses of the charity; whether the interested party participated in the board vote on the transaction; if competitive bids were sought[;] and whether the transaction is one-time, recurring[,] or ongoing."[50] These standards, however, hint at the utility of a conflict-of-interest policy in the reference to "arm's length procedures established by the charity."[51]

By contrast, the Evangelical Council for Financial Accountability opts for the other approach. One of its best practices requires the organization's members to "avoid conflicts of interest." Having said that, members are allowed to engage in transactions with related parties if (1) a material transaction is fully disclosed in the audited financial statements of the organization, (2) the related party is excluded from the discussion and approval of the transaction, (3) a competitive bid or comparable valuation exists, and (4) the organization's board has demonstrated that the transaction is in the best interest of the entity. The ECFA Standards best practices include (1) adoption of a conflict-of-interest policy covering the governing board and key executives, (2) annual documentation of any potential related-party transactions, and (3) initial approval of all significant related-party transactions and, if continuing, annual reapproval by the board.[52]

Likewise, the Standards for Excellence state that a nonprofit organization should have a conflict-of-interest policy applicable to "all board members and staff, and to volunteers who have significant independent decisionmaking authority regarding the resources of the organization."[53] This policy "should identify the types of conduct or transactions that raise conflict of interest concerns, should set forth procedures for disclosure of actual or potential conflicts, and should provide for review of individual transactions by the uninvolved members of the board of directors." The policy should include a statement that provides "space for the board member, employee, or volunteer to disclose any known interest that the individual, or a member of the individual's immediate family, has in any business entity, [that] transacts business with the organization."[54] This statement should be signed by board members, staff, and volunteers "both at the time of the individual's initial affiliation with the organization and at least annually thereafter."[55]

---

49. BBB Standards, § 5.
50. *Id.*
51. *Id.*
52. ECFA Standards, Standard 6, p. 12.
53. Standards for Excellence, p. 16.
54. *Id.*
55. *Id.*

The IRS, in its draft of good governance principles, stated that the duty of loyalty imposed on directors of charitable organizations "requires a director to avoid conflicts of interest that are detrimental to the charity."[56] According to these principles, the board of a charitable organization "should adopt and regularly evaluate an effective conflict of interest policy" that "requires directors and staff to act solely in the interests of the charity without regard for personal interests," includes "written procedures for determining whether a relationship, financial interest, or business affiliation" results in a conflict of interest, and prescribes a "certain course of action in the event a conflict of interest is identified."[57] Directors and staff "should be required to disclose annually in writing any known financial interest that the individual, or a member of the individual's family, has in any business entity that transacts business with the charity."[58]

The instructions to Form 990 state that a conflict-of-interest policy should define the concept of conflicts of interest, identify the classes of individuals within the organization covered by the policy, facilitate the disclosure of information that may help identify conflicts of interest, and specify procedures to be followed in managing conflicts of interest.[59] For purposes of Form 990 reporting, a *conflict of interest* arises when a person in a position of authority over an organization, such as an officer, director, or manager, may benefit financially from a decision he or she could make in such capacity, including indirect benefits, such as to family members or businesses with which the person is closely associated.[60] For this purpose, a conflict of interest does not include questions involving a person's competing or respective duties to the organization and to another organization, such as by serving on the board of directors of both organizations, that do not involve a material financial interest of, or benefit to, such person.[61] The redesigned Form 990 also asks reporting organizations to describe their practices for monitoring proposed or ongoing transactions for conflicts of interest and dealing with potential or actual conflicts, whether discovered before or after the transaction has occurred.[62]

The Panel on the Nonprofit Sector states in its 33 Principles that an organization should "adopt and implement policies and procedures to ensure that all conflicts of interest, or the appearance thereof, within the organization and the board are appropriately managed though disclosure, recusal, or other means."[63] A conflict-of-interest policy "must be consistent with the laws of the state in which the nonprofit is organized and should be tailored to specific organizational needs and characteristics."[64] This policy "should require full disclosure of all potential conflicts of interest within the organization" and "should apply to every person who has the ability to influence decisions of the organization, including board and staff members and parties related to them."[65]

---

56. "Good Governance Practices for 501(c)(3) Organizations," (February 2, 2007), § 4.
57. *Id.*
58. *Id.*
59. Form 990 instructions, Part VI, line 12a.
60. *Id.*
61. *Id.*
62. Form 990, Part VI, Section B, line 12c.
63. 33 Principles, § 3.
64. *Id.*
65. *Id.*

Conflicts of interest are not inherently illegal or unethical, but they must be handled appropriately. The person with the actual or potential conflict of interest should disclose the conflict and then recuse himself or herself from further participation in any decision-making involving the conflict. Nonprofit organizations should maintain records, such as minutes from meetings, documenting any noted conflicts and the method in which the conflict was addressed to demonstrate the conflict was properly handled.

Disclosures of conflicts of interest, actual or potential, are necessary for board members to carry out their fiduciary duty of loyalty to an organization. An important element of a conflict-of-interest policy is an annual disclosure statement signed by each board member, officer, and key employee, disclosing all relationships, family and business, that could give rise to a conflict. The IRS, in its LifeCycle Educational Tool principles, encourages organizations to require the individuals covered by the conflict-of-interest policy to make periodic, written disclosures of any known financial interest that the individual, or member of the individual's family, has in entities transacting business with the nonprofit.[66] These statements should be periodically reviewed by the organization to determine instances of potential conflicts. The redesigned Form 990 asks whether a tax-exempt organization's officers, directors, trustees, and key employees are required to disclose or update at least annually their interests that could give rise to conflicts of interest, such as a list of family members, substantial business or investment holdings, and other transactions or affiliations with businesses and other organizations and those of family members.[67]

(c) Whistleblower Policy

Under the Sarbanes-Oxley Act, all organizations, including nonprofit organizations, are subject to the act's protection of whistleblowers.[68] A whistleblower policy demonstrates an organization's efforts to comply with these provisions.

In its draft of good governance principles, the IRS stated that the board of directors of a charitable organization "should adopt an effective policy for handling employee complaints and establish procedures for employees to report in confidence suspected financial impropriety or misuse of the charity's resources."[69] More recently, in its LifeCycle Educational Tool principles, the IRS "encourages the board of directors to adopt" such a policy.[70] The Evangelical Council for Financial Accountability recommends a whistleblower policy in its best practices standards.[71]

The redesigned Form 990 asks if a reporting organization has a written whistleblower policy, which it describes as a policy that "encourages staff and volunteers to come forward with credible information on illegal practices or violations of adopted policies of the organization, specifies that the organization will protect the individual from retaliation, and identifies those staff or board members or outside parties to whom such information can be reported."[72] The Panel on the Nonprofit Sector states

---

66. LifeCycle Educational Tool principles, § 4.B.
67. Form 990, Part VI, Section B, line 12b; Form 990 instructions, Part VI, Section B, line 12b.
68. 18 U.S.C. § 1513(e).
69. § 2.
70. § 4.G.
71. ECFA Standards, p. 10.
72. Form 990 instructions, Part VI, lines 13 and 14.

that an organization "should establish and implement policies and procedures that enable individuals to come forward with information on illegal practices or violations of organizational policies."[73] This whistleblower policy "should specify that the organization will not retaliate against, and will protect the confidentiality of, individuals who make good-faith reports."[74] The Panel recommended that "[i]nformation on these policies . . . be widely distributed to staff, volunteers[,] and clients, and should be incorporated both in new employee orientations and ongoing training programs for employees and volunteers."[75] These policies "can help boards and senior managers become aware of and address problems before serious harm is done to the organization" and "can also assist in complying with legal provisions that protect individuals working in charitable organizations from retaliation for engaging in certain whistle-blowing activities."[76]

(d)   Document Retention and Destruction Policy

All organizations, including tax-exempt entities, are subject to the Sarbanes-Oxley Act's provisions regarding document destruction.[77] In addition, most versions of good governance principles recommend this type of policy. The IRS's draft of good governance principles stated that an "effective charity" will "adopt a written policy establishing standards for document integrity, retention, and destruction."[78] (A charitable organization, however, can be effective, presumably programmatically, in the absence of a document retention and destruction policy.) According to the IRS, this type of policy, which "should include guidelines for handling electronic files," should "cover backup procedures, archiving of documents, and regular check-ups of the reliability of the system."[79]

The redesigned Form 990 asks if a filing organization has a written document retention and destruction policy, and describes such a policy as one that "identifies the record retention responsibilities of staff, volunteers, board members, and outsiders for maintaining and documenting the storage and destruction of the organization's documents and records."[80] In addition, the Form 990 instructions advise that a document retention and destruction policy "should address the length of time specific types of documents must be retained, as well as when it is permissible or required to destroy certain types of documents" and that the "policy should contain specific procedures to ensure document destruction is immediately halted if any official investigation of the organization is under way or anticipated."[81]

The Panel on the Nonprofit Sector states in one of its principles that a charitable organization should "establish and implement policies and procedures to protect and preserve the organization's important documents and business records."[82] The Panel observed that a document-retention policy "is essential for protecting the

---

73. 33 Principles, § 4.
74. *Id.*
75. *Id.*
76. *Id.*
77. 18 U.S.C. § 1519.
78. "Good Governance Practices for 501(c)(3) Organizations," § 9.
79. *Id.*
80. Form 990, Part VI, line 14.
81. Form 990 instructions, Part VI, lines 13 and 14.
82. 33 Principles, § 5.

organization's records of its governance and administration, as well as business records that are required to demonstrate legal compliance."[83] This type of policy "also helps to protect against allegations of wrongdoing by the organization or its directors and managers."[84]

(e) Executive Compensation Policy

The Evangelical Council for Financial Accountability standards include adoption of an "executive compensation philosophy statement" as a best practice.[85] According to the Standards for Excellence Institute, the board or a committee of it "should hire the executive director, set the executive's compensation," and "periodically review the appropriateness of the overall compensation structure of the organization."[86]

The IRS's view, in its draft of good governance principles, was that a "successful charity pays no more than reasonable compensation for services rendered."[87] (Again, however, there is no correlation between the success of a charitable organization, presumably from a program standpoint, and whether the compensation it pays is reasonable; a charity can pay excessive compensation to, for example, its chief executive and nonetheless be a successful organization in terms of program outcomes.) Charities, said the IRS, "may pay reasonable compensation for services provided by officers and staff."[88]

The Panel on the Nonprofit Sector states that the board of a charitable organization should "hire, oversee, and annually evaluate the performance of the chief executive officer of the organization, and should conduct such an evaluation prior to any change in that officer's compensation," unless a multiyear contract is in force or the change consists solely of routine adjustments for inflation or the cost of living.[89] The Panel stated that "[o]ne of the most important responsibilities of the board . . . is to select, supervise, and determine a compensation package that will attract and retain a qualified chief executive."[90] The organization's governing documents should require the full board to evaluate the executive's performance and approve his or her compensation.

An executive compensation policy should refer to the rebuttable presumption of reasonableness, which is a procedure found in the intermediate sanctions law applicable to public charities and social welfare organizations.[91] If the three elements of the procedure can be satisfied, payments of compensation or other transactions between a public charity or social welfare organizations and its insiders are presumed to be reasonable, and the burden of proof is shifted to the IRS to prove that compensation is not reasonable. While there may be circumstances where meeting the rebuttable presumption is not practicable, if at all possible, charitable organizations will want to invoke the rebuttable presumption of reasonableness for the protection it affords its executives and those determining their compensation.

---

83. *Id.*
84. *Id.*
85. EFCA Standards, p. 10.
86. Standards for Excellence, p.
87. "Good Governance Practices for 501(c)(3) Organizations," § 8.
88. *Id.*
89. 33 Principles, § 13.
90. *Id.*
91. Treasury Regulation § 53.4958-6(c).

A nonprofit organization may wish to establish a compensation committee to assess, evaluate, and recommend the compensation of the organization's top officials. A compensation committee should be independent, meaning that it should be composed of individuals whose compensation is not being evaluated by the committee.[92]

(f) Joint Venture Policy

Nonprofit organizations are increasingly participating in joint venture arrangements with other nonprofit, and sometimes for-profit, entities. Sometimes these joint ventures are organized as separate legal entities (typically as partnerships or limited liability companies taxed as partnerships), or less formally as joint ventures. Most of the entities that have written good governance principles have not addressed the matter of a joint venture policy. This policy is principally the subject of federal tax law considerations. An organization in this position is to evaluate its participation in joint venture arrangements and take the requisite steps to safeguard its tax-exempt status. This policy requirement is targeted at public charities that enter into joint ventures and partnerships with taxable entities.

Typically, a joint venture with a nonprofit entity that has the same tax-exempt status does not pose a concern with an organization's own exempt status, as both parties will need to operate the joint venture in a manner that protects each member's exempt status. With a joint venture between an exempt organization and a for-profit entity or an individual, both parties will not necessarily be concerned with operating the joint venture in furtherance of exempt purposes. If not structured carefully, these arrangements can jeopardize an organization's exempt status by ceding control of the arrangement to the other partner(s) or, less severely, result in unrelated business income to the nonprofit organization. Recent court decisions and IRS rulings in this area provide that a nonprofit organization can protect its exempt status by maintaining a controlling position in the joint venture and taking steps to ensure that the joint venture will be conducted solely in furtherance of the nonprofit organization's exempt purposes.

The redesigned Form 990 requests information on whether a tax-exempt organization is participating in a joint venture, and if so, whether it has adopted a written policy or procedure requiring the organization to evaluate its participation in joint venture arrangements under applicable federal tax law, and taken steps to safeguard the organization's exempt status with respect to such arrangement.[93] Some examples of *safeguards* include control over the venture or arrangement sufficient to ensure that the venture furthers the exempt purposes of the organization; requirements that the venture or arrangement give priority to exempt purposes over maximizing profits for the other participants; requirements that it not engage in activities that would jeopardize the organization's exemption; and a requirement that all contracts entered into with the organization be on terms that are arm's length or more favorable to the organization.[94]

---

92. See Reg. §53.4958-6(a)(1) for a description of an authorized body to approve compensation to establish the rebuttable presumption of reasonableness under the intermediate sanctions. The procedure requires that only persons without a conflict of interest with respect to the compensation arrangement may participate in the decision-making process.
93. Form 990, Part VI, lines 16a and 16b.
94. Form 990 instructions, Part VI, line 16.

(g) Documentation of Meetings

According to the Evangelical Council for Financial Accountability standards, as a best practice, organizations should "properly document the proceedings of all board and board committee meetings in order to protect the organization" and board minutes "should identify all voting board members as present or absent to clearly document a quorum."[95] The Standards for Excellence state that a board should maintain written "meeting minutes reflecting the actions of the board, including reports of board committees when acting in the place of the board" and that the minutes should be "distributed to board and committee members."[96]

On the redesigned Form 990, an organization is asked whether it contemporaneously documented by any means permitted by state law every meeting held or written action undertaken during the year by the governing body and each committee with authority to act on behalf of the governing body.[97] For Form 990 purposes, documentation may include minutes, strings of e-mails, or similar writings that explain the action taken, when it was taken, and who made the decision.[98] *Contemporaneous* typically means by the later of either the next meeting of the governing body or committee or 60 days after the date of the meeting or written action.[99] In the IRS LifeCycle Educational Tool principles, the IRS encourages the governing bodies and "authorized sub-committees" to take steps to ensure that minutes of their meetings are contemporaneously documented and that actions taken by written action or outside of meetings are similarly documented.[100]

(h) Policy Concerning Chapters, Affiliates, and Branches

The IRS, in connection with the annual information return, asks organizations that have chapters, branches, or affiliates whether they have a policy or procedure governing the activities of these affiliated organizations, to ensure that their operations are "consistent" with those of the principal organization.[101] Some organizations have formal agreements with their chapters, which encompass this aspect of the affiliation; many organizations, however, do not. This new information return question is likely to provide an incentive for organizations that have chapters or the like to implement this type of policy. For Form 990 reporting purposes, *written policies and procedures governing the activities of chapters, branches, and affiliates to ensure their consistency* are documents used by the organization and its local units to address the policies, practices, and activities of the local unit.[102] These policies and procedures may include required provisions in the chapter's articles of organization or bylaws, a manual provided to chapters, a constitution, or similar documents. Organizations with affiliates

---

95. ECFA Standards, p. 9.

96. Standards for Excellence, p. 14.

97. Form 990, Part VI, lines 8a and 8b.

98. Form 990 instructions, Part VI, line 8.

99. See Form 990 instructions, Part VI, Section A, line 8. Also Reg. § 53.4958-6(c)(3)(ii) for the requirement of concurrent documentation necessary to invoke the rebuttable presumption of reasonableness under the intermediate sanctions.

100. LifeCycle Educational Tool principles, § 4.E.

101. Form 990, Part VI, line 9b.

102. Form 990 instructions, Part VI, line 9b.

may also wish to address standards of conduct, permissible activities, and approved use of the national or parent organization's name in the policy.

Regardless of whether the chapters or affiliates are organized as separate entities, a tax-exempt entity with branches, chapters, or affiliates should have some standardization and consistency regarding the branches, chapters, and affiliates, given their common mission and goals, as well as the public perception that the organizations are all part of one entity, despite what may otherwise be true as a matter of law. In addition, an exempt organization that is a central organization in a group exemption[103] should ensure that its chapters and affiliates are generally subject to its control and do not engage in activities that jeopardize its exempt status.

(i)   Annual Information Return Review Policy

The IRS requires an organization to describe, on the redesigned Form 990, the process, if any, it uses to have the return reviewed.[104] This review may be by one or more members of the board, one or more officers, one or more staff members, and/or the organization's lawyer. In addition, an organization may have a committee, such as an audit committee or finance committee, that is responsible for the review of its annual information return. The IRS recognizes that practices for review of the annual information return "differ widely."[105] An organization is well-advised to have some procedure in place for review of its information return by its board of directors or an independent committee, prior to filing the return with the IRS.

An additional question on the annual return inquires as to whether a copy of the final Form 990, as filed, was provided to the organization's governing body, whether in electronic form or otherwise.[106] As a matter of practice, tax-exempt organizations should consider circulating a copy of their information return (Form 990 or Form 990-PF) to the entire board of directors for review prior to filing and giving board members an opportunity to provide comments. Because the question on Form 990 asks whether each board member received a copy of the final Form 990 as "ultimately filed with the IRS,"[107] any changes that result from the circulation of the information return to the governing body will require a redistribution of the revised Form 990 to respond "yes" to the question. It is not necessary for any board member to undertake a review of the tax-exempt organization's Form 990 to answer the question "yes," provided each member receives a copy of the form.[108]

(j)   Gift Acceptance Policy

The Standards for Excellence state that a charitable organization should have policies governing the acceptance and disposition of charitable gifts, including procedures to determine any limits on individuals or entities from which the organization will accept a gift, the purposes for which contributions will be accepted, the type of property that will be accepted, and whether an "unusual or unanticipated" gift will be

---

103. See *Law of Tax-Exempt Organizations,* § 25.6.

104. Form 990, Part VI, line 10.

105. LifeCycle Educational Tool principles, § 5.B.

106. Form 990, Part VI, Section A, line 10.

107. Form 990 instructions, Part VI, Section A, line 10.

108. *Id.*

accepted in view of the organization's mission and "organizational capacity."[109] Gift acceptance policies often give details regarding how long an organization will retain property it receives that it is unable to use in furtherance of its exempt purposes, and how it will dispose of the property.

The IRS has launched an examination program pertaining to charitable contributions of certain successor member interests, involving the questionable use of limited liability companies, ostensibly done to inflate the value of contributed property for deduction purposes. The agency has developed a prototype document that it is sending to various charities, asking pointed questions that charitable organizations should ponder when considering whether to accept an "unconventional" charitable contribution. These questions include a request for a summary of the economic rights the charity anticipates, the nature of the legal advice obtained in connection with the gift, whether the organization has "guidelines" for accepting "unusual" gifts, and whether the gift transaction was reviewed by the organization's board.[110]

The redesigned Form 990 asks tax-exempt organizations if they have implemented a gift acceptance policy that requires the review of nonstandard contributions.[111] A *nonstandard contribution* includes a contribution of an item that is not reasonably expected to be used to satisfy or further the organization's exempt purpose (aside from the need of such organization for income or funds) and for which (1) there is no ready market to which the organization may go to liquidate the contribution or convert it to cash, and (2) the value of the item is highly speculative or difficult to ascertain.[112]

(k) Conservation Easements Policy

Few charitable organizations have the need for a policy as to conservation easements, simply because it is not common for entities to receive this type of property by gift. For a charitable contribution of a conservation easement (or certain other conservation properties) to be deductible, however, the charitable donee must be *qualified* to receive and maintain the property.[113] A policy in this context, therefore, will focus on the organization's ability to properly maintain the conservation property and enforce the terms of the easement (and perhaps other restrictions) placed on it.

The redesigned Form 990 asks whether a filing organization has a written policy regarding how the organization will monitor, inspect, respond to violations and enforce conservation easements.[114] The question must be answered only if a tax-exempt organization reports that it received or held a conservation easement.

(l) International and Domestic Grantmaking Policy

If an organization engages in grantmaking activities, it should consider adoption of a policy and procedures summarizing the substance of these activities; the potential grantees involved (including their location); the application process for potential

---

109. Standards for Excellence, p. 28.
110. See *Law of Tax-Exempt Organizations* § 27.15(j) (2009 Cum. Supp.); *New Form 990* § 19.1(x).
111. Form 990, Schedule M, line 31.
112. Form 990 instructions, Schedule M, line 31.
113. IRC § 170(h).
114. Form 990, Schedule D, line 5.

grantees; and the due diligence the organization will undertake before and after the grant is made, such as investigation of the grantee and the required reporting for the grant. If the organization's activities involve international grantmaking, the policy should be formulated taking into account the concerns of the federal government that donations to U.S. charities are being funneled overseas to fund terrorism. Organizations can look to the U.S. Department of Treasury's "Anti-Terrorist Financing Guidelines: Voluntary Best Practices for U.S.-Based Charities,"[115] which were finalized in 2006, for guidance in determining their international grantmaking procedures. As the title suggests, the guidelines are voluntary and do not create any new legal requirements for tax-exempt organizations. The guidelines state that they "are designed to assist charities that attempt in good faith to protect themselves from terrorist abuse," and acknowledge that certain aspects will not be applicable to every charity, charitable activity, or circumstance.

Tax-exempt entities can also review the private foundation expenditure responsibility rules[116] for further guidance on procedures for international grantmaking. In addition, organizations can determine whether potential charitable recipients are recognized as charitable entities by the IRS or engage in an equivalency determination process to determine whether the recipient is the equivalent of a U.S. charity. Such process is common practice for private foundations, which are treated as making taxable expenditures if they do not either engage in expenditure responsibility with respect to foreign grants or make equivalency determinations regarding foreign grantees.[117]

(m) Charity Care Policy

The only type of nonprofit organization that needs to concern itself with a charity care policy is a tax-exempt hospital, which must state on its Form 990 whether it has such a policy.[118] This type of policy should describe how the organization will provide *charity care*, a controversial topic that generally means free or discounted health services made available to individuals who meet the organization's criteria for assistance and are thereby deemed unable to pay for all or a portion of the services.[119] It is the view of the IRS that the concept of charity care does not include (1) bad debt or uncollectible charges that the hospital recorded as revenue but wrote off due to failure to pay by patients who did not qualify for charity care, or the cost of providing that care; (2) the difference between the cost of care provided under Medicaid or other means-tested government programs or under Medicare and the revenue derived from the programs; or (3) contractual adjustments with third-party payors.[120]

(n) Community Benefit Report

Community benefit reports are prepared by tax-exempt hospitals to communicate with the public about what the hospitals do to promote health in their communities.

---

115. See § 3.6.
116. Reg. § 53.4945-5(b). See *Private Foundations*, § 9.6.
117. See Rev. Proc. 92-94, 1992-2 C.B. 507, for a description of the equivalency determination process.
118. Form 990, Schedule H, Part I, line 1a.
119. Form 990 instructions, Schedule H, line 1.
120. *Id.*

A community benefit report can be used for fundraising, conveying information to donors, assisting with media and press relations, and communicating with lawmakers and regulators. Often, a hospital's community benefit report is part of a larger annual report. On the redesigned Form 990, exempt hospitals must disclose whether they prepare an annual community benefit report.[121]

(o) Debt Collection Policy

Likewise, only tax-exempt hospitals need be concerned with a debt collection policy; this type of policy pertains to the collection of amounts owed by patients. The redesigned Form 990 contains a question regarding whether an exempt hospital has a written debt collection policy, and if so, whether the policy contains provisions on the collection practices to be followed for patients who are known to qualify for charity care or financial assistance.[122] The latter includes provisions such as procedures for internal review of accounts prior to initiation of legal action or continuing a collection action undertaken by an outside agency.[123]

(p) Investment Policy

Oddly, none of the organizations that promulgate good governance principles have focused on the terms of a nonprofit organization's investment policy. The closest in this regard is the Panel on the Nonprofit Sector's principles, which state that the board of a charitable organization "must institute policies and procedures to ensure that the organization (and, if applicable, its subsidiaries) manages and invests its funds responsibly, in accordance with all legal requirements."[124]

The IRS, in its LifeCycle Educational Tool principles, focuses on a policy for investing in only certain types of investments, namely "joint ventures, for-profit entities, and complicated and sophisticated financial products or investments or investments that require financial and investment expertise and, in some cases, the advice of outside investment advisors."[125] The IRS further encourages charities making these investments to "adopt written policies and procedures requiring the charity to evaluate its participation in these investments and to take steps to safeguard the organization's assets and exempt status if they could be affected by the investment arrangement."[126] Further, the IRS states it will review compensation arrangements with investment advisors to see that they comply with federal tax law.[127]

An investment policy should primarily address two elements. One concerns the nature of the organization's portfolio, stating the vehicles and properties in which the organization will invest (or, in some instances, will not invest). This includes stocks, bonds, real estate, partnership and limited liability company interests, and investment in funds. The other element is the general balance of the portfolio, stipulating the percentages of investments in equities, interest-bearing instruments, foreign investment property, and the like. The policy can also address the selection and

---

121. Form 990, Schedule H, Part I, line 6a.
122. Form 990, Schedule H, Part III, lines 9a and 9b.
123. Form 990 instructions, Schedule H, Part III, line 9b.
124. 33 Principles, § 21.
125. LifeCycle Educational Tool principles, § 4.C.
126. *Id.* See § 6.3(f) for a discussion of these safeguards.
127. *Id.*

ongoing review of and decisions regarding an investment manager for the organization's assets.

(q) Fundraising Policy

Organizations engaged in fundraising activities should consider having a fundraising policy. The ECFA Standards and Best Practices require that, in fundraising materials, representations of fact, descriptions of the organization's financial condition, and narrative information about events be "current, complete, and accurate."[128] "[M]aterial omissions or exaggerations of fact" are not permitted.[129] Member organizations are exhorted to "not create unrealistic donor expectations of what a donor's gift will accomplish."[130] Organizations are asked to make efforts to "avoid accepting a gift from or entering into a contract with a prospective donor which would knowingly place a hardship on the donor, or place the donor's wellbeing in jeopardy."[131] The ECFA standards also address the compensation paid to outside fundraisers and require the organization to honor statements made in fundraising appeals.[132]

Along these lines, the Standards for Excellence state that solicitation materials should be "accurate and truthful and should correctly identify the organization, its mission, and the intended use of the solicited funds."[133] All statements made by a charitable organization in its fundraising appeals "about the use of a contribution should be honored."[134] A charitable organization "must honor the known intention of a donor regarding the use of donated funds" and should respect the privacy of donors and "safeguard the confidentiality of information that a donor reasonably would expect to be private."[135] These standards likewise address the topic of fundraisers' compensation, including a prohibition on compensation on the basis of a "percentage of the amount raised or other commission formula," and mandate that a charitable organization should contract only with those persons who are "properly registered with applicable regulatory authorities."[136]

In its LifeCycle Educational Tool principles, the IRS "encourages charities to adopt and monitor policies to ensure that fundraising solicitations meet federal and state law requirements and solicitations materials are accurate, truthful, and candid."[137] Charities are further encouraged to keep fundraising costs reasonable and to inform donors and the public about fundraising costs and practices.[138]

The position of the Panel on the Nonprofit Sector in its 33 Principles is that solicitation materials and other communications addressed to prospective donors and the public "must clearly identify the organization and be accurate and truthful."[139] The Panel states that a prospective donor "has the right to know the name of anyone

---

128. EFCA Standards and Best Practices, p. 3.
129. *Id.*
130. *Id.*
131. EFCA Standards and Best Practices, p. 4.
132. ECFA Standards and Best Practices, pp. 3-4.
133. Standards of Excellence, p. 26.
134. *Id.*
135. *Id.*, pp. 26-27.
136. *Id.*, p. 28.
137. LifeCycle Educational Tool principles, § 4.D.
138. *Id.*
139. 33 Principles, § 27.

soliciting contributions, the name and location of the organization that will receive the contribution, a clear description of its activities, the intended use of the funds to be raised, a contact for obtaining additional information, and whether the individual requesting the contribution is acting as a volunteer, employee of the organization, or hired solicitor."[140] (The derivation of this right, ostensibly possessed by prospective contributors, to know the names of everyone soliciting contributions is not clear.)

In the Panel's view, contributions "must be used for purposes consistent with the donor's intent, whether as described in the relevant solicitation materials or as specifically directed by the donor."[141] The Panel states that solicitations should "indicate whether the funds they generate will be used to further the general programs and operations of the organization or to support specific programs or types of programs."[142] The Panel advises charitable organizations to "carefully review the terms of any contract or grant agreement before accepting a donation."[143]

An organization must, according to the Panel, "provide donors with specific acknowledgments of charitable contributions, in accordance with [federal tax law] requirements, as well as information to facilitate the donor's compliance with tax law requirements."[144] The Panel notes that not only is this type of acknowledgment generally required by law, but "it also helps in building donors' confidence in and support for the activities they help to fund."[145]

(r) Expense Reimbursement Policy

The ECFA best practices recommend that organizations adopt a policy with respect to "accountable expense reimbursements."[146] Form 990 (Schedule J) asks whether a tax-exempt organization follows a written policy regarding payment, reimbursement, or provision of business expenses and whether the organization requires substantiation prior to reimbursing or allowing expenses by its top officials. It is prudent for a non-profit organization to adopt an accountable plan for income tax reasons, as well as for good governance purposes. Expenses paid or incurred by an employee under a reimbursement or other expense allowance arrangement with an employer are excludable from the employee's gross income if the arrangement meets the requirements of an *accountable plan*.[147] A reimbursement or other expense allowance arrangement qualifies as an accountable plan by meeting certain requirements as to business connection, substantiation, and returning amounts in excess of substantiated expenses.[148]

An arrangement meets the *business connection* requirement if it provides advances, allowances (including per-diem allowances, allowances only for meals and incidental expenses, and mileage allowances), or reimbursements only for deductible business expenses. These allowances and the like must be paid or incurred by the employee in connection with the performance of services as an employee of the

---

140. *Id.*
141. 33 Principles, § 28.
142. *Id.*
143. *Id.*
144. Principles, § 29.
145. *Id.* See § 5.19 for additional information on fundraising policies.
146. ECFA Standards and Best Practices, p. 10.
147. IRC § 61(a)(2)(A); Reg. § 1.62-2(c).
148. Reg. § 1.62-2(c)(2).

employer. The payment may include amounts charged directly or indirectly to the payor through credit card systems or otherwise.[149]

A *substantiation* requirement covers reimbursements for travel, entertainment, use of a passenger automobile, and certain other business expenses.[150] Substantiation of the amount of a business expense in accordance with certain other federal tax rules is treated as substantiation of the amount of an expense for purposes of the accountable plan rules.[151] For example, for business expenses other than travel, entertainment, use of a personal vehicle, gifts, and certain property, an employee must submit information sufficient to enable an employer to identify the specific nature of each expense and to conclude that the expense is attributable to the employer's business activities.[152] For expenses relating to travel and entertainment, an employee must substantiate the amount, time, place, business purpose, and (with respect to entertainment) the business relationship to the persons entertained.[153]

The rules concerning *return of excess amounts* are satisfied if the employee is required to return to the payor, within a reasonable period of time, any amount paid under the arrangement in excess of the substantiated expenses.[154] The accountable plan rules state that an expense substantiated to the payor within 60 days after it is paid or incurred, or an amount returned to the payor within 120 days after an expense is paid or incurred, will be treated as having occurred within a reasonable period of time.[155]

The treatment of reimbursements is different under a nonaccountable plan. If a plan does not qualify as an accountable plan, all amounts reimbursed to an employee, even business expenses, can be included in an employee's gross income, must be reported as wages or other compensation, and are subject to withholding and employment taxes.[156] The employee can then deduct, as a business expense, the amounts that are properly treated as business expenses, provided the employee can substantiate the expenses, but the employee can deduct them only as miscellaneous itemized deductions subject to the appropriate limitations (such as the limitations on the deduction of expenses attributable to meals and entertainment, and the 2% floor for miscellaneous itemized deductions). If an employer provides a nonaccountable plan, an employee who receives payments under the plan cannot compel the payor to treat the payments as paid under an accountable plan by voluntarily substantiating the expenses and returning any excess to the payor.[157] Thus, it is important that an organization's expense reimbursement procedures meet the requirements of an accountable plan to avoid having its employees include reimbursable amounts in their income.

The intermediate sanctions rules address accountable and nonaccountable plans.[158] If an arrangement constitutes an accountable plan, reimbursements of

---

149. Reg. § 1.62-2(d).
150. These expenses are the subject of IRC § 274(d).
151. Reg. § 1.62-2(e).
152. Reg. § 1.62-2(e)(3).
153. Reg. § 1.274-5T(b).
154. Reg. § 1.62-2(f).
155. Reg. § 1.62-2(g)(2).
156. Reg. § 1.62-2(c)(5).
157. Reg. § 1.62-2(c)(3).
158. Reg. § 53.4958-4(a)(4)(ii).

expenses incurred by a disqualified person that are paid by a tax-exempt organization to the disqualified person are disregarded as compensation under the intermediate sanctions rules.[159] If, however, a plan is not an accountable plan, all amounts paid by an exempt organization to a disqualified person may be subject to the intermediate sanctions rules. Furthermore, if amounts are paid under a nonaccountable plan and are not contemporaneously substantiated as an employee's compensation, the reimbursed amounts result in an automatic excess benefit transaction, regardless of whether the reimbursements are reasonable, any other compensation the disqualified person receives is reasonable, and the aggregate of the reimbursements and any other compensation the disqualified person may have received is reasonable.[160]

(s) Policy Regarding Tax-Exempt Bond Compliance

Tax-exempt organizations that are the beneficiary of tax-exempt bond financing may want to have a policy that requires the organization to act in compliance with the terms and conditions of their tax-exempt bond financing. This policy should strive to ensure compliance with the private use and arbitrage provisions to which the tax-exempt bond financing is subject. On the redesigned Form 990, the IRS asks if an organization has "adopted management practices and procedures to ensure the post-issuance compliance of its tax-exempt bond liabilities."[161]

(t) Code of Ethics

The ECFA suggests, as a best practice, that organizations adopt a "stewardship philosophy statement."[162] The IRS, in its draft of good governance principles, stated that the public "expects a charity to abide by ethical standards that promote the public good."[163] According to the IRS, the board of directors of a charitable organization "bears the ultimate responsibility for setting ethical standards and ensuring [that] they permeate the organization and inform its practices."[164] To that end, the board "should consider adopting and regularly evaluating a code of ethics that describes behavior it wants to encourage and behavior it wants to discourage."[165] This code of ethics "should be a principal means of communicating to all personnel a strong culture of legal compliance and ethical integrity."[166]

In its LifeCycle Educational Tool principles, the IRS does not give as much emphasis to a code of ethics as in its prior good governance publication, but notes that a "code of ethics will serve to communicate and further a strong culture of legal compliance and ethical integrity to all persons associated with the organization."[167] The Form 990 does not ask about a code of ethics.

---

159. *Id.*
160. Reg. § 53.4958-4(c)(1); Bauer and Henzke, "'Automatic' Excess Benefit Transactions Under IRC 4958," IRS Continuing Professional Education Text (2004).
161. Form 990, Schedule K, Part III, line 7.
162. ECFA Standards and Best Practices, p.10.
163. "Good Governance Practices for 501(c)(3) Organizations," § 2.
164. *Id.*
165. *Id.*
166. *Id.*
167. LifeCycle Educational Tool principles, § 4.G.

The Panel on the Nonprofit Sector advises that an organization should have a "formally adopted, written code of ethics with which all of its directors or trustees, staff[,] and volunteers are familiar and to which they adhere."[168] This principle is predicated on the thought that "[a]dherence to the law provides a minimum standard for an organization's behavior."[169] The adoption of a code of ethics "helps demonstrate the organization's commitment to carry out its responsibilities ethically and effectively."[170] The code should be "built on the values that the organization embraces, and should highlight expectations of how those who work with the organization will conduct themselves in a number of areas, such as the confidentiality and respect that should be accorded to clients, consumers, donors, and fellow volunteers and board and staff members."[171]

(u) Audit Committee

So far, only California, as part of the Nonprofit Integrity Act of 2004, requires nonprofit organizations to have an audit committee, and it is required only if a nonprofit organization has gross revenues in excess of $2 million.[172] In its LifeCycle Educational Tool principles, the IRS does not affirmatively recommend an audit committee, but sets forth that a "board may establish an independent audit committee to select and oversee an independent auditor."[173] The IRS further states that an audit committee is generally responsible for selecting the organization's independent auditor and reviewing its performance, with "a focus on whether the auditor has the competence and independence necessary to conduct the audit engagement, the overall quality of the audit, and in, particular, the independence and competence of the key personnel on the audit engagement teams."[174] The IRS further encourages all charities to implement steps that will ensure the continuing independence of its auditors.[175] On the redesigned Form 990, the IRS asks whether an organization has a committee that "assumes responsibility for oversight of the audit, review, or compilation of its financial statements and selection of an independent accountant."[176] This question must be answered only if the organization indicates that its financial statements were compiled or reviewed by an independent accountant or that its financial statements were audited by an independent accountant.[177]

The Panel on the Nonprofit Sector advises that every charitable organization that has its financial statements audited, regardless of whether it is legally required to undergo the audit, "should consider establishing an audit committee composed of independent board members with appropriate financial expertise."[178] The Panel observes that an audit committee can provide the board with increased assurance that the audit has been appropriately conducted by reducing possible conflicts of

---

168. 33 Principles, § 2.
169. *Id.*
170. *Id.*
171. *Id.*
172. California Government Code § 12586(e).
173. LifeCycle Educational Tool principles, § 5.A.
174. *Id.*
175. *Id.*
176. Form 990, Part XI, line 2c.
177. Form 990, Part XI, lines 2a and 2b.
178. 33 Principles, § 21.

interest between outside auditors and the organization's paid staff.[179] The Panel also notes that if permitted by state law, an organization's board can appoint nonvoting, nonstaff advisors rather than board members to the audit committee.[180]

§ 6.4 COLLEGES AND UNIVERSITIES

In 2008, IRS began an inquiry into the practices of the tax-exempt higher education community. The IRS sent a 33-page compliance questionnaire[181] to 400 public and private colleges and universities, focusing on unrelated business activities, endowment funds, and executive compensation. From the questions, colleges and universities can easily glean the policies and procedures the IRS, at least, thinks they should have in place.

The questionnaire first asks for general information about the college or university, including whether it has a written conflict-of-interest policy governing the board, top management officials, and full-time faculty (for private institutions) or a state statute that explicitly governs conflicts of interest for these same persons (for public institutions) and whether it makes its audited financial statements available to the public. Private institutions are asked whether they have a written policy that is designed to ensure that transactions with related noncharitable organizations, taxable or tax-exempt, are made at arm's length; the institutions must indicate whether the policy applies to the provision of goods or services, lending of money, rental of property, transfers of assets, cost-sharing and expense-reimbursement arrangements, licensing arrangements, shared employees, and other transfers of assets, liabilities, or funds. Public institutions are asked whether they are subject to a state statute designed to ensure that these transactions are made at arm's length. Similar questions are asked regarding controlled and related entities.

The questionnaire requests information on the organization's activities, including whether the organization conducts activities through a joint venture, whether the organization conducts the activities using a third-party manager/operator, and whether the organization relies on an independent accountant or counsel to provide advice on business activities. The questionnaire also requires detailed breakdowns of income and expenses for various types of business activities.

With respect to endowment funds, the questionnaire asks whether the organization has an investment committee to oversee investment of its endowment fund assets and asks about the use and approval of investment advisors and their recommendations, the methods used to compensate internal and external investment managers, whether this compensation was approved by the board of directors or a board committee, and how the funds are managed (including whether they are invested in alternative or foreign investments). There are also questions relating to the size of the organization's endowment funds, the restrictions placed on the endowment funds, and the use for which the endowment funds were distributed.

The executive compensation portion of the questionnaire requires all recipients to provide detailed disclosure of the compensation of the institutes' top officials and the benefits they may receive. The remaining questions, which must be answered only by

---

179. *Id.*
180. *Id.*
181. IRS Form 14018, Colleges and Universities Compliance Questionnaire (September 2008).

private schools, include questions as to whether the entity used a process intended to satisfy the rebuttable presumption of reasonableness in setting compensation,[182] whether the entity has a formal written compensation policy, whether it used an outside consultant to provide comparable data to determine executive compensation, and disclosure regarding the person within the college or university who sets the compensation for the officers, directors, trustees, and key employees.

The questionnaire effectively serves as a roadmap of the policies and procedures the IRS believes colleges and universities should have in place regarding the subject matters addressed. The project originally began as a proposed inquiry into the unrelated trade or business activities of colleges and universities, but grew into an investigation, too, of the endowment and executive compensation practices of these institutions. Especially with the executive compensation portion, the questionnaire clearly lays out the issues on which the IRS is focused, which includes the methodology used by private institutions to set compensation and ensure that it is reasonable. Colleges and universities that were fortunate enough not to have received the questionnaire should be mindful of its questions, and may wish to undertake answering the questionnaire as a form of self-audit.

§ 6.5 OTHER POLICIES

There are numerous other policies that are recommended by the various published good governance guidelines. The ECFA standards recommend the adoption of policies concerning board confidentiality, donor confidentiality, and ownership of intellectual property. The ECFA also recommends adoption of stewardship and executive compensation philosophy statements and a "vision statement communicating a compelling and inspirational hope for the future of the organization."[183] Some sets of good governance principles provide that a nonprofit organization have a policy of compliance with all applicable federal, state, and local laws. This latter type of policy can be problematic, even if the organization is aware of all applicable law. For example, it is doubtful that a charitable organization that engages in nationwide fundraising is registered in compliance with the solicitation ordinances of every city and county in the country.

The Panel on the Nonprofit Sector, as part of its battery of proposed policies, states that a charitable organization's board "should ensure that the organization has adequate plans to protect its assets—its property, financial[,] and human resources, programmatic content and material, and its integrity and reputation—against damage or loss."[184] The board "should review regularly the organization's need for general liability and directors' and officers' liability insurance, as well as take other actions necessary to mitigate risks."[185] The Panel notes that the board is "responsible for understanding the major risks to which the organization is exposed, reviewing those risks on a periodic basis, and ensuring that systems have been established to manage them."[186] The Panel observes that the "level of risk to which the

---

182. See §§ 4.2(c) and 8.4(f).
183. ECFA Standards, p. 10.
184. 33 Principles, § 6.
185. *Id.*
186. *Id.*

organization is exposed and the extent of the review and risk management process will vary considerably based on the size, programmatic focus, geographic location, and complexity of the organization's operations."[187]

There is no end to the number of policies that a nonprofit organization can adopt. An organization, should, however, be somewhat selective with its policies, adopting only those that make sense for the organization and that reflect practices and procedures that the organization will implement and in which it will engage. At a minimum, there are certain "core" policies that organizations should consider adopting, such as a conflict-of-interest policy, whistleblower policy, document retention and destruction policy, and a travel and reimbursement policy. In addition, a nonprofit organization should keep minutes of the meetings of its governing body and committees, have a process for reviewing its information return prior to submission, circulate a copy of its information return to the governing body prior to its filing with the IRS, have a mission statement that has been adopted by the board, and consider invoking the rebuttable presumption of reasonableness in setting executive compensation. In determining whether to adopt other suggested policies, nonprofit organizations should focus on their activities and specific reporting requirements, paying close attention to questions on the IRS information return that the organization files and to the policies that need to be adopted and implemented to respond in an affirmative manner to the relevant questions.

---

187. *Id.*

CHAPTER SEVEN

Nonprofits in the Spotlight: Governance Case Studies

Many nonprofit organizations have recently found themselves the subject of attention and investigations, spearheaded by various sources—Senator Charles Grassley and the staff of the Senate Finance Committee, state attorneys general, public watchdog groups, and/or the media. While the specific allegations of misconduct vary, the boards of nonprofit organizations often find themselves the subject of attack. Poor governance, lack of oversight, absence of transparency, and the failure to exercise a "duty of curiosity" have all been alleged in these matters. This chapter discusses some of the nonprofit organizations (typically public charities) that have found themselves under the spotlight for their perceived poor governance practices, and what the organizations have done to avert this attention and regain public trust.

§ 7.1 THE AMERICAN NATIONAL RED CROSS

The American National Red Cross (Red Cross) is a humanitarian organization chartered by Congress in 1900 "to act in matters of relief."[1] The Red Cross is an instrumentality of the United States and a body corporate and politic of the District of Columbia.[2] Its purposes include providing volunteer aid in time of war to the sick and wounded of the armed forces, helping the United States fulfill its treaty obligations under the Geneva Convention, and acting as an intermediary in communications between families and their relatives who are members of the armed forces of the United States.[3]

Over the years, the Red Cross has endured criticism for its performance in addressing many different disasters. In the late 1980s, the Red Cross fell under attack for its responses to a California earthquake and Hurricane Hugo. The Red Cross was later the subject of a Congressional hearing regarding the safety of its blood supply. The Red Cross was sharply criticized for its handling of the aftermath of the September 11, 2001, attacks on the World Trade Center and elsewhere, and was accused of being inadequate in its responses to the devastation caused by Hurricanes

---

1. American Red Cross Charter, 36 U.S.C. §§ 300101 (Charter), § 2, available at www.redcross.org/images/pdfs/charter.pdf.
2. Charter, § 1(a).
3. Charter, § 2.

Katrina and Rita in 2005.[4] Critics of the Red Cross pointed to its governance structure and board inaction for its inefficiencies.

In response to the criticism, the Governance Committee of the Board of Governors of the Red Cross commissioned a governance audit of the organization, which culminated in a report, dated October 2006, entitled "American Red Cross Governance for the 21st Century" (Red Cross Report). The Red Cross Report developed a set of governance recommendations intended to reflect best practices in the nonprofit sector. It contains a statement from Ira Millstein, the Senior Associate Dean for Corporate Governance of the Yale School of Management, who said the following about the report:

> It is a scholarly review of "corporate governance" best practices as they should be applied to not for profits, generally. . . . It is made more relevant because it is based on the reality of an actual case study—the American Red Cross. It is certain to become must reading for all in the field.[5]

Because it is Congressionally chartered, the Red Cross could not amend its charter to make the recommended changes to its governance structure. Instead, the Red Cross worked with members of Congress to cause the report's recommendations to be enacted into law through the passage of the American National Red Cross Modernization Act of 2007 (Act).[6] The purpose of the Act was to amend the congressional charter of the American Red Cross to modernize its structure, enhance the ability of the board of governors to support the mission of the Red Cross, and "for other purposes." Below is a listing of the Act's specific governance changes for the Red Cross. The changes focus on reducing the board size from 50 members to a more manageable 20-person maximum, having staggered terms for board members to provide continuity and preserve institutional knowledge among the board members while at the same time imposing term limits, authorizing committees to carry out certain board functions, and delineating the functions of the governing body to provide clarity and direction to the board. Specifically, the main actions of the Act were to

- Reduce the board size to no less than 12 and no more than 25 by 2009 and no more than 20 by 2012.
- Cause the board to have staggered terms.
- Impose term limits on board members.
- Authorize an executive committee.
- Establish an advisory committee.
- Disallow proxy voting by the board of directors.

The Act also outlines the board's responsibilities, as follows:

- Reviewing and approving the mission statement for the American National Red Cross
- Approving and overseeing the corporation's strategic plan and maintaining strategic oversight of operational matters

---

4. Schwinn, "Red Cross Proposes Sweeping Governance Changes," *Chron. of Phil.* (October 30, 2006).
5. Red Cross Report, Foreword.
6. Pub. L. No. 110-26, 110th Cong,, 1st Sess. (2007); 36 U.S.C. § 300101. See § 3.11.

- Selecting, evaluating, and determining the level of compensation of the corporation's chief executive officer

- Evaluating the performance and establishing the compensation of the senior leadership team and providing for management succession

- Overseeing the financial reporting and audit process, internal controls, and legal compliance

- Holding management accountable for performance

- Providing oversight of the financial stability of the corporation

- Ensuring the inclusiveness and diversity of the corporation

- Ensuring the chapters of the Red Cross are geographically and regionally diverse

- Providing oversight of the projection of the brand of the corporation

- Assisting with fundraising on behalf of the corporation

The above listing of board functions and duties can serve as a checklist for all nonprofit governing bodies.

§ 7.2   THE SMITHSONIAN INSTITUTION

The Smithsonian Institution (Smithsonian) is organized as a charitable trust, with the U.S. government serving as trustee. The Smithsonian is the entity created by Congress to house the assets bequeathed to the United States by Englishman John Smithson when he died in 1829. The Smithsonian is a public trust for the benefit of all humankind. The Smithsonian's charter provides for a Board of Regents to govern the trust. Members of the Board of Regents are drawn from all three branches of government and from the private sector. The Chief Justice of the Supreme Court, the Vice President of the United States, three members of the Senate, and three members of the House of Representatives make up eight members of the Board of Regents. The other nine members must be U.S. citizens. Amending the Smithsonian's charter requires action by Congress, with concurrence by the President.

In the mid-2000s, the Smithsonian found itself the subject of criticism from Congress and the media for its lack of transparency relating to confidential business contracts and the compensation of its senior executives, especially its then-acting Secretary, Lawrence Small. In addition, senior executives were viewed as having divided attention to the Smithsonian, due to serving on a number of outside boards of directors for which they received compensation. More criticism came after the Board of Regents received a report from the Smithsonian's Acting Inspector General on executive compensation and a confidential outside audit of Secretary Small's expenses that identified a number of unauthorized or unsupported transactions.[7] Despite the report's findings, the Regents concluded that the expenses were for

---

7. According to one account, these expenses totaled approximately $90,000 and included charter jet travel and transactions that "might be considered lavish or extravagant" and were in addition to $160,000 for redecoration of Small's offices and $1.15 million in housing allowances over a six-year period for agreeing to use his house for Smithsonian functions. See Grimaldi, "Smithsonian Documents Detail Chief's Expenses," *Washington Post* (March 19, 2007).

legitimate business purposes and retroactively approved the expenses. Senator Charles Grassley (R-Iowa), ranking member of the Senate Finance Committee, sent the Smithsonian a letter of inquiry and launched an investigation, alleging an "anything goes" culture at the Smithsonian[8] and a Board of Regents that was "turning a blind eye to very serious issues."[9]

In response to this criticism and investigation, the Smithsonian formed a Governance Committee to comprehensively review the organization's policies and practices, and the method by which the Board of Regents conducts its oversight of the entity. The board simultaneously established an Independent Review Committee to review the issues arising from the Inspector General's report, the response by the Board of Regents, and related Smithsonian practices identified by Senator Grassley.

Both the Governance Committee and the Independent Review Committee identified weaknesses in the Smithsonian's governance practices. The Independent Review Committee stated in its report that governance weaknesses were the "root cause" of the Institute's problems. The Independent Review Committee report concluded that "failure to take voluntary action will lead, ultimately, to action by Congress, state legislatures, and the courts to impose reforms from without, just as it did in the corporate world."[10]

The Governance Committee, as it stated in its report,[11] identified the governance weaknesses to be threefold. First, the Board of Regents "did not routinely receive, nor did they demand, the information necessary to support vigorous deliberation and well-reasoned decision-making." Second, "critical relationships necessary to allow key staff to bring forward or highlight important issues and concerns to the Board were lacking." Third, "with monitoring systems failing to raise the necessary 'red flags,' the Regents' ability to provide critical oversight and required compliance with policies and internal controls was crippled."

After identifying these weaknesses, the Governance Committee issued a 108-page report[12] outlining 25 suggested recommendations for the Smithsonian to improve its governance and accountability. The Governance Committee's report was divided into three areas of focus: (1) recommendations to reinforce the foundation of integrity and responsibility; (2) recommendations to promote a constructive partnership, and (3) recommendations to strengthen the culture of accountability.

As to the first area, reinforcing the foundation of integrity and responsibility, the report recommended:

- The Smithsonian's operations and activities will reflect its status as a public trust administered on behalf of American people.

- The Smithsonian will remain committed to the highest standards of ethical conduct.

- The Smithsonian will conduct its business with an ethos of transparency.

---

8. Letter to Chief Justice Roberts dated February 21, 2007, as reported in Memorandum from Senator Charles Grassley, R-Iowa, Ranking Member, U.S. Senate Committee on Finance (July 7, 2008), http://finance.senate.gov.

9. Trescott, "Group Asks Gonzales to Review Small's Conduct." *Washington Post* (February 28, 2007).

10. "A Report to the Board of Regents of the Smithsonian Institution" (June 18, 2007).

11. "Report of the Governance Committee to the Board of Regents" (June 14, 2007).

12. *Id.*

As to promoting a constructive partnership, the report recommended:

- The Governance Committee will further examine the appropriate structure and composition of the board, and report its findings and recommendations to the board.

- The Smithsonian will have a description of the Regents' duties and responsibilities to establish clear expectations.

- The Smithsonian will adopt specific duties and responsibilities of the Chancellor and Chair of the Board, and separate these positions in the Smithsonian's bylaws.

- The Board will have at least four meetings a year, including an executive session without staff, and will prepare minutes of all meetings, including the executive sessions.

- The Smithsonian will develop an orientation program for new Regents and develop, and regularly administer, a process to assess the effectiveness of the Board, Board committees, and individual Regents.

- Each committee will review its role, function, and charter, which will be revised and updated as necessary, and new leadership will be appointed for each Board-established committee.

- The Compensation and Human Resources Committee will create a process that follows best practices in executive compensation and recommend a compensation package for the next general secretary.

- The Facilities Revitalization Committee will be a standing committee of the Board.

- The Governance Committee (to be renamed the Governance and Nominating Committee) will assume the responsibilities of the Nominating Committee to strengthen board development and integrate the nominating and governance process.

- The Smithsonian's general counsel will attend board and board committee meetings (either in person or by delegate) and regularly report to the Board of Regents and relevant board committees in executive session, and has the right and obligation to bring to the Board or relevant Board committee any information on legal or compliance matters that the general counsel reasonably believes should be brought to their attention.

- The Smithsonian's Chief Financial Officer will have direct access to the Board, will attend Board and relevant Board committee meetings, will regularly report to the Board of Regents, the Audit and Review Committee, and/or other relevant Board committees in executive session, and will have the right and obligation to bring directly to the Board and/or the relevant Board committee any information on financial or compliance matters that the Chief Financial Officer reasonably determines should be brought to their attention.

- The Audit and Review Committee will document the expectations for, and reporting relationship of, the Inspector General to the Board of Regents, who is expected to bring directly to the Board and/or the relevant Board committee information on all matters the Inspector General determines should be brought to their attention.

- The Governance Committee will oversee an examination of options to more effectively engage the Smithsonian's advisory boards and report its findings to the Board.

As to strengthening the culture of accountability, the report recommended:

- The Secretary will develop a code of ethics to foster a culture of ethical conduct, which will be presented to the Board for review and approval.

- To embrace a spirit of increased openness, the Regents will provide an opportunity for input through an annual public forum and other appropriate mechanisms, as well as launch a public Web page that includes information about the Smithsonian's structure, membership, functions of the Board, meetings agendas, and summaries of meeting minutes.

- To foster an "ethos of transparency," the Secretary will develop a strategy to increase available information about the Board and Smithsonian activities and operations and to enhance communications with the Board, which should include the following components:

  ○ Enhanced use of the Internet to make information about the Smithsonian widely available

  ○ Mechanisms to foster communication among senior management, the Board of Regents, staff, and other stakeholders

  ○ A framework to ensure effective Congressional outreach and information

  ○ A communications plan to ensure that all constituencies are routinely informed of important decisions and current issues and have opportunities to provide comments or information to the Board and management and consideration of a public ombudsman

  ○ Whistleblower procedures and hotlines

  ○ Plans for monitoring and measuring these efforts, including benchmarking the Smithsonian's efforts against evolving best practices

- The Secretary will develop a policy on disclosure of the Smithsonian's records, which embraces the principles of disclosure reflected in the Freedom of Information Act.

- Senior executives cannot serve on for-profit boards, to avoid appearances of conflict of interest or divided loyalty.

- The Smithsonian will avoid conflicts of interest for staff members with a leave accrual system and general counsel review of conflicts and of outside activity requests.

- The operations of Smithsonian Business Ventures (a subsidiary of the Smithsonian) will follow established Smithsonian policies, except in specific preapproved circumstances.

- The Board will adopt policies regarding travel and expenses, representational activities, and special events.

- The Finance and Investment Committee will review the Smithsonian's federal and trust budget formulation and monitoring process to ensure the committee and the Board of Regents have adequate opportunities to provide strategic direction in the development of budget priorities and meaningful oversight of the Smithsonian's budget and financial resources.

- The Audit and Review Committee will review the Smithsonian's financial reporting systems and internal controls to ensure that appropriate systems and controls are in place to enable the committee and the board to provide meaningful oversight of the accuracy and integrity of the Smithsonian's financial statements and reports.

- The Compensation and Human Resources Committee will review the Smithsonian's philosophy and rationale for senior trust employee compensation to present a unified compensation philosophy and structure to the Board.

- The Secretary will develop a contracting policy to include principals and practices that will ensure that all Smithsonian contracting activities are conducted with integrity, fairness, and openness and in a manner that best achieves the Smithsonian's mission requirements.

The situation with the Smithsonian illustrates what can happen when a board is comprised mainly of individuals who do not have the time to carry out their board duties zealously and effectively and when the organization has a chief executive who controls and limits the flow of information to the board. In the Smithsonian's case, it resulted in little accountability by the executives of the organization to the Board of Regents. And although the Board of Regents took steps to increase its effectiveness, the organization was still plagued by executives taking advantage of the institution.[13]

§7.3   AMERICAN UNIVERSITY

The American University, a tax-exempt private university in Washington, D.C., found itself subject to media attention over the compensation and spending habits of its president, Benjamin Ladner. This attention began with an anonymous letter, which led to an investigation by the American University into the president's personal and travel expenses. American University then commissioned a law firm to prepare a report of the expenses of the president, which included expenses for a personal chef, a chauffeur, and an engagement party for his son.[14] The spending also included payments for professional development trips to France, Italy, and Britain for the president's chef and salary expenses paid to a social secretary who performed personal services for the president and his wife.[15] In all, the report on the personal and travel expenses of the president and his wife questioned more than $500,000 in expenses over a three-year period.[16]

---

13. See "Smithsonian Official Resigned in Wake of Ethics Probe," *WashingtonPost.com* (April 15, 2008).
14. Romano, "AU Scandal Atypical in Post-Enron Era, College Presidents Say," *Washington Post* (October 9, 2005).
15. Janofsky, "American University Chief Is Investigated Over Spending," *New York Times* (September 23, 2005).
16. Kinzie and Strauss, "'$500,000 in Ladner Spending Itemized," *Washington Post* (September 22, 2005).

While the board suspended the university's president (who later resigned), it also proceeded to award him a lucrative severance package, including a pretax sum of $950,000 and $2.75 million in benefits earned during his 11-year tenure with the university.[17] Not all board members were in favor of the severance package; four trustees resigned in the aftermath of the decision. The board's actions prompted more criticism of American University and led to an investigation of the university by Senator Charles Grassley, the senior ranking official on the Senate Finance Committee. In his letter to American University, Senator Grassley demanded documents to determine whether the university had sufficient transparency regarding its highly compensated officers, directors, trustees, and employees, stating that the university could be a "poster child of why review and reform are necessary."[18]

Two trustees issued an apology for the board's performance regarding the situation with the university's president, stating that the board lacked a "clear understanding" of the president's compensation and contracts with the university.[19] The IRS subsequently commenced an audit of the institution, focusing principally on the reasonableness of compensation paid to university officials.

The Board of Trustees of the American University authorized a Governance Committee to make recommendations for governance changes. The Board of Trustees unanimously approved and implemented the recommendations, which included bylaw revisions, adoption of a university-wide whistleblower policy, and adoption of a conflict-of-interest policy.[20]

§7.4 J. PAUL GETTY TRUST

The J. Paul Getty Trust (Trust), a California nonprofit trust, is one of the richest cultural organizations in the country. The Trust found itself under investigation by the California Attorney General after newspaper articles alleged misuse of funds by the trust's president, Barry Munitz. The Attorney General's office issued a report that found that Mr. Munitz used Trust employees to run personal errands, used Trust funds to pay travel expenses for his wife, made gifts of artwork to retiring trustees who were supposed to serve without compensation, and incurred extravagant travel expenses, including first-class air travel, luxury hotels, and meals at five-star restaurants.[21]

The board of trustees, following the reports of questionable expenses and gifts to retiring board members, implemented a number of policy and procedural changes.[22] The reforms included policies that restrict travel expenses, prevent the payment of spousal travel, bar the use of employees for personal purposes, and prohibit gifts to

---

17. Williams, "Senate Investigates Board of American University Over Compensation of President and Other Financial Matters," *Chron. of Phil.* (October 28, 2005).
18. Letter from Senator Charles E. Grassley to Thomas Gottshalk, Acting Chair of the Board, American University (October 27, 2005).
19. *Id.*
20. Memorandum to Campus Community from Gary Abramson, Chairman, Board of Trustees (June 9, 2006).
21. "Attorney General Lockyer Issues Report Criticizing Getty Trustees, Former President Munitz for Improper Spending and Legal Violations," Office of the Attorney General News Release (October 2, 2006).
22. Watt and Kennedy, "California Attorney General Appoints Overseer of Reforms at J. Paul Getty Trust," *New York Times* (October 3, 2006).

trustees.[23] Even though the Attorney General determined that the former president and the Trust's trustees violated their legal duties, he declined to take action against them. Instead, he appointed an Overseer of Reforms to oversee the Trust for two years and report to the Attorney General on whether the Trust's plans for reform are being followed.[24]

§7.5 UNIVERSITY-AFFILIATED MEDICAL CENTERS

Motivated by critical media reports about the M.D. Anderson Cancer Center (Anderson Center), which is affiliated with the University of Texas, and the University of Chicago Medical Center, Senator Grassley, as ranking member of the Senate Finance Committee, wrote to these two centers, seeking an abundance of information.[25] He noted in his letter to the Anderson Center that he is "working to see that tax-exempt hospitals provide benefits to the public commensurate with benefits and subsidies they receive" from federal, state, and local governments.

All tax-exempt charitable healthcare institutions should review the questions posed by Senator. Grassley in his two letters. The senator's letter to the Anderson Center requested a list of all of its facilities in the United States and abroad, identification of the jurisdiction in which each facility is incorporated, copies of audited financial statements, a list of its outstanding tax-exempt bond issuances, and a summary of the purpose of each. The questions, hereafter described, are broken down in six categories: financial assistance; uncompensated case and charity care; insurance coverage; billing and collections; transactions with interested persons; and philanthropy and fundraising. While the questions on charity care and billings and collections are unique to hospitals, all charities should be mindful of the questions in the other categories.

(a) Financial Assistance

Questions posed about the Anderson Center's financial assistance program included the following (many of which entail follow-up questions):

- Provide a copy of the Center's financial assistance policy, or explain why such a policy does not exist.

- Indicate whether the policy provides for free or discounted care to any patients.

- Provide a description of the criteria for eligibility for such care, including income or asset thresholds.

- Does the Center budget amounts for free or discounted care?

---

23. "Attorney General Lockyer Issues Report Criticizing Getty Trustees, Former President Munitz for Improper Spending and Legal Violations," Office of the Attorney General News Release (October 2, 2006).
24. Watt and Kennedy, "California Attorney General Appoints Overseer of Reforms at J. Paul Getty Trust," *New York Times* (October 3, 2006).
25. Letter to Dr. John Mendelsohn, President, University of Texas M.D. Anderson Cancer Center from Senator Charles E. Grassley (July 23, 2008), available at http://finance.senate.gov/press/Gpress/2008/prg090208.pdf and Letter to James L. Madara, M.D., Chief Executive Officer from Senator Charles E. Grassley (August 29, 2008), available at http://finance.senate.gov/press/Gpress/2008/prg090208A.pdf.

- Does the Center prominently display its financial assistance policy and otherwise promote it?
- Are admissions or billing staff required to explain the financial assistance policy to patients who qualify for the assistance?
- Does the Center train staff on the financial assistance policy?

(b)   Uncompensated Care and Charity Care

- Provide a detailed breakdown of the uncompensated care provided by the Center in each of the previous five years.
- Provide a breakdown of how much of the Center's uncompensated care costs are attributable to bad debt, variations from Medicare or Medicaid reimbursements, or free or discounted care.
- Describe the Center's methodology for calculating costs when determining variations from Medicare or Medicaid reimbursements.
- Explain the extent to which any shortfall between Medicare reimbursements and Medicare allowable costs is deemed to be charity care.

(c)   Insurance Coverage

- List the top five insurance companies with which the Center has contracts.
- Describe how the Center chooses the insurance companies with which it contracts.
- Explain how the Center's hospital calculates charges for patients without insurance, limited insurance, or with insurance plans in which the Center does not participate.

(d)   Billing and Collections

- Provide a copy of the Center's "upfront payment policy."
- How many patients of the Center were required to provide upfront payments, and what was the amount of the upfront payment in each case?
- Does this policy provide for waivers from its requirements?
- What is the Center's policy regarding billing and collections staff entering a patient's room while the patient is undergoing examination?
- What is the Center's policy regarding billing and collection staff informing patients of other tax-exempt organizations that can assist patients to manage their medical debt?
- Provide a copy of the Center's debt collection policy.
- What is the Center's policy on the collection practices to be followed for patients who are known to qualify for financial assistance?
- How many lawsuits has the Center, or its hired collection agencies, filed against patients in the preceding five calendar years?

- Provide the total amount and percentage breakdown of the accounts referred to hired collection agencies that were closed due to receipt of payment in each of the previous three years.

(e) Transactions with Interested Persons

- This letter poses questions about officers, directors, trustees, and key employees, and their compensation and reimbursements.
- Does the Center have a conflict-of-interest policy?
- What procedures are used to monitor and enforce the policy?
- Does the Center have a written policy governing contracts, joint ventures, or other financial arrangements with officers, directors, trustees, key employees, or other physicians?

(f) Philanthropy and Fundraising

- If any portion of the Center's funding is from private foundations, provide the source and purpose of each grant.
- Indicate what portion of annual fund revenue was dedicated to patient care and how the funds were used for patient care.
- Does the hospital solicit contributions for charity care or for providing care for the uninsured or underinsured?
- Explain why the Center does not solicit endowment funds for charity care or other financial assistance programs.
- Provide the total value of all assets in the Center's endowment funds.
- What portion of the Center's operating expenses, if any, are covered by endowment funds?

§7.6 LESSONS LEARNED

The foregoing is a discussion of charitable organizations that found themselves under the spotlight for poor governance. These organizations are not alone in their issues; many other organizations over the years have found themselves in similar situations. The United Way of the National Capital Area suffered a financial accountability scandal that resulted in the replacement of its board and the conviction of its executive director for stealing the nonprofit's funds.[26] Senator Grassley launched a two-year investigation of the Nature Conservancy that questioned and reviewed the charity's real estate dealings, which often involved buying property and services from corporations whose executives served on the nonprofit's board and selling land to its own

---

26. Lawton, "Struggling to Regain Image, UW Changes Methods," *Washington Business Journal* (September 21, 2007).

trustees, allowing the buyers to "claim significant tax breaks."[27] The investigation led to the board's restructuring and a ban on certain practices, such as lending money to insiders and selling land to its trustees.[28]

The Baptist Foundation of Arizona filed for bankruptcy due to aggressive investment strategies that left it unable to fulfill promises to its investors.[29] The Statue of Liberty Foundation received attention for allegedly paying its executives excessive amounts while the Statue of Liberty remained unopened.[30] The trustees of Adelphi University in New York received criticism for ignoring, for four years, the recommendation of the university's auditors that they disclose conflicts of interest.[31] These conflicts included the university's purchase of services, such as insurance and advertising services, from companies run by Adelphi University trustees.[32] (While such conflict situations are not illegal, they should be addressed in a manner that involves full disclosure, recusal by the interested parties, and deliberation and decision-making by persons without a financial interest in the proposed arrangements.)

These are only some of the many organizations that have been scrutinized, and the investigations will likely continue in the future. Senator Grassley, for one, shows no sign of slowing down in his examination of public charities. In late 2007, Grassley sent letters to six Christian media ministries requesting information about their expenses, the compensation paid to their executives, and the benefits received by ministry staff. Senator Grassley complimented one of the ministries for undertaking voluntary governance reforms after the Senate Finance Committee investigation began, stating that "[s]elf-reform can be faster and more effective than government regulation," and that it is the "hallmark" of his oversight of other public charities, including the American Red Cross and the Smithsonian.[33] Senator Grassley also stated that the scrutiny of public charities by the Senate Finance Committee "has resulted in self-corrective measures" by the nonprofit sector.[34]

In 2008, the IRS began an inquiry into the practices of the tax-exempt higher education community. The IRS sent a 33-page compliance questionnaire[35] to 400 colleges and universities focusing on unrelated business, endowment funds, and executive compensation.[36] The questions on endowment funds appear to be the result of Senator Grassley's interest in the ever-increasing endowments of colleges and universities that, arguably, are not being used for charitable purposes but instead are being

---

27. Stephens and Ottaway, "Senators Question Conservancy's Practices," *Washington Post* (June 8, 2005).
28. *Id.*
29. Smith, "Baptist Foundation of Arizona Plans Bankruptcy Law–Debt Restructuring," *Wall Street Journal* (November 8, 1999).
30. Miller, "Self-Auditing—A Futile Endeavor or a Credible Safeguard Against Scandal for New York Nonprofits?" *Responsive Philanthropy* (Fall 2004).
31. Lambert, "Adelphi Trustees Ignored Auditor's Advice," *New York Times* (September 1, 1996).
32. *Id.*
33. Memorandum to Reporters and Editors, Senator Chuck Grassley—Iowa, Ranking Member, United States Senate Committee on Finance (July 7, 2008), available at http://finance.senate.gov.
34. *Id.*
35. IRS Form 14018, Compliance Questionnaire Colleges and Universities (September 2008).
36. See § 6.4 for further discussion of IRS Form 14018, Compliance Questionnaire, Colleges and Universities (September 2008).

invested indefinitely.[37] Many of the questionnaire's inquiries involve disclosure of the institutions' governing policies and procedures.

This chapter discusses only a few of the many examples of nonprofit organizations receiving negative publicity and scrutiny that might have been avoided if the organizations involved had implemented better governance procedures. There are certain common denominators among the governance practices of the nonprofit organizations that found themselves in these unfavorable situations. In most situations, the organizations were governed by disengaged boards of directors that were not exercising adequate oversight and were not requesting or receiving the information necessary to have been alerted of the conduct of bad actors. These governing bodies should have been questioning the acts of the charities' executives, overseeing the spending practices of the organizations, exercising their duties to govern the organizations, and providing oversight that the nonprofit entities needed to be well governed. Board members also needed to be paying closer attention to the financial situation of the organizations, the major transactions in which they were engaging, and the qualifications, effectiveness, and compensation of the organizations' chief executive officers.

In many instances, the boards of the organizations having issues were too large to effectively govern the organization. A large board can cause board members to feel disengaged from the organization, which in turn leads to inaction by a board. One of the most egregious examples was the 50-person board of directors of the American Red Cross, which will eventually be reduced to no more than 20 members.[38]

Nonprofit organizations not wishing to find themselves under the spotlight of an investigation should be auditing their governance practices and internal controls, and taking self-corrective measures where needed. The legal audit checklist in this book[39] is designed to serve as a useful tool in this regard.

---

37. One of the questions requires the institutions to report the average amount of their endowment assets per full-time equivalent student. See IRS Form 14018, line 46.
38. See § 7.1.
39. See Chapter 9.

CHAPTER EIGHT

Law for Nonprofit Board
Members: A Primer

Much more is required than the few pages of this chapter to summarize the federal and state law applicable to nonprofit organizations. Nonetheless, the following synopsis of this body of law is provided to supply members of nonprofit boards with sufficient information to understand the basics of nonprofit law, in furtherance of their governance responsibilities, and to be in a position to ask informed questions of legal counsel.

§8.1 NONPROFIT ORGANIZATIONS

A fundamental precept is the concept of the *nonprofit organization*. This term does not mean an organization that is prohibited by law from earning a profit (that is, an excess of gross earnings over expenses). In fact, it is quite common for nonprofit (and tax-exempt) organizations to generate profits. Rather, the definition of nonprofit organization essentially relates to requirements as to what must be done with the profit earned or otherwise received. This fundamental element of the law is subsumed in the doctrine of private inurement.[1]

This concept in law of a nonprofit organization is best understood through a comparison with the concept of a *for-profit* organization. A fundamental distinction between the two types of entities is that the for-profit organization has owners that hold the equity in the enterprise, such as stockholders of a corporation. The for-profit organization is operated for the economic benefit of its owners; the profits of the business undertaking are passed through to them, such as by the payment of dividends on shares of stock. That is what is meant by the term *for-profit organization*: It is an entity that is designed to generate a profit for its owners. The transfer of the profits from the organization to its owners is private inurement—the inurement of net earnings to them in their private (personal) capacity. For-profit organizations are expected to engage in private inurement.

By contrast, a nonprofit organization is not permitted to distribute its profits (net earnings) to those who control it, such as directors and officers. That is why the private inurement doctrine is the substantive defining characteristic that distinguishes nonprofit organizations from for-profit organizations for purposes of the

---

1. See § 8.4(d).

law. There are thus two categories of profit: one is at the *entity* level and one is at the *ownership* level. Both nonprofit and for-profit organizations can yield entity-level profit; the distinction in law between the two types of entities pivots on the latter category of profit.

§8.2 TAX-EXEMPT ORGANIZATIONS

A nonprofit organization is not necessarily a tax-exempt organization, although most nonprofit entities qualify for some classification as an exempt entity. Whether a nonprofit organization is entitled to tax exemption, initially or on a continuing basis, is a matter of law. If a nonprofit organization qualifies for a tax exemption at the federal and/or state law levels, it is entitled to the exemption. (There is, however, no constitutional law right to an exemption.)

Some categories of nonprofit organizations that are eligible for tax-exempt status at the federal law level are required, by law, to apply to the Internal Revenue Service (IRS) for *recognition* of that exemption. This is generally accomplished by filing an application for recognition of exemption (usually Form 1023 or 1024). Most charitable organizations, certain employee benefit organizations, and credit counseling organizations that desire exemption as social welfare organizations are required to apply in a timely fashion for recognition of exemption. Political organizations must, to be exempt, file a notice with the IRS (Form 8871).

Additional rules apply with respect to *group exemptions*. This is a regime by which organizations that are affiliated with a central tax-exempt organization can be exempt without each member of the group having to apply to the IRS for recognition of exemption.

The IRS can revoke a recognition of tax exemption for good cause, such as a change in the law, but an organization that has been recognized by the IRS as being exempt generally can rely on that determination as long as there are no substantial changes in its character, purposes, or methods of operation. If material changes occur, the organization should notify the IRS and may have to undergo a reevaluation of its exempt status.

In a law sense, there is no such thing as a tax-exempt organization. Nearly all exempt organizations are subject to tax on unrelated business income. Many types of exempt organizations can have some or all of their investment income taxed if they engage in political activities. Public charities can incur taxes if they undertake legislative or political campaign activities. Private foundations are potentially subject to a variety of excise taxes. Social clubs, political organizations, and certain other nonprofit entities are required to pay tax on their net investment income. Even with complete exemption from federal taxation, a nonprofit organization may have exposure to state or local income, sales, use, or property taxation; each state has laws regarding qualification for these exemptions.

§8.3 CATEGORIES OF TAX-EXEMPT ORGANIZATIONS

There are in excess of 70 categories of tax-exempt nonprofit organizations. Board members of nonprofit organizations generally need be aware of only the principal types.

(a)   Charitable and Like Organizations

Tax exemption is provided for a variety of charitable organizations, including those that provide relief for the poor or distressed; promote health; lessen the burdens of government; advance education, science, or religion; promote social welfare; and promote youth sports and protection of the environment.[2] Exemption also is available for cruelty prevention organizations, amateur sports organizations, public safety testing organizations, cooperative hospital service organizations, cooperative educational service organizations, and charitable risk pools. Limitations apply as to private inurement, private benefit, and impermissible advocacy (namely, substantial legislative activities and any political campaign activity).

(b)   Religious Organizations

Tax exemption is provided for churches and similar institutions, conventions or associations of churches, integrated auxiliaries of churches, religious orders, apostolic organizations, and other religious organizations, including certain communal groups and retreat facilities.

(c)   Private Schools

Tax exemption is provided for private schools, albeit with a variety of requirements, including the necessity of a disseminated policy as to nondiscrimination on the basis of race. A *school* is an educational institution that has a regular faculty, a regularly enrolled student body, a curriculum, and a place where the educational activities are regularly carried on.

(d)   Other Educational Organizations

Tax exemption is provided for formal educational organizations, such as schools, colleges, and universities, as well as for organizations that instruct individuals or the public. The term *educational* is not well-defined; the federal tax law distinguishes it from *propagandizing*.

(e)   Scientific Organizations

Tax exemption is provided to organizations that engage in scientific research in the public interest. There can be controversy as to whether an activity involves *research* as opposed to *commercial testing*.

(f)   Amateur Athletic Sports Organizations

Tax exemption is provided to organizations that promote sports for the benefit of youth.

---

2. These are the organizations the tax exemption of which is based on the well-known IRC § 501(c)(3).

(g) Social Welfare Organizations

Tax exemption is provided to organizations that operate for the promotion of social welfare (such as civic leagues), in the sense of benefiting those in a community; this category of organizations may include advocacy organizations.

(h) Labor Organizations

Tax exemption is provided for organizations that engage in collective action to better the working conditions of individuals engaged in a common pursuit. The principal type of this category of tax-exempt organization is the union.

(i) Agricultural and Horticultural Organizations

Tax exemption is provided for organizations that engage in activities to improve the grade of agricultural or horticultural products and develop a higher degree of efficiency in the activity.

(j) Business Leagues

Tax exemption is provided for business leagues, namely, associations of persons united by common interests, as well as chambers of commerce, boards of trade, real estate boards, and professional football leagues. The principal categories of tax-exempt organizations in this context are trade and business associations, and professional societies. The general purpose of these associations is to promote betterment of the conditions within the line of business they represent.

(k) Social Clubs

Tax exemption is provided for organizations that provide pleasure and recreation for the benefit of their members. These tax-exempt organizations, which include country clubs and hobby clubs, are required to pay tax on their net investment income.

(l) Fraternal Societies

Tax exemption is provided for fraternal beneficiary organizations operating under the lodge system and providing certain benefits to their members and for domestic fraternal societies operating under the lodge system that devote their net earnings to charitable purposes.

(m) Veterans' Organizations

Tax exemption is provided for organizations of past or present members of the U.S. armed forces, or related auxiliaries or foundations, in which at least 75% of the members are past or present members of the U.S. armed forces and substantially all of the other members are spouses or otherwise related to the members.

(n) Political Organizations

Tax exemption is provided for parties, committees, associations, funds, and other organizations operated primarily for the purpose of accepting contributions or making expenditures, usually for the purpose of assisting one or more individuals in getting elected to public office or preventing a candidate from becoming elected to a public office.

(o) Other Tax-Exempt Organizations

Other types of nonprofit organizations that are eligible for tax exemption under the federal tax law are title-holding organizations, credit unions, small insurance companies, various mutual and cooperative organizations, crop financing entities, health maintenance organizations, homeowners' associations, and a variety of employee benefit funds.

§ 8.4 TAX-EXEMPT ORGANIZATIONS LAW BASICS

Eight principles of law at the federal level comprise the basics of the law of tax-exempt organizations, particularly for charitable entities.

(a) Primary Purpose Test

The primary purpose of an organization determines (in part) whether it can qualify as a tax-exempt organization and, if so, which category of exemption is applicable. The focus in this context is on purposes, not activities. Use of the term *exclusively* in the statutes has been interpreted by the courts to mean *primarily*.

(b) Organizational Test

The federal tax regulations contain an organizational test, applicable to charitable organizations, that focuses on the content of an organization's statement of purposes and the necessity of a dissolution clause. Although there is no formal organizational test for any of the other types of tax-exempt organizations, these tests are inherent in each category of exemption.

(c) Operational Test

The federal tax regulations contain an operational test, applicable to charitable organizations, that focuses on how an organization functions in relation to the applicable requirements for tax-exempt status. (These requirements fundamentally are avoidance of private inurement, substantial legislative activity, and political campaign activity.) Although there is no formal operational test for any of the other types of tax-exempt organizations, these tests are inherent in each category of exemption.

(d) Private Inurement Doctrine

The doctrine of private inurement is one of the most important sets of rules constituting the federal law of tax-exempt organizations. This doctrine is a statutory criterion for federal income tax exemption for several categories of exempt organizations, including charitable entities.

The private inurement doctrine requires that a tax-exempt organization subject to it be organized and operated so that, in antiquated language, ''no part of . . . [its] net earnings . . . inures to the benefit of any private shareholder or individual." What this doctrine means is that none of the income or assets of a tax-exempt organization subject to the private inurement doctrine may be permitted to directly or indirectly unduly benefit an individual or other person who has a close relationship with the organization when that person is in a position to exercise a significant degree of control over the entity.

The purpose of the private inurement rule is to ensure that the tax-exempt organization involved is serving exempt rather than private interests. It is thus necessary for an organization subject to the doctrine to be in a position to establish that it is not organized and operated for the benefit of persons in their private capacity, informally referred to as *insiders*, such as the organization's founders, trustees, directors, officers, members of their families, entities controlled by these individuals, or any other persons having a personal and private interest in the activities of the organization.

The doctrine of private inurement does not prohibit transactions between a tax-exempt organization subject to the doctrine and those who have a close relationship with it. Rather, the private inurement doctrine requires that these transactions be tested against a standard of *reasonableness*. The standard calls for a roughly equal exchange of benefits between the parties; the law is designed to discourage a disproportionate share of the benefits of the exchange flowing to an insider.

The private inurement doctrine does not prohibit the payment of compensation to employees of a charitable organization, provided the compensation is reasonable and not excessive. The reasonableness standard focuses essentially on comparability of data—that is, how similar organizations, acting prudently, transact their affairs in comparable instances. Thus, the regulations pertaining to the business expense deduction, addressing the matter of the reasonableness of compensation, provide that it is generally just to assume that reasonable and true compensation is only such amount as would ordinarily be paid for like services by like enterprises under like circumstances.

The sanction for violation of the private inurement doctrine is revocation (or denial) of the tax-exempt status of the organization involved.[3]

(e)   Private Benefit Doctrine

A tax-exempt organization's charitable status can be revoked if there is a finding that the organization is serving a private, rather than a public, benefit. To be exempt, a charitable organization must establish that it is not organized or operated for the benefit of private interests such as designated individuals, the organization's creator or the creator's family members, shareholders of the organization, or persons controlled, directly or indirectly, by such private interests.

The prohibition against private benefit is not limited to situations where benefits accrue to an organization's insiders. An organization's conferral of benefits on "disinterested persons" (i.e., persons who are not insiders) may cause it to serve a private interest. Unlike the private inurement doctrine, the private benefit doctrine permits incidental private benefit. This is an important distinction, inasmuch as, technically, any amount of private inurement may jeopardize a charitable organization's tax-exempt status, while an incidental amount of private benefit is allowable.

---

3. Also see § 1.6(b).

The sanction for violation of the private benefit doctrine is revocation (or denial) of the tax-exempt status of the organization involved.[4]

(f)   Intermediate Sanctions Rules

The intermediate sanctions rules emphasize the taxation of persons who engaged in impermissible private transactions with certain types of tax-exempt organizations, rather than revocation of the tax-exempt status of these entities. With this approach, tax law sanctions—structured as penalty excise taxes—may be imposed on those persons who improperly benefited from the transaction and on certain managers of the organization who participated in the transaction knowing that it was improper. These taxes are applied to the amount of the excess benefit derived from the transaction. The taxes consist of an *initial* tax and an *additional* tax. The law as to excess benefit transactions applies with respect to tax-exempt public charities and exempt social welfare organizations. These entities are collectively termed, for this purpose, *applicable tax-exempt organizations*.

A person who has a close relationship with an applicable tax-exempt organization is a *disqualified person*. A disqualified person generally is a person who has, or is in a position to have, some type or degree of control over the operations of the applicable tax-exempt organization involved. The term *disqualified person* is defined under the intermediate sanctions rules as (1) any person who was, at any time during the five-year period ending on the date of the transaction involved, in a position to exercise substantial influence over the affairs of the organization (whether by virtue of being an organization manager or otherwise), (2) a member of the family of an individual described in the preceding category, and (3) an entity in which individuals described in the preceding two categories own more than a 35% interest.

At the heart of the intermediate sanctions regime is the *excess benefit transaction*. In general, an excess benefit transaction is a transaction in which an economic benefit is provided by an applicable tax-exempt organization, directly or indirectly, to or for the use of a disqualified person, and the value of the economic benefit provided by the organization exceeds the value of the consideration (including the performance of services) received for providing the benefit. The difference between the value provided by the exempt organization and the consideration (if any) it received from the disqualified person is an *excess benefit*.

An excess benefit transaction includes a payment of unreasonable (excessive) compensation by an applicable tax-exempt organization to a disqualified person with respect to it. The value of services, in the intermediate sanctions setting, is the amount that ordinarily would be paid for like services by like organizations under like circumstances. Compensation in this context includes all economic benefits (other than certain disregarded benefits) provided by an applicable tax-exempt organization, to or for the use of a person, in exchange for the performance of services, including all forms of cash and noncash compensation.

A key component of the intermediate sanctions rules is the *rebuttable presumption of reasonableness*. When activated, this presumption shifts the burden of proof to the IRS, which must then prove that an element of a transaction or arrangement was unreasonable. (The IRS can rebut this presumption with appropriate facts of its own.)

---

4. Also see § 1.6(b).

This presumption comes into play where the decision to engage in the transaction was made by an independent board or board committee, the board considered appropriate data as to comparability, and the decision was properly and timely documented (including in minutes).

The intermediate sanctions rules entail an initial tax, which is 25% of the excess benefit, payable by the disqualified person or persons involved. The transaction must be undone by placing the parties in the same economic position they were in before the transaction was entered into; this is "correction" of the transaction. If the initial tax is not paid in a timely manner and the transaction is not properly corrected in a timely manner, an additional tax may have to be paid; this tax is 200% of the excess benefit.

(g) Commensurate Test

Pursuant to an infrequently used commensurate test, the IRS may assess whether a charitable organization is maintaining program activities that are commensurate in scope with its financial resources. The IRS has announced, however, that it is going to make greater use of this test.

(h) Public Policy Doctrine

Tax exemption as a charitable organization is available only where the organization is operating in conformance with federal public policy. For example, pursuant to this body of law, a private school cannot be tax-exempt if it has a racially discriminatory policy as to the admission of students.

§8.5 LEGISLATIVE ACTIVITIES LAW

Considerable law restricts the ability of nonprofit organizations to engage in lobbying; these rules are principally directed at charitable organizations.

(a) Charitable Organizations

Tax-exempt public charities may engage in legislative activities to the extent that lobbying is not a *substantial* part of their overall functions. This rule is known as the *substantial part test*. Thus, an insubstantial portion of an exempt organization's activities may constitute lobbying; the term *insubstantial* in this context remains undefined. These rules apply with respect to attempts to influence a legislative branch, usually in connection with the development of legislation.

A mechanical test for measuring allowable lobbying, the *expenditure test*, may be elected. Pursuant to this rule, generally 20% of an organization's expenditures may be for lobbying; several exceptions from the concept of lobbying are available under these rules. Excessive lobbying may lead to the imposition of excess taxes and/or revocation of exemption. More stringent rules are applicable to private foundations.

(b) Social Welfare Organizations

There are no federal tax law limitations on attempts to influence legislation by tax-exempt social welfare organizations, other than the general requirement that the organization primarily engage in efforts to promote social welfare.

(c) Associations (Business Leagues)

There are no federal tax law limitations on attempts to influence legislation by tax-exempt business leagues, other than the general requirement that the organization primarily engage in activities appropriate for these organizations. The federal tax law, however, includes rules restricting the tax deductibility of dues paid to these organizations to the extent a portion of the dues is used for lobbying.

(d) Other Exempt Organizations

There are no federal tax law limitations on attempts to influence legislation by any other types of tax-exempt organizations, other than the general requirement that the organization primarily engage in efforts to advance its exempt purpose.

§ 8.6 POLITICAL ACTIVITIES LAW

The federal tax law generally discourages political campaign activity by nonprofit, tax-exempt organizations. There is an absolute prohibition on political campaign activity by charitable organizations—a rule that is frequently violated.

(a) Charitable Organizations

A charitable organization, to be tax-exempt, may not participate or intervene in a political campaign on behalf of or in opposition to a candidate for public office. This absolute prohibition encompasses political campaign contributions, endorsements, use of facilities, and signage on organization property. Leaders of charitable organizations may, however, engage in political activity in their personal capacity. Political activity may lead to the imposition of excess taxes and/or revocation of exemption. More stringent rules are applicable to private foundations.

(b) Social Welfare Organizations

A tax-exempt social welfare organization can engage in political campaign activity without jeopardizing its exemption, but this type of activity cannot be its primary function.

(c) Associations (Business Leagues)

There are no federal tax law limitations on political campaign activity by tax-exempt business leagues, other than the general requirement that the organization primarily engage in activities appropriate for these organizations. The federal tax law, however, includes rules restricting the tax deductibility of dues paid to these organizations to the extent that a portion of the dues is used for political activity.

(d) Political Organizations

Most political organizations have as their primary exempt function the involvement in political campaign activity, either in support of or in opposition to one or more candidates for public office.

(e)   Other Exempt Organizations

The federal tax law is silent as to the extent to which other types of tax-exempt organizations can engage in political campaign activity in relation to their eligibility for exempt status.

§8.7   PUBLIC CHARITIES AND PRIVATE FOUNDATIONS

The realm of charitable organizations is divided into two classes: public charities and private foundations.

(a)   Rebuttable Presumption

Every tax-exempt charitable organization is presumed to be a *private foundation*, a term that is not expansively defined in the federal tax law. This presumption may be rebutted by a showing that the entity is a *public charity*. Because of this presumption, a charitable organization that loses its public charity status becomes, by operation of law, a private foundation.

(b)   Definition of Private Foundation

Generically, a private foundation is a charitable entity that is funded from one source, has ongoing funding in the form of investment income, and makes grants, usually to public charities, for charitable purposes. More technically, a private foundation is an exempt charitable organization that is not a public charity. There are three basic types of charitable organizations that are not private foundations: the institutions,[5] publicly supported charities,[6] and supporting organizations.[7] A fourth form of public charity is the public safety testing organization.

(c)   Institutions

Certain tax-exempt *institutions* are classified as public charities. The principal types of institutions are churches, certain other religious organizations, formal educational institutions, hospitals, medical research organizations, and governmental units.

(d)   Publicly Supported Organizations

Publicly supported charitable organizations are forms of public charities. The *donative* type of publicly supported charity normally receives a substantial part of its support (other than exempt function revenue) in the forms of contributions or grants from the public or one or more governmental units. The term *substantial* in this context means at least one-third. Generally, support from a member of the public cannot, to be public support, exceed 2% of the total amount of support the organization received during the measuring period, which is the entity's most recent five years (including its current year).

---

5. See § 8.7(c).
6. See § 8.7(d).
7. See § 8.7(e).

The *service provider* type of publicly supported charity normally receives more than one-third of its support in the form of contributions, grants, membership fees, and fee-for-service revenue from *permitted sources*, and normally does not receive more than one-third of its support in the form of gross investment income and net unrelated business income. Permitted sources do not include disqualified persons with respect to the organization. Public support for these organizations is determined for a measuring period, which is the entity's most recent five years (including its current year).

(e) Supporting Organizations

Supporting organizations are forms of public charities. Essentially, a *supporting organization* must be organized and operated exclusively for the benefit of, to perform the functions of, or to carry out the purposes of one or more qualified supported organizations. Typical functions of a supporting organization are fundraising, operation of separate programs, and maintenance of an endowment fund. There are four basic types of supporting organizations: Type I, II, or III (either functionally integrated or not). Stringent law provisions are directed at Type III supporting organizations, particularly those that are not functionally integrated with a supported organization.

A grant-making private foundation may not treat as a qualifying distribution[8] an amount paid to a Type III supporting organization that is not a functionally integrated Type III supporting organization or to any other type of supporting organization if a disqualified person with respect to the foundation directly or indirectly controls the supporting organization or a supported organization of the supporting organization. An amount that does not count as a qualifying distribution under this rule is regarded as a taxable expenditure.[9]

A Type III supporting organization must apprise each organization that it supports of information regarding the supporting organization in order to help ensure the responsiveness by the supporting organization to the needs or demands of the supported organization(s). A Type III supporting organization that is organized as a trust must established to the satisfaction of the IRS that it has a sufficiently close and continuous relationship with the supported organization so that the trust is responsive to the needs or demands of the supported organization.

A supporting organization must annually demonstrate that one or more of its disqualified persons (other than its managers and supported organization(s)) do not, directly or indirectly, control it. This is done by means of a certification on its annual information return.

Generally, a supported organization of a supporting organization is a public charity that is classified as one of the institutions[10] or is a publicly supported charity.[11] Under certain circumstances, however, a tax-exempt social welfare organization,[12] labor organization,[13] or business league (association)[14] can qualify as a supported organization.

---

8. See § 8.7 (f)
9. *Id.*
10. See § 8.7(c).
11. See § 8.7(d).
12. See § 8.3(g).
13. See § 8.3(h).
14. See § 8.3(j).

(f) Private Foundation Rules

Private foundations are subject to a battery of rules prohibiting self-dealing with disqualified persons, excess business holdings, jeopardizing investments, and taxable expenditures, and mandating an income payout in the form of qualifying distributions. The sanctions for violating these rules include a series of excise taxes. These taxes are reported on Form 4720.

(g) Donor-Advised Funds

A donor-advised fund, while not a separate legal entity, is often seen as an alternative to a private foundation. A *donor-advised fund* is a fund or account (1) that is identified by reference to one or more donors, (2) that is owned and controlled by a sponsoring organization, and (3) to which a donor or a donor advisor has advisory privileges with respect to the distribution or investment of amounts held in the fund or account by reason of the donor's status as a donor. A *sponsoring organization* is a public charity[15] that maintains one or more donor-advised funds. Various distributions from a donor-advised fund can give rise to a tax.

§8.8 REPORTING RULES

Nonprofit, tax-exempt organizations are subject to many reporting rules.

(a) Annual Information Returns

Nearly every organization that is exempt from federal income taxation is required to annually file an information return with the IRS. For most tax-exempt organizations, this return is Form 990.[16] Small exempt organizations can file Form 990-EZ. Private foundations file Form 990-PF. Political organizations may file Form 990 and/or 1120-POL. Homeowners' associations file Form 1120-H. Black lung benefit trusts file Form 990-BL. Very small organizations are required to electronically file Form 990-N (the e-postcard). Some exceptions to this filing requirement are available.

(b) Unrelated Business Income Tax Returns

A tax-exempt organization with unrelated business income is generally required to file an income tax return, reporting the income, expenses, and any tax due (Form 990-T).

(c) Split-Interest Trust Returns

A split-interest trust is required to annually file a return (generally Form 1041A, perhaps Form 5577) with the IRS.

(d) Nonexempt Charitable Trust Returns

A nonexempt charitable trust is required to annually file a return (Form 1041A, perhaps 5577) with the IRS.

---

15. See § 8.7.
16. See Chapter 4.

(e) Apostolic Organizations' Returns

Apostolic organizations are required to annually file a partnership return with the IRS (Form 1065).

(f) State Annual Reports

Nonprofit organizations, particularly nonprofit corporations, are generally required to file annual reports with the state in which they are formed, headquartered, and/or do business.

(g) Charitable Solicitation Act Reports

Charitable and other types of nonprofit organizations that engage in fundraising are generally required to file annual reports with each state in which they solicit funds.[17]

(h) Disposition of Gift Property Rules

A charitable organization that disposes of charitable gift property within three years of the date of the gift is generally required to report the transaction (on Form 8282) to the IRS.

§ 8.9 DISCLOSURE RULES

In general, a tax-exempt organization is required to make available to the public copies of its application for recognition of exemption (if any) (e.g., Form 1023) and supporting documents. Likewise, in general, a tax-exempt organization is required to make available to the public copies of its three most recent annual information returns (if any) (e.g., Form 990). Tax-exempt charitable organizations must make available to the public copies of their three most recent unrelated business income tax returns (if any) (Form 990-T).[18]

§ 8.10 UNRELATED BUSINESS RULES

One of the principal aspects of the law of tax-exempt organizations is the body of law concerning the conduct of unrelated business, which may never cause income taxation.

(a) Requirement of Business

A *business* of a tax-exempt organization is an activity that is carried on for the production of income from the sale of goods or the performance of services. Nearly every undertaking of an exempt organization, including its programs, is a business. Businesses of exempt organizations are, for this purpose, either related or unrelated.

---

17. See § 8.16.
18. Also see § 4.3.

(b) Regularly Carried On Rule

A business of a tax-exempt organization, to be considered an unrelated business, must be regularly carried on. Generally, this element of regularity is measured annually; if a season is involved, that is the measuring period.

(c) Substantially Related Standard

A business of a tax-exempt organization, to be considered a related business, where the conduct of the business activity has a causal relationship to the achievement of an exempt purpose (other than through the production of income) and the causal relationship is substantial.

(d) Exceptions as to Activities

Various exceptions from treatment as unrelated business are available for activities of tax-exempt organizations, including volunteer-conducted businesses, convenience businesses, sales of gift items, certain entertainment activities, the conduct of trade shows, certain hospital services, the dissemination of low-cost articles, and the exchanging or rental of mailing lists.

(e) Exceptions as to Income

Various exceptions (in the form of *modifications* of the general rule) from treatment as unrelated business income are available for certain types of income received by tax-exempt organizations, including dividends, interest, annuities, royalties, rent, capital gains, and research income.

(f) Social Clubs' and Like Organizations' Rules

Special unrelated business rules are applicable to social clubs, veterans' organizations, voluntary employees' beneficiary associations, and supplemental unemployment benefit trusts.

(g) Unrelated Debt-Financed Income Rules

In computing a tax-exempt organization's unrelated business taxable income, there must be included with respect to each debt-financed property that is unrelated to the organization's exempt function—as an item of gross income derived from an unrelated trade or business—an amount of income from the property subject to tax in the proportion to which the property is financed by the debt.

(h) Tax Computation

The unrelated income tax rates payable by most tax-exempt organizations are the corporate rates. In computing unrelated business taxable income, exempt organizations may deduct expenses that are directly connected with the carrying on of the trade or business. A specific deduction is available, as is a charitable deduction. Taxable unrelated business income is reported on Form 990-T.[19]

---

19. See § 8.8(b).

§ 8.11 SUBSIDIARIES

It is common for nonprofit, tax-exempt organizations to have one or more subsidiaries. Generically, this type of arrangement is known as *bifurcation*: a splitting of functions that might otherwise be conducted by one organization so that, for law, management, or other reasons, some of the functions are conducted by one entity and the balance of the functions are conducted by the other entity. If one or more subsidiaries exist, the board members should know why; if there are no subsidiaries, the board members should, from time to time, deliberate and seek advice as to whether a subsidiary might be of advantage to the nonprofit organization.

As will be discussed, a subsidiary may be a tax-exempt organization or it may be a for-profit organization. Before addressing those distinctions, however, there are six law aspects of the parent–subsidiary relationship that the board should consider, irrespective of the type of subsidiary: the form of the subsidiary, the nature of control of the subsidiary, funding of the subsidiary (initially and on an ongoing basis), day-to-day management of the subsidiary, revenue flow from the subsidiary to the parent, and, perhaps, liquidation of the subsidiary.

- *Form.* If the subsidiary is a nonprofit organization, the legal forms are nonprofit corporation, unincorporated association, trust, or limited liability company.[20] If the subsidiary is a for-profit organization, the choices basically are for-profit corporation or limited liability company. Matters can become more complicated where the nonprofit parent is not the sole owner of the for-profit subsidiary.

- *Control.* If the subsidiary is a nonprofit organization, the parent will control it by overlapping governing boards, membership (where the parent is the sole member of the subsidiary), appointments, ex officio positions, or some combination of the foregoing. If the subsidiary is a for-profit organization, the control feature will be manifested by ownership, either by stock in the corporation or membership interest in the limited liability company.

- *Funding.* The parent must decide how much money (or property), if any, to transfer to the subsidiary and should understand the federal tax consequences of the transfer. If the subsidiary is a for-profit entity, the transfer may be in the nature of a capitalization, such as in exchange for stock or membership interest. The parent may make loans to the subsidiary.

- *Management.* If the parent organization is unduly involved in the day-to-day management of the subsidiary, the activities of the subsidiary may be attributed to the parent. This type of attribution usually causes federal tax problems, either in the form of endangering tax exemption or of unrelated business income taxation.

- *Revenue flow.* Revenue can flow from a subsidiary to a nonprofit parent in two basic ways: payment of net earnings (usually in the case of a for-profit subsidiary) or payment for services or assistance (such as rent or interest). The second category of these payments may be taxable to the parent as unrelated business

---

20. See § 1.2(a).

income.[21] A special rule (set to expire at the close of 2009) exempts certain types of revenue from a subsidiary from unrelated business income taxation.

- *Liquidation.* If the subsidiary is terminated and liquidated into the parent, the subsidiary may have to pay income tax on the capital gain resulting from the transfer of assets that have appreciated in value to the parent.

If the subsidiary is a tax-exempt charitable organization, it may be a supporting organization.[22] Typical parents of charitable subsidiaries are social welfare organizations,[23] associations (business leagues),[24] and labor organizations.[25] A charitable organization may be the parent of a charitable subsidiary, such as a "foundation" related to a domestic public charity[26] or a fundraising entity affiliated with a foreign charitable organization.

A charitable organization may be the parent entity, where the subsidiary is a tax-exempt, noncharitable entity. Two common examples are the lobbying arms (social welfare organizations) of public charities and certification organizations (business leagues) associated with public charities.

Other arrangements involving nonprofit, tax-exempt parents and nonprofit, exempt subsidiaries are those using title-holding companies,[27] political action committees and other political organizations[28] (but not by charitable organizations[29]), and various types of employee benefit funds.[30]

Some of these subsidiaries may be for-profit, taxable entities, usually used to conduct substantial unrelated business. Particular consideration needs to be given to choice of entity in this context; a standard corporation (C corporation) is likely to be the answer, in that flow-through entities (such as S corporations and limited liability companies) can give rise to tax dilemmas for the charitable parent. In some instances, revenue received by an exempt organization parent from its subsidiary is taxable as unrelated business income.

§ 8.12 JOINT VENTURES

Nonprofit, tax-exempt organizations may participate in partnerships and other forms of joint ventures, such as those using limited liability companies. Most of the law in this area concerns public charities as general partners or members in these ventures. Ventures may be whole-entity or ancillary. The IRS is particularly sensitive to the potential for private inurement or private benefit in these circumstances.

The term *partnership* generally has a technical meaning; partnerships are recognized forms of business entities, either as general partnerships or limited partnerships. The term *joint venture*, however, is much broader; a nonprofit organization can

---

21. See § 8.10.
22. See § 8.7(e).
23. See § 8.3(g).
24. See § 8.3(j).
25. See § 8.3(h).
26. See § 8.7.
27. See § 8.3(o).
28. See § 8.3(n).
29. See § 8.6.
30. See § 8.3(o).

be involved in a joint venture with one or more other nonprofit entities or one or more for-profit entities. On occasion, the joint venture form can be imposed on an arrangement between a nonprofit organization and one or more other organizations by operation of law.

A public charity (or perhaps another form of tax-exempt organization) can be a (or the) general partner in a general partnership and not endanger its exempt status where (1) the participation of the exempt organization in the partnership is in furtherance of an exempt purpose, (2) the exempt organization is insulated from the day-to-day responsibilities of being the general partner, and (3) the limited partners are not receiving an unwarranted economic benefit from the partnership.

The federal tax law recognizes the concept of the *whole-entity joint venture*. This type of vehicle was started by tax-exempt healthcare institutions, which placed the entirety of the institution in a venture (unlike most joint ventures, where only a portion of nonprofit resources are involved). The other venturer(s) may be nonprofit or for-profit. Where it is the latter, the IRS and the courts will look to see whether the exempt venturer has "ceded control" over its operations to the for-profit venturer. If it has, the nonprofit organization will likely lose its tax-exempt status, on the basis of violation of the private benefit doctrine.[31]

The federal tax law developed in the context of whole-entity joint ventures is being applied to other ventures involving nonprofit organizations, where less than the entire entity is placed in the venture. These are termed *ancillary joint ventures*. It may be that an ancillary joint venture is wholly in furtherance of charitable or other exempt purposes, in which case tax exemption is not at issue. Or, the involvement of an exempt organization in an ancillary joint venture may be, from the organization's standpoint, incidental, thus eliminating any private benefit doctrine problems.[32] This open question remains: What happens when a tax-exempt, charitable organization is involved in an ancillary joint venture, to more than an insubstantial extent, and loses control of its resources in the venture to a for-profit co-venturer? The logical, albeit perhaps harsh, answer is that the organization would lose its exempt status.

The joint venture vehicle of choice these days, when tax-exempt organizations are involved, is the limited liability company. These companies, which can have one or more members, are generally treated, for federal tax law purposes, as partnerships, which means that they are not taxed but are flow-through entities, causing their members to be the organizations that are taxable on the venture's income. While for-profit venturers tend to favor this approach, to avoid double taxation, tax-exempt organizations usually want to avoid it, so as not to have unrelated business income (but rather nontaxable dividends, if the venture does not further exempt purposes). For this reason, some tax-exempt organizations place a for-profit corporation in the joint venture, rather than themselves, to serve as a "blocker" entity to escape tax and perhaps to avoid jeopardizing exempt status.

The single-member limited liability company is usually disregarded for tax purposes. This feature allows a tax-exempt organization to place activities in a limited

---

31. See § 8.4(e).
32. *Id.*

liability company to protect against legal liability, yet still treat them for federal tax purposes as activities directly conducted by the exempt organization.

§ 8.13   OTHER ASPECTS OF LAW OF EXEMPT ORGANIZATIONS

Seven other aspects of the law of tax-exempt organizations warrant mention for the edification of the members of the board of nonprofit organizations.

(a)   Gaming

In general, the conduct of gaming (or gambling) activity by a tax-exempt organization constitutes an unrelated business or a nonexempt function that may jeopardize the organization's exempt status. An exception in the unrelated business context is available for the conduct of bingo games, where they are lawful under state law.

(b)   Withholding of Taxes

As is the case with for-profit employers, nonprofit organization employers are required to withhold income and other taxes and remit them to the appropriate government. Members of the board of nonprofit organizations can be personally liable for these taxes owed (and not paid by the organization) to the federal government.

(c)   Unemployment Tax

Tax-exempt organizations (other than charitable entities) generally are required to pay the federal unemployment tax with respect to their employees.

(d)   Nonexempt Membership Organizations

Special rules apply that can limit the deductibility of expenses in computing taxable income, in situations where a nonprofit organization is a nonexempt membership entity.

(e)   Maintenance of Books and Records

Tax-exempt organizations are required to keep records sufficiently showing gross income, expenses, and disbursements, and providing substantiation for their annual information returns. The IRS frequently revokes the exempt status of organizations that do not maintain adequate records.

(f)   Personal Benefit Contracts

The federal tax law denies a charitable contribution deduction in connection with, and imposes penalties on tax-exempt organizations that engage in transactions involving, certain personal benefit contracts.

(g)   Commerciality Doctrine

Tax-exempt organizations, particularly public charities, that operate in a commercial manner (that is, in the same manner as for-profit entities) may have their exemption revoked. Commercial activity may alternatively be considered an unrelated business.[33] Factors as to commerciality include the extent of the sale of goods and services to the public, pricing policies, and competition with for-profit businesses.

§ 8.14   CHARITABLE GIVING RULES

The federal tax law is replete with detailed rules concerning the charitable contribution deduction, for income, gift, and estate tax purposes.

(a)   Charitable Deduction

The federal tax law provides for an income tax charitable contribution deduction for gifts to charitable and certain other types of tax-exempt organizations. These deductible contributions may be made in the form of money or property. Various percentage limitations may restrict the amount of a charitable contribution deduction in a year. Many special rules apply in this context for particular types of charitable gifts, such as those of inventory, scientific research property, vehicles, and intellectual property. These rules can limit the amount of the charitable deduction, sometimes confining it to the amount of the donor's basis in the property.

(b)   Property Valuation

In connection with charitable contributions of property, often the major issue affecting the deductibility of the gift is the matter of the fair market value of the property at the time of its contribution. Various "accuracy related" penalties can apply with respect to an overvaluation of property in this context.

(c)   Gift Restrictions

A gift may be made to charity that involves the imposition of conditions or restrictions. In many instances, such a restriction is lawful (such as for scholarships, a form of research, or for an endowment). A restriction or condition may, however, be unlawful, result in unwarranted private benefit, or reduce or eliminate the amount of the allowable charitable deduction.

(d)   Split-Interest Trusts

Contributions may be made to charity by means of a split-interest trust. The resulting charitable contribution deduction (if any) is based on the value of the partial interest contributed to the charity by means of the trust. For a charitable deduction to be available in this context, various requirements must be satisfied, such as those for charitable remainder trusts, pooled income funds, and other types of gifts of remainder interests. These vehicles are used in the realm of the type of charitable fundraising known as *planned giving*. If a charitable organization does not have a planned giving program, the board member may wish to inquire as to why that is the case.

---

33. See § 8.10.

(e) Charitable Remainder Trusts

The *charitable remainder trust* is the mainstay of a typical planned giving program. This term is nearly self-explanatory: the entity is a trust, in which has been created a remainder interest that is destined for one or more charitable organizations. One or more income interests are also created by means of this type of trust. These trusts, if they qualify under the federal tax law, are tax-exempt entities.

A qualified charitable remainder trust must provide for a specified distribution of income, at least annually, to one or more beneficiaries (at least one of which is not a charitable organization) for life or for a term of no more than 20 years, with an irrevocable remainder interest to be held for the benefit of, or paid over to, the charitable organization. The manner in which the income interests in a charitable remainder trust are ascertained depends on whether the trust is a charitable remainder annuity trust or a charitable remainder unitrust.

In the case of the *charitable remainder annuity trust*, the income payments are a fixed amount (hence the term *annuity*). With a *charitable remainder unitrust*, the income payments are in an amount equal to a fixed percentage of the fair market value of the assets in the trust. Conventionally, once the income interest expires, the assets in a charitable remainder trust are distributed to the charitable organization that is the remainder beneficiary. The assets (or a portion of them) may, however, be retained in the trust; if this type of a retention occurs, the trust will likely be classified as a private foundation.[34]

(f) Nonexempt Charitable Trusts

The federal tax law provides special rules for certain nonexempt charitable trusts; these entities are usually subject to one or more of the private foundation rules.

§ 8.15 FEDERAL LAW AS TO FUNDRAISING

The federal tax law includes five bodies of law that pertain to fundraising.

(a) Special Events

Special events are social occasions (such as annual balls, games of chance, and sports events) for the benefit of charities that use ticket sales and underwriting to generate revenue. These events, however, may raise federal tax law issues, such as unrelated business and inappropriate gaming. Special event fundraising is the subject of specific reporting rules as part of the annual information return.

(b) Gift Substantiation Rules

For a charitable contribution of $250 or more to be deductible, certain substantiation requirements must be met. This principally entails a written communication from the charitable donee to the donor, containing specified information. Other charitable gift substantiation rules may arise in other contexts, such as with respect to contributions of vehicles or intellectual property.

---

34. See § 8.7(b).

(c) Quid Pro Quo Contribution Rules

The federal tax law imposes certain disclosure requirements on charitable organizations that receive *quid pro quo contributions*, which are payments made partially as a contribution and partially in consideration for goods or services provided by the donee organization. Penalties apply for violation of these rules.

(d) Noncharitable Organizations Gifts Disclosure

The federal tax law imposes certain disclosure requirements in connection with contributions to tax-exempt organizations other than charitable entities. These rules, targeted principally at exempt social welfare organizations, are designed to prevent circumstances where donors are led to believe that the gifts are deductible when they are not. Penalties apply for violation of these rules.

(e) Appraisal Requirements

A contribution deduction is not available, in an instance of a gift of property with a value in excess of $5,000, unless certain appraisal requirements are satisfied, including an obtaining by the donor of a *qualified appraisal*, the preparation of an *appraisal summary*, and use of the services of a *qualified appraiser*.

§ 8.16 STATE LAW AS TO FUNDRAISING

Many states have elaborate laws—charitable solicitation acts—that apply to charitable and other nonprofit organizations that engage in fundraising in their jurisdictions. These laws require charitable organizations soliciting gifts to register with and annually report to the state. Fundraising consultants and paid solicitors may also have registration and reporting requirements; bonds may also be necessitated. These laws can impose several other requirements, such as dictation of the contents of a contract between a charity and a professional fundraiser.

§ 8.17 IRS AUDITS

The IRS, of course, has the authority to examine—audit—nonprofit, tax-exempt organizations. Until recently, this has not been a priority for the IRS. With more appropriations from Congress, considerable prodding from members of Congress, and an energetic Commissioner of Internal Revenue, IRS audits of exempt organizations have been steadily increasing. Today, IRS audit activity involving exempt organizations is at an all-time high. Thus, managers of nonprofit organizations are on notice that the chance of their organization getting audited, while inherently slight, is statistically greater than ever.

(a) Organization of IRS

The leadership of nonprofit organizations, and those who represent these entities, should understand the organization of the IRS. Among the many reasons for this is to gain a perspective on the IRS audit function. Generally, an IRS audit is less traumatic if the overall process is understood.

The IRS is an agency (bureau) of the Department of the Treasury. One of the functions of the Treasury Department is assessment and collection of federal income and other taxes. Congress has authorized the Secretary of the Treasury to, in the language of the Internal Revenue Code, undertake what is necessary for "detecting and bringing to trial and punishment persons guilty of violating the internal revenue laws or conniving at the same." This tax assessment and collection function has largely been assigned to the IRS.

The IRS Web site proclaims that the agency's mission is to "provide America's taxpayers with top quality service by helping them understand and meet their tax responsibilities and by applying the tax law with integrity and fairness to all." The function of the IRS, according to its site, is to "help the large majority of compliant taxpayers with the tax law, while ensuring that the minority who are unwilling to comply pay their fair share."

The IRS is headquartered in Washington, D.C.; its operations there are housed principally in its National Office. An Internal Revenue Service Oversight Board is responsible for overseeing the agency in its administration and supervision of the execution of the nation's internal revenue laws. The chief executive of the IRS is the Commissioner of Internal Revenue. The National Office is organized into four operating divisions; the pertinent one is the Tax Exempt and Government Entities (TE/GE) Division, headed by the Commissioner (TE/GE). Within the TE/GE Division is the Exempt Organizations Division, which develops policy concerning and administers the law of tax-exempt organizations. The components of this Division are Rulings and Agreements, Customer Education and Outreach, Exempt Organizations Electronic Initiatives, and Examinations.

The Examinations Office, based in Dallas, Texas, focuses on tax-exempt organizations' examination programs and review projects. This office develops the overall exempt organizations enforcement strategy and goals to enhance compliance consistent with overall TE/GE strategy, and implements and evaluates exempt organizations examination policies and procedures. Two important elements of the Examinations function are the Exempt Organizations Compliance Unit and the Data Analysis Unit.

(b) Reasons for IRS Audits

The reasons for an IRS examination of a nonprofit, tax-exempt organization are manifold. Traditionally, the agency has focused on particular categories of major exempt entities, such as healthcare institutions, colleges and universities, political organizations, community foundations, and private foundations. Recent years have brought more targeted examinations, such as those involving credit counseling entities and down-payment assistance organizations.

An examination of a tax-exempt organization may be initiated on the basis of the size of the organization or the length of time that has elapsed since a prior audit. An examination may be undertaken following the filing of an annual information return or a tax return, inasmuch as one of the functions of the IRS is to ascertain the correctness of returns. An examination may be based on a discrete issue, such as compensation practices or political campaign activity. Other reasons for the development of an examination include media reports, a state attorney general's inquiry, or other third-party reports of alleged wrongdoing.

(c) IRS Audit Issues

The audit of a nonprofit, tax-exempt organization is likely to entail one or more of the following issues:

- The organization's ongoing eligibility for exempt status[35]
- Public charity/private foundation classification[36]
- Unrelated business activity[37]
- Extensive advocacy undertakings[38]
- One or more excise tax issues
- Whether the organization filed required returns and reports
- Payment of employment taxes[39]
- Involvement in a form of joint venture[40]

(d) Types of IRS Examinations

There are four basic types of IRS examinations of nonprofit, tax-exempt organizations. A compliance check is not technically an audit. Also, there are special procedures for inquiries and examinations of churches.

Common among the types of IRS examinations of tax-exempt organizations are *field examinations,* in which one or more revenue agents (typically, however, only one) review the books, records, and other documents and information of the exempt organization under examination, on the premises of the organization or at the office of its representative. IRS procedures require the examiner to establish the scope of the examination, state the documentation requirements, and summarize the examination techniques (including interviews and tours of facilities).

The IRS's office/correspondence examination program entails examinations of tax-exempt organizations by means of office interviews and/or correspondence. An *office interview* case is one where the examiner requests an exempt organization's records and reviews them in an IRS office; this may include a conference with a representative of the organization. This type of examination is likely to be of a smaller exempt organization, where the records are not extensive and the issues not particularly complex. A *correspondence examination* involves an IRS request for information from an exempt organization by letter, fax, or e-mail communication.

Office or correspondence examinations generally are limited in scope, usually focusing on no more than three issues, conducted by lower-grade examiners. The import of these examinations should not be minimized, however. A correspondence examination can be converted to an office examination. Worse, an office examination can be upgraded to a field examination.

---

35. See § 8.3.
36. See § 8.7.
37. See § 8.10.
38. See §§ 8.5, 8.6.
39. See § 8.13(c).
40. See § 8.12.

For years, one of the mainstays of the IRS tax-exempt organizations examination effort was the *coordinated examination program* (CEP), which focused not only on exempt organizations but also on affiliated entities and arrangements (such as subsidiaries, partnerships, and other joint ventures) and collateral areas of the law (such as employment tax compliance and tax-exempt bond financing). The CEP approach (which was much dreaded), involving relatively sizeable teams of revenue agents, was concentrated on large, complex exempt organizations, such as colleges, universities, and healthcare institutions. Exempt organizations management could expect the CEP exercise to span about three years, with the IRS agents decamping in offices at the exempt organization, to which they would daily directly commute.

The CEP approach was abandoned in 2003 and replaced by the *team examination program* (TEP). Both the CEP and TEP initiatives nonetheless share the same objective, which is to avoid a fragmenting of the exempt organization examination process by using multiple agents. The essential characteristics of the TEP approach that differentiates it from the CEP approach are that the team examinations are being used in connection with a wider array of exempt organizations, the number of revenue agents involved in an examination is somewhat smaller, and the revenue agents are less likely to semipermanently carve out office space in which to live at the exempt organization undergoing the examination. The TEP agents, however, are still likely to want an office for occasional visits and storage of computers and documents.

A TEP case generally is one where the annual information return of the tax-exempt organization involved reflects either total revenue or assets greater than $100 million (or, in the case of a private foundation, $500 million). Nonetheless, the IRS may initiate a team examination where the case would benefit (from the government's perspective) from the TEP approach or where there is no annual information return filing requirement. IRS examination procedures include a presumption that the team examination approach will be used in all cases satisfying the TEP criteria.

In a TEP case, the examination will proceed under the direction of a case manager. One or more tax-exempt organizations revenue agents will be accompanied by others, such as employee plans specialists, actuarial examiners, engineers, excise tax agents, international examiners, computer audit specialists, income tax revenue agents, and/or economists. These examinations may last about two years; a postexamination critique may lead to a cycling of the examination into subsequent years. The IRS examination procedures stipulate the planning that case managers, assisted by team coordinators, should engage in when launching a team examination; these procedures also provide for the exempt organization's involvement in this planning process.

The foregoing types of IRS audits are those normally used to examine nonprofit, tax-exempt organizations. The IRS, however, has within it a Criminal Investigation Division, the agents of which occasionally are involved in exempt organizations examinations.

(e) Compliance Checks

An overlay to the IRS program of examinations of tax-exempt organizations is the agency's *compliance check projects*, which focus on specific compliance issues. These projects, orchestrated by the Exempt Organizations Compliance Unit, are a recent invention of the IRS; they are designed to maximize the agency's return (gaining data and assessing compliance) on its investigation efforts. In a pronouncement issued in early 2008, the IRS stated that its exempt organizations examination and compliance-check processes are among the "variety of tools at [the agency's] disposal to make certain that tax-exempt organizations comply with federal tax law designed to ensure they are entitled to any tax exemption they may claim."

Usually, in the commencement of these projects, the IRS contacts exempt organizations only by mail to obtain information pertaining to the particular issue. An exempt organization has a greater chance of being a compliance check target than the subject of a conventional audit. A compliance check, however, can blossom into an examination.

As of early 2009, nine compliance check projects are in play, with varying levels of intensity.

The IRS announced, in 2004, an Executive Compensation Compliance Initiative. The agency then stated that it was going to "identify and halt" the practice of some tax-exempt organizations of paying excessive compensation and other benefits to insiders. This program entailed contact (compliance check letters) with 1,223 public charities and private foundations. More than 100 of these organizations became the target of formal examinations.

As it turned out, the IRS found less wrongdoing (unreasonable compensation) than initially contemplated. Thus, in a preliminary report on its findings (2007), the agency wrote that "examinations to date do not evidence widespread concerns other than reporting." (More than 30% of these compliance check recipients were required to amend their annual information returns.) Cryptically, the IRS concluded that, "although high compensation amounts were found in many cases, generally they were substantiated based on appropriate comparability data." (Translation: *high* compensation is not necessarily *excessive* compensation.) Of the examinations, 25 resulted in proposed excise tax assessments pursuant to the intermediate sanctions rules (over $4 million) and the self-dealing rules (over $16 million).

These compliance checks continue. Inquiries into compensation levels are part of other compliance checks and usually are embedded in every examination of a tax-exempt organization.

The IRS began a Political Activities Compliance Initiative, starting with the 2004 election campaign, in response to various allegations of participation by charities, including churches, in political campaigns in violation of the tax law.[41] This initiative continued with the 2006 and 2008 election cycles, and may be anticipated to remain in place.

The effort with respect to the 2004 campaign caused the IRS to review 166 cases. For the most part, either no violations were found or the IRS helped organizations correct their activities by issuing *written advisories*. Revocation of exemption was proposed in three instances. There were 237 cases in connection with the 2006 elections. No exemption revocations have been reported as a result of these cases, although the IRS uncovered about $300,000 in inappropriate campaign contributions (about one-half of which have been refunded). The IRS monitored exempt organizations' involvement in the 2008 campaign.

---

41. See § 8.6.

The IRS, in 2006, initiated a Hospital Compliance Project, the purpose of which is to study tax-exempt hospitals and assess how these institutions believe they are providing a community benefit, as well as to determine how exempt hospitals establish and report executive compensation. This massive effort, involving 487 hospitals, commenced with the mailing of a 9-page questionnaire containing 81 questions. Information was requested regarding the type of hospital and patient demographics, governance, medical staff privileges, billing and collection practices, and categories of programs that might constitute community benefit, such as uncompensated care, medical education and training, medical research, and other community programs conducted by hospitals.

The IRS has been processing the data gathered from these questionnaires. In a preliminary report (2007), the agency observed that "there is variation in the level of expenditures hospitals report in furtherance of community benefit." (The report did not address the point that the law does not include a uniform definition of *community benefit*.) This report also noted that "there is considerable variation in how hospitals report uncompensated care." (The term *uncompensated care* was deliberately not defined in the questionnaire because the IRS wanted to learn how the exempt hospital community is applying it.) Hospitals, according to the report, also "vary in how they measure and incorporate bad debt expense and shortfalls between actual costs and Medicare or Medicaid reimbursements into their measures, and whether they use charges or costs in their measures."

The IRS, in early February 2009, made public the final results of its study of tax-exempt hospitals. This report's "key community benefit findings" included the fact that there is considerable diversity in the demographics, community benefit activities, and financial resources among the respondent hospitals. In particular, significant differences were observed by the IRS between the critical-access hospitals and the high-population hospitals, and between the smallest and largest hospitals based on revenue size. The average and median percentages of total revenues reported as community benefit expenditures were 9 percent and 6 percent, respectively. Among the community types, these percentages were lowest for rural hospitals (both critical-access and non-critical-access institutions) and highest for high-population hospitals. The percentage spent on reported community benefit expenditures generally increased with revenue size.

Uncompensated care was the largest reported community benefit expenditure for each of the study's demographics, other than for a group of 15 hospitals reporting large medical research expenditures (93 percent of all research expenditures reported by the study's respondents). Overall, the average and median percentages of uncompensated care as a percentage of total revenues were 7 percent and 4 percent, respectively. Uncompensated care accounted for 56 percent of aggregate reported community benefit expenditures. The next largest categories of community benefit expenditures, ranked as a percentage of total community benefit expenditures, were medical education and training (23 percent), research (15 percent), and community programs (6 percent). The expenditure mix, however, varied by community type and revenue size. Additionally, the group of 15 hospitals reporting large medical research expenditures materially impacted the overall numbers in this area. For example, when the research group is disregarded, the percentage of total community benefit expenditures reported as spent on uncompensated care increases from 56 percent to 71 percent, and that spent on medical research decreases from 15 percent to one percent.

The final report summarizes the executive compensation information arising from the questionnaires and compensation examinations conducted as part of the study. The reported data was analyzed based on community type and revenue size. The key findings are that nearly all hospitals in the study reported compliance with important elements of the rebuttable presumption procedure available to establish compensation of certain persons.[42] The results did not vary materially by demographic. The examinations confirmed widespread use by the examined hospitals of comparability data and independent personnel to review and establish executive compensation amounts.

The average and median total compensation amounts reported as paid to the top management official by respondents to the questionnaire were $490,000 and $377,000, respectively. By community type, the largest amounts were reported by high-population and other urban and suburban hospitals, while critical-access hospitals reported the smallest amounts paid. Average and median total compensation paid increased with revenue size. This report concluded that, although "many of the compensation amounts reported may appear high to some, nearly all examined amounts were upheld as established pursuant to the rebuttable presumption process and within the range of reasonable compensation."

Another of the ongoing IRS compliance initiatives, one that is relatively low-key these days, is a project concerning compliance with the intermediate sanctions reporting rules. The annual information return asks questions about exempt organizations' participation in excess benefit transactions. When one of these returns, lacking answers to these questions, is received by the IRS, an exempt organizations law specialist in the National Office may contact the organization, seeking the response(s).

Another low-key ongoing IRS compliance initiative is a project concerning the reporting of fundraising costs. From time to time, IRS reviewers of annual information returns will come across a return that reflects a considerable amount of gifts and grants, and little or no fundraising expense. This anomaly is likely to perplex the reviewer, who may contact the organization for an explanation. The IRS may also advise the organization that its subsequent annual information returns may be reviewed, from this perspective, by personnel in the Exempt Organizations Compliance Unit.

The IRS, in 2007, undertook a compliance check initiative, this one targeting charitable organizations that are engaged in tax-exempt bond financing. The agency has concluded (based on about 40 audits in fiscal year 2006) that there is a lack of compliance with certain record-retention rules. The IRS is currently surveying about 500 charitable organizations in this regard.

The IRS has embarked on a project inquiring as to charitable contributions of interests in limited liability companies, involving questionable transactions concerning successor member interests in these companies. This program is unique in that instead of a mailing of letters or questionnaires, the IRS developed and is sending (starting in late 2007) a prototype information document request (IDR). This IDR (11 single-spaced pages) includes some pointed questions.

The IRS has launched a compliance check project, by the mailing of questionnaires, to the nation's community foundations. Concerned that these foundations may be wandering outside of their legal bounds, the IRS is asking detailed questions

---

42. See § 8.4(f), fifth paragraph.

about these foundations' "area of service" (in that they are, after all, *community* foundations), revenues, assets, investments, grantmaking, business relationships, fees paid, and staff.

The most recent compliance initiative has targeted about 400 tax-exempt colleges and universities, both public and private. By means of dissemination of a compliance check questionnaire, the IRS is looking at how institutions of higher education (1) report income and expenses on their annual information returns, (2) calculate and report losses on their unrelated business income tax returns, (3) allocate income and expenses in calculating their unrelated business taxable income, (4) invest and use their endowment funds, and (5) (once again) determine executive compensation.[43]

§8.18 BANKRUPTCY

As a consequence of the nation's economic difficulties, including those caused by the recession that began in 2008, there is an increase in bankruptcy filings by public charities and other nonprofit organizations. These filings are both made in accordance with the bankruptcy code, specifically, Chapter 7 (liquidations) and Chapter 11 (reorganizations). These bankruptcies are the result of declining contributions, inability to borrow, increasing expenses, and, in some instances, impending IRS (for payroll taxes) and other liens.

---

43. See § 6.4.

CHAPTER NINE

Governance Legal Audit

On occasion, a lawyer is called on to conduct an audit of the structure and operations of a nonprofit organization to determine whether—or the extent to which—the organization is in compliance with federal and state law, including emerging governance concepts. This undertaking is referred to as the *governance legal audit*. Other subjects that may be reviewed, albeit often outside the context of a legal audit, include accounting principles, ethics enforcement programs, and compliance with watchdog agency standards.

The lawyer embarking on a legal audit of a nonprofit organization is hereby provided with checklists to assist in this endeavor to the extent it pertains to governance matters (which it largely will). Thus, the emphasis here is on aspects of the legal audit, although obviously much of what is offered is usable by planners other than lawyers (such as accountants, fundraisers, management consultants, and the management of nonprofit organizations).

§9.1 INVENTORY OF BASICS

- What is the nonprofit organization's formal name?

- Does the organization operate under a different name? If so, what is it?

- Are the organization and the lawyer conducting the legal audit satisfied that this name is (or these names are) the most appropriate name(s) for the organization?[1]

- What is the organization's mailing address?

- What is the organization's e-mail address?

- Does the organization have a Web site? If so, what is the address?

- When the organization was established, was consideration given to forming it as a for-profit organization? If so, what were the reasons for creating the entity as a nonprofit organization?

- What is, or are, the organization's primary purpose or purposes?[2]

- Does the organization's articles of organization[3] appropriately reflect these purposes?

---

1. See *Law of Tax-Exempt Organizations* § 4.8.
2. See *id.* § 4.4.
3. See *id.* § 4.2.

- When was the organization's statement of purposes in the articles[4] most recently written, amended, or reviewed?
- Does the organization have a procedure for periodic review of its statement of purposes?
- What are the organization's activities?[5]
- How does this list of activities correlate with Form 990, Part III?
- Have any material activities been added or terminated in the previous three years?
- If so, how are these developments reflected in relation to Form 990, Part VI, question 76?
- What is the organization's principal state of operation? Why was that state selected?
- What is the organization's legal form?[6]
- What is the date of formation of the organization?
- What is the type of the organization's articles of organization?[7] Provide a copy of the document.
- Have the articles of organization been reviewed to be certain that all of the requisite provisions are in the document?[8]
- Why was this legal form selected?
- If the organization is not incorporated, why?
- Does the organization have members? If so, describe.
- Does the organization have committees? If so, describe.
- Does the organization have bylaws? If so, provide a copy of the document.
- If so, have the bylaws been reviewed to be certain that all of the requisite provisions are in the document?[9]
- Is the organization in compliance with state and local filing requirements, such as annual corporate and fundraising reports?
- How is the organization funded?
- Does the organization indemnify any person?[10] If so, describe.
- Does the organization provide any form of guarantee? If so, describe.
- Does the organization have any insurance coverage?[11] If so, describe.
- If the organization is incorporated, who is the registered agent?

---

4. See *id*. § 4.3(a).
5. See *id*. § 4.5(a).
6. See *id*. § 4.1.
7. See § 1.2(b).
8. See § 1.2(b).
9. See § 1.2(c).
10. See § 2.6(b).
11. See § 2.6(c).

- Does the organization do business in one or more states other than the state in which it is located? If so, what are those other states?

- If so, is the organization in compliance with the initial and ongoing filing requirements of the other state(s)? [The lawyer should review these documents.]

- If so, and if the organization is incorporated, who is the registered agent in the other state(s)?

- Is the organization under the scrutiny of a watchdog agency?[12] If so, explain.

- Has the organization ever undergone an Internal Revenue Service (IRS) audit?[13] If so, what was (were) the outcome(s)?

- Has the organization ever received a private ruling from the IRS? If so, describe the circumstances and provide a copy of the ruling.

- Has the organization previously undergone a legal audit? If so, what was (were) the outcome(s)?

§ 9.2 GOVERNANCE

- What is the name of the nonprofit organization's governing board (generically referred to as the *board of directors*)?[14]

- Identify the individuals who comprise the organization's board of directors.

- How are these individuals selected?[15]

- Identify the organization's officers.[16]

- How are these individuals selected?[17]

- Identify the organization's key employees.[18]

- On what basis were these individuals determined to be key?

- Are the proceedings of the meetings of the board of directors reflected in minutes?[19] [The minutes, at least those of recent meetings, should be reviewed by the lawyer conducting the legal audit.]

- Are the proceedings of other meetings (most likely, those of committees) reflected in minutes? [If so, these should be reviewed by the lawyer.]

- Are minutes reviewed by a lawyer before circulation of them to the board of directors (and/or other body)?

- Does the full board of directors vote on the compensation of the organization's chief executive officer and/or other personnel?

---

12. See § 3.3.
13. See *Law of Tax-Exempt Organizations* § 26.6; Hopkins, *IRS Audits of Tax-Exempt Organizations: Policies, Practices, and Procedures* (Hoboken, NJ: John Wiley & Sons, 2008).
14. See § 1.3(a).
15. See § 1.3(c).
16. See § 2.2(b).
17. See § 2.2(c).
18. See § 2.3.
19. See § 2.7(d).

- Does the full board of directors review the organization's annual information return before it is filed?[20]

- Does the organization have a mission statement?[21] If so, was the policy adopted by the board?[22] If so, provide a copy.

- Does the organization have a business plan? If so, provide a copy.

- Does the organization have a case statement? If so, provide a copy.

- Does the organization have an employees' handbook? [If so, the lawyer should review it.]

§ 9.3 POLICIES AND PROCEDURES

- Does the organization have a code of ethics?[23] If so, provide a copy.

- Does the organization have a conflict-of-interest policy?[24] Is this policy required by law? If such a policy is in place, provide a copy.

- If so, do the appropriate individuals annually sign affirmation statements? [If so, the lawyer should review these.]

- Does the organization have a whistleblower policy?[25] If such a policy is in place, provide a copy.

- Does the organization have a document destruction and retention policy?[26] If such a policy is in place, provide a copy.

- Does the organization have an investment policy?[27] If such a policy is in place, provide a copy.

- Does the organization have a gift acceptance policy (if applicable)?[28] If such a policy is in place, provide a copy.

- Does the organization have a policy as to preservation of its tax-exempt status (if applicable)?[29] If such a policy is in place, provide a copy.

- Does the organization have a policy as to use of subsidiaries and involvement in joint ventures?[30] If such a policy is in place, provide a copy.

- If the organization is a tax-exempt hospital, does it have charity care, community benefit, and billing policies?[31] If such policies are in place, provide copies.

---

20. See § 6.3(i).
21. See § 5.15.
22. See § 6.3(a).
23. See § 5.16.
24. See § 4.2(a).
25. See § 4.2(b).
26. *Id.*
27. See § 6.3(p).
28. See § 6.3(j).
29. See § 6.3(f).
30. *Id.*
31. See §§ 6.3(m)-(o).

- Does the organization accept gifts of conservation easements? If so, does it have a policy as to acceptance and maintenance of these easements?[32] If such a policy is in place, provide a copy.

- Does the organization have a policy concerning executive compensation?[33]

- Does the organization have a policy concerning chapters, affiliates, and branches?[34]

- Does the organization have a policy as to grantmaking?[35]

- Does the organization have a travel and expense reimbursement policy?[36]

- Does the organization have a tax-exempt bond compliance policy?[37]

- Does the organization have an audit committee?[38]

- Does the organization have a policy as to board review of its annual information returns?[39]

- Does the organization currently have a business relationship with one or more directors? If so, discuss.

- Does the organization currently have a business relationship with one or more officers? If so, discuss.

- Has the board of directors reviewed the operations of the organization in light of corporate governance principles? If so, what was the outcome?

- Does each member of the board of directors have a board book?[40] [If so, the lawyer should review it.]

- Does the board of directors have an e-mail communications system?[41] If so, is there a policy as to when this system should not be used?

- Is there a policy as to board members' attendance at meetings?[42]

- Do board members read materials about nonprofit boards?[43]

- Do board members attend seminars about nonprofit organization management and law?[44]

- Does the board of directors periodically have retreats?[45]

---

32. See § 6.3(k).
33. See § 6.3(e).
34. See § 6.3(h).
35. See § 6.3(l).
36. See § 6.3(r).
37. See § 6.3(s).
38. See § 6.3(u).
39. See § 6.3(i).
40. See § 2.7(a).
41. See § 2.7(c).
42. See § 2.7(e).
43. See § 2.7(k).
44. See § 2.7(l).
45. See § 2.7(m).

§9.4 EXTERNAL RELATIONSHIPS

- Does the nonprofit organization use the services of one or more lawyers? If so, describe.

- Does the organization use the services of one or more accountants? If so, describe.

- Does the organization use the services of a fundraising consultant (individual) or company?[46] If so, describe.

- Does the organization use the services of a professional solicitor?[47] If so, describe.

- Does the organization use the services of a management company?[48] If so, describe.

- Does the organization use the services of any other independent contractor? If so, describe. [Examples are investment advisors, lobbyists, public relations consultants, and political campaign consultants.]

- Is the organization a party to a lease(s)? If so, provide a copy(ies).

- Is the organization a party to any other contract(s)? If so, provide a copy(ies).

- Does the organization have a formal relationship with another tax-exempt organization(s)?[49] If so, describe?

- Does the organization have a for-profit subsidiary?[50] If so, discuss.

- Is the organization a partner in a partnership?[51] If so, discuss.

- Is the organization a member of another type of joint venture?[52] If so, discuss. [See below.]

- Is the organization a member of a limited liability company?[53] If so, discuss.

- Is the organization the sole member of a limited liability company?[54] If so, discuss.

- Is the organization the beneficiary of a trust(s)?[55] If so, discuss.

- Is the organization the beneficiary of an insurance policy(ies)? If so, discuss.

- Is the organization referenced in one or more wills or estate plans? If so, discuss.

---

46. See *Law of Fundraising* § 3.6.
47. See *id.* § 3.7.
48. See § 2.4.
49. See, e.g., *Law of Tax-Exempt Organizations* § 12.3(c), Chapter 28.
50. See *id.*, Chapter 29; § 8.11.
51. See *Law of Tax-Exempt Organizations*, Chapter 30; § 8.12.
52. See *id.*
53. See *id.* §§ 31.4-31.6; § 1.2(d).
54. See *Law of Tax-Exempt Organizations* § 31.6; § 1.2(d).
55. See § 1.2(a).

§9.5   TAX-EXEMPT STATUS

- Is the nonprofit organization tax-exempt under federal income tax law? If so, pursuant to which section of the Internal Revenue Code?

- Is the organization exempt from the payment of state and/or local tax? If so, describe. [This includes sales, use, tangible personal property, intangible personal property, and real property taxation.]

- Has the organization's federal income tax exemption been recognized by the IRS?[56] If so, provide a copy of the determination letter or ruling.

- Does the organization have a copy of its application for recognition of exemption?[57] If so, provide a copy.

- If the organization's tax exemption has not been recognized by the IRS, should consideration be given to acquisition of that recognition?

- Is the organization subject to the federal unrelated business income tax?[58] If not, explain.

- Is the organization's net investment income subject to federal taxation?[59] If yes, explain.

- If the organization is exempt from federal income taxation by reason of IRC § 501(c)(3), what is the primary reason for that exemption (charitable, educational, religious, scientific, or other)?[60]

- If the organization provides benefits, services, and/or products for a fee, how is that fee determined?[61]

- Is there any content on the organization's Web site that may pertain to the organization's tax-exempt status?

- If an application for recognition of exempt status is in preparation, is it being prepared or reviewed by a lawyer?

- Subsequent to the issuance of a determination letter or ruling as to exempt status by the IRS, have there been any material changes in the activities of the organization? If so, describe.

- Subsequent to the issuance of such a document, have there been any amendments to the organization's governing instruments? If so, describe.

- Subsequent to the issuance of such a document, has there been any change in the organization's legal form? If so, describe.

- Is the organization a central organization in connection with the group exemption rules?[62] If so, describe.

---

56. See *Law of Tax-Exempt Organizations* § 3.2; § 8.7.
57. See *id.*, Chapter 25.
58. See *id.*, Chapter 24; § 8.10.
59. See, e.g., *Law of Tax-Exempt Organizations* § 15.5.
60. See *id.*, Part Three.
61. See *id.* §§ 4.11, 24.2(e).
62. See *id.* § 25.6.

- Is the organization a subordinate organization in connection with the group exemption rules?[63] If so, describe.

§9.6 PRIVATE INUREMENT DOCTRINE

- Is the nonprofit organization subject to the private inurement doctrine?[64]
- The insiders with respect to the organization[65] are the following persons: [Insert list.]
- Is the organization's board an independent board or a captive board?
- Does the organization pay compensation to an insider?[66]
- If so, is the organization assured that the amount and terms of the compensation are reasonable?
- What is the basis for that assurance?[67]
- Is the compensation based, in whole or in part, on the revenue flow of the organization?[68]
- Is the organization borrowing money from an insider?[69]
- If so, is the organization assured that the terms of the arrangement are reasonable?
- If so, what is the basis for that assurance?
- Is the organization lending money to an insider?[70]
- If so, is the organization assured that the terms of the arrangement are reasonable?
- If so, what is the basis for that assurance?
- Is the organization renting property to an insider?[71]
- If so, is the organization assured that the terms of the arrangement are reasonable?
- If so, what is the basis for that assurance?
- Is the organization renting property from an insider?[72]
- If so, is the organization assured that the terms of the arrangement are reasonable?
- If so, what is the basis for that assurance?

---

63. *Id.*
64. See *id.*, Chapter 20; § 83(d).
65. See *Law of Tax-Exempt Organizations* § 20.3.
66. See *id.* § 20.4.
67. See *id.* § 20.4(b).
68. See *id.* § 20.4(c).
69. See *id.* § 20.5(b).
70. *Id.*
71. See *id.* § 20.5(a).
72. *Id.*

- Is the organization making facilities or services available to an insider?
- If so, is the organization assured that the terms of the arrangement are reasonable?
- If so, what is the basis for that assurance?
- Is the organization selling property to an insider?[73]
- If so, is the organization assured that the terms of the transaction are reasonable?
- If so, what is the basis for that assurance?
- Is the organization purchasing property from an insider?[74]
- If so, is the organization assured that the terms of the transaction are reasonable?
- If so, what is the basis for that assurance?
- Is the organization a partner in a partnership involving an insider?[75]
- If so, is the organization assured that the terms of the arrangement are reasonable?
- If so, what is the basis for that assurance?
- Is the organization a member of another type of joint venture involving an insider?[76]
- If so, is the organization assured that the terms of the arrangement are reasonable?
- If so, what is the basis for that assurance?
- Is the organization taking the position that a benefit to an insider is incidental?[77] If so, describe.

§ 9.7 PRIVATE BENEFIT DOCTRINE

- Is the nonprofit organization subject to the private benefit doctrine?[78]
- Does the organization pay compensation?
- If so, is the organization assured that the amount and terms of the compensation are reasonable?
- Is the compensation based, in whole or in part, on the revenue flow of the organization?
- What is the basis for that assurance?
- Is the organization borrowing money?
- If so, is the organization assured that the terms of the arrangement are reasonable?

---

73. See *id*. § 20.5(c).
74. *Id*.
75. See *id*., Chapter 30.
76. *Id*.
77. See *id*. § 20.7.
78. See *id*. § 20.11; § 8.3(e).

- If so, what is the basis for that assurance?
- Is the organization lending money?
- If so, is the organization assured that the terms of the arrangement are reasonable?
- If so, what is the basis for that assurance?
- Is the organization renting property?
- If so, is the organization assured that the terms of the arrangement are reasonable?
- If so, what is the basis for that assurance?
- Is the organization making facilities or services available?
- If so, is the organization assured that the terms of the arrangement are reasonable?
- If so, what is the basis for that assurance?
- Is the organization selling property?
- If so, is the organization assured that the terms of the transaction are reasonable?
- If so, what is the basis for that assurance?
- Is the organization purchasing property?
- If so, is the organization assured that the terms of the transaction are reasonable?
- If so, what is the basis for that assurance?
- Is the organization a partner in a partnership?
- If so, is the organization assured that the terms of the arrangement are reasonable?
- If so, what is the basis for that assurance?
- Is the organization a member of another type of joint venture?[79]
- If so, is the organization assured that the terms of the arrangement are reasonable?
- If so, what is the basis for that assurance?
- Is the organization taking the position that a benefit being provided is incidental? If so, describe.

§9.8 EXCESS BENEFIT TRANSACTIONS

- Is the nonprofit organization subject to the intermediate sanctions rules?[80]
- The disqualified persons with respect to the organization are the following persons:[81] [Insert list.]

---

79. See *Law of Tax-Exempt Organizations* § 20.7(b).
80. See *id.*, Chapter 21; § 8.3(f).
81. See *Law of Tax-Exempt Organizations* § 21.3.

- Does this list include members of the family of disqualified persons? [If not, add to list.]
- Does the list of disqualified persons include entities controlled by disqualified persons? [If not, add to list.]
- Does the organization pay compensation to a disqualified person?[82]
- If so, is the organization assured that the amount and terms of the compensation are reasonable?
- If so, what is the basis for that assurance?
- Is the compensation based, in whole or in part, on the revenue flow of the organization?[83]
- Is the compensation properly documented as such?[84]
- Is the organization borrowing money from a disqualified person?[85]
- If so, is the organization assured that the terms of the arrangement are reasonable?
- If so, what is the basis for that assurance?
- Is the organization lending money to a disqualified person?[86]
- If so, is the organization assured that the terms of the arrangement are reasonable?
- If so, what is the basis for that assurance?
- Is the organization renting property to a disqualified person?[87]
- If so, is the organization assured that the terms of the arrangement are reasonable?
- If so, what is the basis for that assurance?
- Is the organization renting property from a disqualified person?[88]
- If so, is the organization assured that the terms of the arrangement are reasonable?
- If so, what is the basis for that assurance?
- Is the organization making facilities or services available to a disqualified person?[89]
- If so, is the organization assured that the terms of the arrangement are reasonable?
- If so, what is the basis for that assurance?

---

82. See *id.* § 21.4(a).
83. See *id.* § 21.4(b).
84. See *id.* § 21.4(c).
85. See *id.* § 21.4(a).
86. *Id.*
87. *Id.*
88. *Id.*
89. *Id.*

- Is the organization selling property to a disqualified person?[90]

- If so, is the organization assured that the terms of the transaction are reasonable?

- If so, what is the basis for that assurance?

- Is the organization purchasing property from a disqualified person?[91]

- If so, is the organization assured that the terms of the transaction are reasonable?

- If so, what is the basis for that assurance?

- Is the organization a partner in a partnership involving a disqualified person?[92]

- If so, is the organization assured that the terms of the arrangement are reasonable?

- If so, what is the basis for that assurance?

- Is the organization a member of another type of joint venture involving a disqualified person?[93]

- If so, is the organization assured that the terms of the arrangement are reasonable?

- If so, what is the basis for that assurance?

- Is the organization properly treating an economic benefit as consideration for the performance of services? Describe.[94]

- Has the organization indirectly provided an excess benefit?[95] If so, explain.

- Has the organization provided an excess benefit for the use of a disqualified person?[96] If so, explain.

- Has the organization reported an excess benefit transaction on an annual information return? If so, explain.

- Is the organization utilizing the initial contract exception?[97] If so, explain.

- Is the organization using the rebuttable presumption of reasonableness?[98] If so, explain.

- Did an organization manager knowingly participate in an excess benefit transaction?

- Are any penalty excise taxes properly calculated?

---

90. *Id.*
91. *Id.*
92. See *id.*, Chapter 30.
93. *Id.*
94. See *id.* § 21.4(b).
95. See *id.* § 21.6.
96. See *id.* § 21.7.
97. See *id.* § 21.8.
98. See *id.* § 21.9.

- Has an excess benefit transaction been corrected? If so, explain.
- Does the organization have a policy for indemnifying disqualified persons subject to a penalty tax? If so, explain.
- Does the organization maintain insurance coverage for payment or reimbursement of penalty excise taxes? If so, explain.
- Is the organization taking the position that a benefit to a disqualified person is incidental? If so, explain.

§9.9   SELF-DEALING RULES

- Is the nonprofit organization a private foundation?[99]
- The disqualified persons with respect to the organization are the following persons: [Insert list.]
- Is the organization engaging in an act of self-dealing[100] directly with a disqualified person?
- Is the organization engaging in an act of self-dealing indirectly with a disqualified person?
- Is the organization providing an improper benefit for the use of a disqualified person?
- Is the organization relying on the personal services exception?
- Did a foundation manager knowingly participate in a self-dealing transaction?
- Are any penalty excise taxes properly calculated?
- Has a self-dealing transaction been corrected? If so, explain.
- Is the organization taking the position that a benefit to a disqualified person is incidental? If so, explain.

§9.10   ACTIONS BY ORGANIZATION

- What persons are authorized to act on behalf of the nonprofit organization?
- Does the board of directors act by majority vote or unanimous consent?
- When is action taken by an officer considered an act of the organization?
- When is action taken by an employee considered an act of the organization?
- Does the organization have one or more persons designated as agents?
- If so, under what circumstances is the act of an agent considered an act of the organization?

---

99. See *Law of Tax-Exempt Organizations* § 12.1(a); *Private Foundations* § 1.2; § 8.6.
100. See *Private Foundations*, Chapter 5.

§ 9.11 PUBLIC CHARITY CLASSIFICATION

- Is the nonprofit organization a public charity because it is an institution?[101]

- Is the organization a public charity because it is a donative publicly supported charity?[102] [If the answer is no, the following 12 questions are inapplicable.]

  - Has the organization's total amount of support, for these purposes, been properly determined?

  - What is the organization's current public support ratio?

  - Is this ratio above or below one-third of total support?

  - Is the reviewer satisfied that the numbers involved, including the 2% threshold, are accurate?

  - Has there been a determination as to which payments are gifts and which are some other form of revenue?

  - Has there been a determination as to which payments are grants and which are forms of exempt function revenue?

  - Are grants from other donative publicly supported charities properly included in full as public support?

  - Are grants from other charitable organizations, which are described in the donative publicly supported charities rules, properly included in full as public support?

  - Are grants from governmental units properly included in full as public support?

  - Is support from various persons aggregated or not aggregated?

  - Have all gifts and grants been examined in relation to the unusual grant rule? If so, what was the outcome?

  - Has application of the facts-and-circumstances test been analyzed?[103] If so, why? What was the outcome?

- Is the organization a public charity because it is a service-provider publicly supported charity?[104] [If the answer is no, the following 14 questions are inapplicable.]

  - Has the organization's total amount of support, for these purposes, been determined?

  - Has the organization identified all of the disqualified persons with respect to it?

  - Are any calculations as to substantial contributor classification correct?

  - Have all foundation managers been identified?

---

101. See *Law of Tax-Exempt Organizations* § 12.3(a); *Private Foundations* § 15.3; § 8.6(b).
102. See *Law of Tax-Exempt Organizations* § 12.3(b)(i); *Private Foundations* § 15.4; § 8.6(c).
103. See *Law of Tax-Exempt Organizations* § 12.3(b)(ii); *Private Foundations* § 15.4(c).
104. See *Law of Tax-Exempt Organizations* § 12.3(b)(iv); *Private Foundations* § 15.5; § 8.6(c).

- ○ What is the organization's current public support ratio?
- ○ Is this ratio above or below one-third of total support?
- ○ Is the reviewer satisfied that the numbers involved are accurate?
- ○ Has there been a determination as to which payments are gifts and which are some other form of revenue?
- ○ Has there been a determination as to which payments are grants and which are forms of exempt function revenue?
- ○ Are grants from governmental units included in full as public support?
- ○ Is support from various persons aggregated or not aggregated?
- ○ Have all gifts and grants been examined in relation to the unusual grant rule? If so, what was the outcome?
- ○ Has the organization's investment income been calculated?
- ○ Is the investment income amount above or below one-third of total support?
- Is the organization a supporting organization?[105] [If the answer is no, the following 30 questions are inapplicable.]
  - ○ What is the supporting organization's type? Type I ___. Type II___. Type III (functionally integrated)___. Type III (not functionally integrated)___ .
  - ○ Is the organization in compliance with the supporting organization organizational test?
  - ○ Identify the organization's supported entity or entities.
  - ○ Determine whether each of the supported organizations is an institution, a donative publicly supported charity, a service provider publicly supported charity, a supporting organization, a social welfare organization, a labor organization, or a business league.
  - ○ If the relationship between a supported organization and a supporting organization is that of parent and subsidiary (Type I), explain how that relationship is manifested.
  - ○ If the relationship is that of common control (Type II), explain how that relationship is manifested.
  - ○ If the relationship is that of "operated in connection with" (Type III, functionally integrated), explain how that relationship is manifested.
  - ○ If the relationship is that of "operated in connection with" (Type III, nonfunctionally integrated), explain how that relationship is manifested.
  - ○ Is the supported organization(s) formally identified in the supporting organization's articles of organization?
  - ○ How does the supporting organization support or benefit the supported organization(s)?
  - ○ Does this support include the making of grants?

---

105. See *Law of Tax-Exempt Organizations* § 12.3(c); *Private Foundations* § 15.7; § 8.6(d).

○ Does the supporting organization annually provide to each supported organization sufficient information to ensure that the organization is responsive to the needs or demands of the supported organization(s)?

○ Does the supporting organization operate in connection with a supported organization in a country other than the United States?

○ Has the supporting organization received a charitable contribution from a person (other than a qualified supported organization) who, directly or indirectly, controls the governing body of a supported organization?

○ Are the private foundation excess business holdings rules[106] applicable to the supporting organization? If so, is the organization in compliance with these rules?

○ Has a private foundation made a grant to the supporting organization, where a disqualified person with respect to the foundation directly or indirectly controls the supporting organization or a supported organization of the supporting organization?

○ If the organization is a fundraising organization, is it in compliance with federal disclosure requirements?[107]

○ If the organization is a fundraising organization, is it in compliance with applicable state fundraising regulation law?[108]

○ If the organization is a fundraising organization, is it in compliance with applicable local fundraising regulation law?

○ Does the supporting organization conduct program activities or is it engaged in fundraising in support of a supported organization's programs?

○ Does the supporting organization function as a holding company?

○ Is the supporting organization a member of a joint venture?

○ Does the supporting organization have a taxable subsidiary?

○ Has a title-holding company[109] been reviewed as an alternative to the supporting organization?

○ Has a single-member limited liability company[110] been reviewed as an alternative to the supporting organization?

○ Was the supporting organization created by one or more donors (as opposed to one or more supported organizations)?

○ Are one or more supported organizations noncharitable entities?

○ If so, does each noncharitable entity qualify as the type of tax-exempt organization that can use a supporting organization?

---

106. See *Law of Tax-Exempt Organizations* § 12.4(c); *Private Foundations*, Chapter 7.
107. See § 8.9.
108. See § 8.16.
109. See *Tax-Exempt Organizations* § 19.2(a).
110. See *id*. § 31.6.

- ○ If so, does each noncharitable entity satisfy the service provider publicly supported charity rules?

- ○ Is the supporting organization controlled by disqualified persons? If not, where is the control manifested?

- Has the organization's public charity status been reviewed by the IRS? If so, what was the outcome?

- Has the organization's public charity status been changed by IRS ruling? If so, provide a copy of that document.

- Does the organization have a plan for receiving the requisite amount of public support? If so, what is it?

- Does the organization have a contingency plan for avoiding private foundation status if the requisite amount of public support is not received? If so, what is it?

- Does this contingency plan (if any) entail use of a supporting organization? [If so, see above.]

- Have any of the private foundation termination rules been used? If so, explain.

§ 9.12   PRIVATE FOUNDATION RULES

[If the organization is not a private foundation, the questions in this section are inapplicable.]

- Is the organization in compliance with the private foundation organizational test?[111]

- Is the organization in compliance with the self-dealing rules?[112]

- Is the organization in compliance with the minimum distribution requirements?[113]

- Is the organization in compliance with the excess business holdings rules?[114]

- Is the organization in compliance with the jeopardizing investments rules?[115]

- Is the organization in compliance with the taxable expenditures rules as to lobbying activities?[116]

- Is the organization in compliance with the taxable expenditures rules as to political campaign activities?[117]

- Is the organization in compliance with the taxable expenditures rules concerning grants to noncharitable organizations?[118]

---

111. See *Law of Tax-Exempt Organizations* § 12.1(g); *Private Foundations* § 1.7.
112. See *Law of Tax-Exempt Organizations* § 12.4(a); *Private Foundations*, Chapter 5.
113. See *Law of Tax-Exempt Organizations* § 12.4(b); *Private Foundations*, Chapter 6.
114. See *Law of Tax-Exempt Organizations* § 12.4(c); *Private Foundations*, Chapter 7.
115. See *Law of Tax-Exempt Organizations* § 12.4(d); *Private Foundations*, Chapter 8.
116. See *Law of Tax-Exempt Organizations* § 12.4(e); *Private Foundations* § 9.1.
117. See *Law of Tax-Exempt Organizations* § 12.4(e); *Private Foundations* § 9.2.
118. See *Law of Tax-Exempt Organizations* § 12.4(e); *Private Foundations* § 9.6.

- Is the organization in compliance with the taxable expenditures rules concerning grants to individuals?[119]

- Is the organization in compliance with the taxable expenditures rules concerning noncharitable expenditures?[120]

- Is the organization calculating, reporting, and paying the tax on net investment income?[121]

§9.13 DONOR-ADVISED FUNDS

- Does the organization qualify as a sponsoring organization in relation to one or more donor-advised funds?[122]

- Is there uncertainty as to whether a fund maintained by the organization constitutes a donor-advised fund? If so, what is being done to resolve the uncertainty?

- Are any distributions from a donor-advised fund taxable?

- Has a donor, donor advisor, or related party provided advice as to a distribution from a donor-advised fund that resulted in a private benefit to one or more of these persons?

- Are the private foundation excess business holdings rules[123] being complied with in this context?

- Does the sponsoring organization provide donors to its donor-advised funds with contemporaneous written acknowledgments that the organization has exclusive legal control over the funds or assets contributed?

§9.14 ENDOWMENT AND OTHER FUNDS

- Does the organization maintain one or more endowment funds?[124]

- Is there uncertainty as to whether a fund maintained by the organization constitutes an endowment fund? If so, what is being done to resolve the uncertainty?

- Is income from the endowment fund paid to the organization? If so, what is the annual payout rate?

- Does the organization maintain any other types of restricted funds, such as funds for scholarships, fellowships, awards, or research?

---

119. See *Law of Tax-Exempt Organizations* § 12.4(e); *Private Foundations* § 9.3.
120. See *Law of Tax-Exempt Organizations* § 12.4(e); *Private Foundations* § 9.8.
121. See *Law of Tax-Exempt Organizations* § 12.4(f); *Private Foundations*, Chapter 10.
122. See *Law of Tax-Exempt Organizations* § 11.8(e); *Private Foundations*, Chapter 16.
123. See *supra* note 114.
124. See *Law of Tax-Exempt Organizations* § 11.9.

§ 9.15 LEGISLATIVE ACTIVITIES

- Does the nonprofit organization attempt to influence legislation?[125]

- If so, what is the extent of these lobbying activities?

- How is this "extent" measured?

- If the organization is a public charity, is this "extent" of lobbying consistent with its tax-exempt status?[126] If so, why?

- If the organization is a public charity, can its primary objective be attained only by legislative action?

- Does the organization engage in direct lobbying?[127]

- Does the organization engage in grassroots lobbying?[128]

- If the organization is a public charity, is it under the substantial part test?[129] Does it comply with that test?

- Is this organization properly reporting its lobbying activities on its annual information return?[130]

- If the organization is a public charity, is it under the expenditure test?[131] Does it comply with that test?

- Is this organization properly reporting its lobbying activities on its annual information return?[132]

- If the organization has elected the expenditure test,[133] is it relying on one or more exceptions provided by these rules?[134]

- If the organization has not elected the expenditure test, why not?

- If the organization elected the expenditure test, when did it do so? Provide a copy of Form 5768.

- If the organization has elected the expenditure test, does it have mixed-purpose expenditures?[135]

- If the organization has elected the expenditure test, does the organization pay for mass media advertisements?[136]

- If the organization has elected the expenditure test, does it have one or more affiliated organizations?[137]

---

125. See § 8.4.
126. See *Law of Tax-Exempt Organizations*, §§ 22.1–22.4.
127. See *id*. § 22.3(b).
128. *Id*.
129. See, e.g., *id*. § 22.3(c).
130. See *id*. § 22.3(c)(iv).
131. See, e.g., *id*. § 22.3(d).
132. See *id*. § 22.3(d)(ix).
133. See *id*. § 22.3(d)(v).
134. See *id*. § 22.3(d)(iv).
135. See *id*. § 22.3(d)(ii).
136. See *id*. § 22.3(d)(i).
137. See *id*. § 22.3(d)(vii).

- If the organization has elected the expenditure test, is it properly taking into account the lobbying expenditures of affiliated organizations?

- If the organization has elected the expenditure test, does the organization have a separate fundraising unit?[138] If so, are total exempt purpose expenditures properly calculated?

- If the organization is a public charity under the substantial part test, has it paid any tax on excessive lobbying expenditures?[139]

- If the organization is a public charity under the expenditure test, has it paid any tax on excessive lobbying expenditures?

- If the organization is a tax-exempt charitable entity, has it ever had its exemption revoked because of its lobbying activities?

- If the organization is a private foundation, what are its lobbying activities? Is it relying on one or more exceptions?[140]

- If the organization is a public charity, does it use a related tax-exempt social welfare organization to conduct lobbying activities?[141]

- If the answer to the preceding question is yes, is the lawyer conducting the legal audit satisfied that the principles as to bifurcation are being followed?[142]

- If the organization is a public charity and the answer to the question before the preceding one is no, has consideration been given to such use of a social welfare organization?

- If the organization is a tax-exempt social welfare organization, what are its lobbying activities, if any?[143]

- If the organization is a tax-exempt business league, what are its lobbying activities, if any?[144]

- If the organization is a business league, is it in conformity with the rules concerning the deductibility of dues as a business expense?[145]

- If the organization is any other type of tax-exempt organization, what are its lobbying activities, if any?[146]

- Does the organization engage in research? If so, how are the research activities treated in relation to the lobbying rules?[147]

- Does the organization engage in attempts to influence legislation by means of the Internet?[148]

---

138. See *id.* § 22.3(d)(iii).
139. See *id.* § 22.4.
140. See *id.* § 12.4(e); *Private Foundations* § 9.1.
141. See *Law of Tax-Exempt Organizations* § 22.5.
142. See *id.* § 28.1.
143. See *id.* § 22.5.
144. See *id.* § 22.6.
145. See *id.* § 22.6(a).
146. See *id.* § 22.7.
147. See *id.* § 22.6(a).
148. See *id.* § 22.8.

- Does the organization provide a Web site link to one or more other organizations?

- If the organization attempts to influence legislation by means of the Internet, is it in compliance with the foregoing rules?

- Is the organization required to register as a lobbyist under the federal law registration and reporting rules?[149]

§ 9.16   POLITICAL CAMPAIGN ACTIVITIES

- Does the nonprofit organization engage in political campaign activities?[150]

- If so, what is the extent of these political campaign activities?

- Is the organization a public charity? If so, how is it in compliance with the proscription on political campaign activities?[151]

- If the organization is a public charity, is it, in complying with the proscription, relying on the proposition that a candidate is not involved?[152]

- If the organization is a public charity, is it, in complying with the proscription, relying on the proposition that a campaign is not involved?[153]

- If the organization is a public charity, is it, in complying with the proscription, relying on the proposition that a public office is not involved?[154]

- If the organization is a public charity, is it, in complying with the proscription, asserting that an activity is not a participation or intervention in a political campaign?[155]

- Is the organization a social welfare organization? If so, is it in compliance with the rules?[156]

- If the organization is a social welfare organization, does it have a related political organization?

- If the organization is a social welfare organization, has it ever paid (or been requested to pay) the political organizations tax?[157]

- Is the organization a business league? If so, is it in compliance with the rules?[158]

- If the organization is a business league, does it have a related political organization?

---

149. See *id*. § 22.10.
150. See *id*. § 23.2(b)-(f); § 8.5.
151. See *id*. § 23.2.
152. See *id*. § 23.2(d).
153. See *id*. § 23.2(e).
154. See *id*. § 22.2(f).
155. See *id*. § 22.2(b).
156. See *id*. § 23.5.
157. See *id*. § 23.4.
158. See *id*. § 23.7.

- If the organization is a business league, has it ever paid (or been requested to pay) the political organizations tax?[159]

- Is the organization any other type of tax-exempt organization? If so, is it in compliance with the rules?[160]

- If the organization is another type of tax-exempt organization, does it have a related political organization?

- If the organization is another type of tax-exempt organization, has it ever paid (or been requested to pay) the political organizations tax?[161]

- If the organization is a public charity, does it have a related political organization that does not engage in political campaign activities?

- If the organization is a public charity, has it ever paid (or been requested to pay) the political organizations tax?[162]

- If the organization is a public charity, has there ever been an assertion that any of its legislative activities constitute political campaign activities?[163]

- Is the organization itself a political organization?[164]

- Is the organization a private foundation? Is it in compliance with the proscription on political campaign activity?[165]

- If the organization is a public charity, and is affiliated with one or more other tax-exempt noncharitable organizations that engage in political campaign activity, is the lawyer conducting the legal audit satisfied that this activity is not tainting the tax-exempt status of the charitable organization?

- Is the organization taking the position that political campaign activities are being undertaken by an individual in his or her personal capacity and not as a representative of the organization?

- If the organization is a public charity, is it taking the position that it is engaging in permissible voter education activities?[166]

- Does the organization engage in political campaign activities by means of the Internet?[167]

- Does the organization provide a Web site link to one or more other organizations?

- If the organization engages in political campaign activities by means of the Internet, is it in compliance with the political campaign activities rules?

---

159. See *id*. § 23.4.
160. See *id*. § 23.8.
161. See *id*. § 23.4.
162. *Id*.
163. See *id*. § 23.9.
164. See *id*., Chapter 17.
165. See, e.g., *id*. § 12.4(e).
166. See *id*. § 23.2(c).
167. See *id*. § 23.10.

§ 9.17 OTHER FORMS OF ADVOCACY

- Does the nonprofit organization engage in activities such as litigation, demonstrations, picketing, and boycotts?[168]
- If so, does the organization regard these as exempt functions?
- If so, and the organization is a charitable organization, ascertain why these activities are charitable and/or educational in nature.
- If the organization is a charitable organization, is it taking the position that such activities are a means to achievement of exempt ends?[169]
- If the organization is a charitable organization, is it in compliance with the law that it may not engage in activities that are contrary to public policy?[170]
- Has the tax-exempt organization been charged with a violation of civil law?
- Has the tax-exempt organization been charged with a violation of criminal law?
- Is there a basis for either type of charge, if it has not occurred?

§ 9.18 SUBSIDIARIES

- Does the nonprofit organization have one or more subsidiaries?[171]
- If so, identify them.
- If the organization does not presently have a subsidiary, is it contemplating one (or more)?
- Should the organization have one or more subsidiaries?
- Is protection against legal liability a factor?
- Is preservation of tax-exempt status (if applicable) a factor?
- Identify the legal form of each of these subsidiaries (if any).[172]
- Identify the control mechanism used for each of these subsidiaries (if any).[173]

§ 9.19 BIFURCATION BASICS

- Does each of the entities have one or more real and substantial business functions?[174]
- What is the nature of the overlap (if any) of the boards of directors?
- What is the nature of the overlap of officers?

---

168. See *id.* § 23.2(g).
169. See *id.* § 6.3(b).
170. See *id.* § 6.2(a).
171. See *id.*, Chapters 28, 29; § 8.11.
172. See, e.g., *Law of Tax-Exempt Organizations* § 29.1(b).
173. See, e.g., *id.* § 29.1(c).
174. See, e.g., *id.* § 29.2.

- What is the nature of the overlap of employees?
- Are the organizations in the same location?
- Is there a sharing of office space, furniture, and/or equipment?
- Is the parent (exempt) organization involved in the day-to-day management of the subsidiary? If not, why not?
- Can a case be made that the subsidiary is merely an extension of the parent?
- Can a case be made that the parent–subsidiary relationship is a sham?
- If the two organizations were treated as one for tax purposes, what would be the impact on the tax-exempt status of the parent?
- Is there a contract between the organizations concerning fees, reimbursements of costs, employee-sharing, and the like?

§ 9.20 TAX-EXEMPT SUBSIDIARIES[175]

- What is the form of the tax-exempt subsidiary?
- What is the purpose of the exempt subsidiary? Responses include lobbying___, political campaign activity___, fundraising___, certification___, conduct of exempt functions___ (program), and/or maintenance of an endowment___.
- If the activity of the subsidiary is fundraising, does the organization have fundraising as its sole function?
- If the activity of the subsidiary is maintenance of an endowment,[176] does the size of the endowment adversely affect the organization's fundraising ability?
- Is the subsidiary a supporting organization?[177] If so, what type of supporting organization?
- If the subsidiary is a charitable organization and is not a supporting organization, what is the public charity status of the subsidiary?[178]
- If the subsidiary is a charitable organization and is not a supporting organization, why is it not a supporting organization?
- What is the tax-exempt status of the parent? IRC___.
- What is the tax-exempt status of the subsidiary? IRC___.

§ 9.21 TAXABLE SUBSIDIARIES[179]

- Does the nonprofit organization have a taxable subsidiary? [These questions are applicable to each taxable subsidiary, if there are more than one.]

---

175. In general, see *id.*, Chapter 28.
176. See *id.* § 11.9.
177. See § 8.6(d).
178. See § 8.6.
179. In general, see *Law of Tax-Exempt Organizations*, Chapter 29.

- What is the legal form of the subsidiary?

- What is the purpose of the subsidiary?

- If the purpose of the subsidiary is unrelated business, what is the size of the subsidiary in relation to the tax-exempt parent?

- How was the subsidiary capitalized? If money was involved, what was the amount?

- Is a liquidation of the subsidiary being contemplated? If so, what would be the tax consequences?

- Is the subsidiary a partner in or member of a joint venture?

- Is the parent exempt organization a partner in or member of a joint venture? Should that role be performed by the/a subsidiary?

- Is the parent exempt organization contemplating becoming a partner in or member of a joint venture? Should that role be performed by the/a subsidiary?

- Is the organization engaged in social enterprise?[180] If so, describe the inter-relationship with use of a taxable subsidiary (if any).

§ 9.22 REVENUE FROM SUBSIDIARY[181]

- Does the subsidiary pay revenue to the tax-exempt parent organization?

- If so, what is the nature of this revenue? Categories include dividend___, interest___, rent___, royalty___, annuity___, capital gain___, or grant___.

- Does the parent organization pay tax on some or all of the revenue received from the subsidiary?

- If no, should tax be paid? Is there a basis for an exemption?

- Is the parent organization using the special carve-out exception available during 2006–2009?[182]

- If the parent is a charitable organization, what is the impact (if any) of revenue from the subsidiary on the parent's public charity status?

§ 9.23 JOINT VENTURE BASICS[183]

- Is the nonprofit organization a partner in a partnership or a member of any other form of joint venture?

---

180. See *id.* § 4.12.
181. See, in general, *id.* §§ 28.6, 29.7.
182. See *id.* § 29.7(d).
183. See, in general, *id.*, Chapter 30; § 8.12.

- If so, what is the legal form of this joint venture?

- What is the documentation associated with the formation of the venture and the exempt organization's participation in it?

- Why did the nonprofit organization become involved in the venture?

- If it is a partnership, is the nonprofit organization a general partner or a limited partner?

- If the nonprofit organization is a tax-exempt organization, is the business being conducted by the joint venture related or unrelated?

- Are there facts that suggest that the nonprofit organization may be deemed to be involved in a joint venture?

- Is the aggregate approach rule being followed?

- Has the nonprofit organization given consideration to use of a subsidiary as a participant in the venture?

§ 9.24 JOINT VENTURES—OTHER ELEMENTS

- How does the nonprofit organization's involvement in the venture further its exempt purposes (if it is tax-exempt)?

- If the organization is (or will be) a general partner in the venture, what are the ways by which the organization is (or will be) insulated from the day-to-day responsibilities of general partner (see above list of factors)?

- Is the rate of return on the capital investment of the limited partners reasonable?

- If the nonprofit organization is a charitable entity, does the documentation make it clear that the fulfillment of charitable purposes by the venture takes precedence over the maximization of profit?

- Has the venture itself entered into a contract, particularly a management contract? If so, with whom?

- What is the extent of the charitable organization's resources that are (or will be) transferred to the venture? All, a primary portion, or an insubstantial portion?

- Is there an argument that the charitable organization has lost control of itself to one or more for-profit co-venturers?

- Have management contracts, leases, royalty agreements, and the like been reviewed to see if a joint venture lurks in the facts?

- Is there potential for application of the doctrines of private benefit, private inurement, and/or intermediate sanctions?

- Is the business in the venture related or unrelated to the purposes of the exempt organization?

- Do any of the unrelated business income modification rules apply?

§ 9.25 UNRELATED BUSINESS ANALYSIS[184]

- Is the nonprofit organization subject to the unrelated business rules?
- What are the businesses (programs and other endeavors) that are conducted by the organization?
- What definition of the term *business* is being used in this analysis?
- Identify undertakings of the organization that do not qualify as businesses (if any).
- Is the fragmentation rule being properly applied by the organization?
- Identify each business that is regularly carried on.
- Is a business of the organization conducted only on a seasonal basis?
- Has the organization outsourced any of its activities?
- If so, does the contract involved provide that the other party to the contract is an agent of the tax-exempt organization?
- Does the organization expend any preparatory time? How extensive is this amount of time?
- Ascertain each business that is related to the organization's exempt purposes. What is the rationale for the relatedness?
- Ascertain each business that is substantially related to the organization's exempt purposes. What is the rationale for the substantiality?
- Ascertain each business that is unrelated to the organization's exempt purposes.
- Is any of the income from one or more unrelated businesses sheltered from unrelated business income taxation by statute? If so, identify the law(s).
- Are one or more unrelated business activities sheltered from unrelated business income by statute? If so, identify the law(s).
- Does the organization engage in fundraising?
- If so, are any of the fundraising activities unrelated businesses?
- Does the organization have unrelated debt-financed income?
- Does the organization receive income from a controlled entity?
- Is the organization correctly ascertaining the expenses that can be deducted in computing unrelated business taxable income?
- Is the organization conducting an unrelated business at a loss, where the loss can be offset against gain from one or more other unrelated businesses?
- How much unrelated business activity can the exempt organization engage in without endangering its tax-exempt status?
- Should one or more unrelated businesses be transferred to another organization?

---

184. In general, see *Law of Tax-Exempt Organizations*, Chapter 24; § 8.10.

- If so, what should the form of that organization be?

- Is the organization contemplating an unrelated business that should be initiated in another organization?

- If so, what should the form of that organization be?

§ 9.26 COMMERCIALITY DOCTRINE[185]

- Does the organization engage in activities that compete with for-profit organizations?

- What factors does the organization take into account in determining the amount of its fees?

- Does the organization advertise one or more of its activities?

- Does the organization have a catchphrase, slogan, jingle, or the like?

- Does the organization have employees?

- If so, are they provided any special training?

- Does the organization use the services of volunteers?

- Does the organization receive any charitable contributions?

- What is the outcome when the commerciality doctrine is applied to the organization?

§ 9.27 ANNUAL INFORMATION RETURNS[186]

- Is the nonprofit organization required to file annual information returns with the IRS?

- If so, which return is the appropriate one? Form 990___. Form 990-EZ___. Form 990-PF___. Form 990-N___. Other___.

- If not, what is the basis for the nonfiling exception? Church___. Other religious organization___. Affiliate of a governmental unit___.

- Is the lawyer conducting the legal audit satisfied that these returns are accurate?

- Does a lawyer, on an ongoing basis, evaluate the content of the organization's Web site?

- For example, in the case of reporting by charitable organizations, are the appropriate distinctions being made between contributions, grants, and exempt function income?

- Likewise, are the appropriate distinctions being made between direct public support and indirect public support?

---

185. In general, see *Law of Tax-Exempt Organizations* § 4.11; § 8.13(f).
186. In general, see *Law of Tax-Exempt Organizations* § 27.2; § 8.8(a).

- Likewise, is revenue from one or more special events being properly reported?
- Likewise, is the organization accurately reporting its expenses on a functional basis?
- Likewise, has the organization adequately stated its primary purpose?
- Likewise, is the organization accurately (and fully) reporting its program service accomplishments?
- Likewise, has the organization properly identified all of its key employees?
- Likewise, is the organization properly answering the question as to the conduct of any activities not previously reported to the IRS?
- Likewise, is the organization properly answering the question as to any changes in the organization's organizing or governing documents?
- Likewise, has the organization properly answered the question as to the making of any political expenditures?
- Likewise, has the organization properly answered the question as to compliance with the public disclosure (inspection) requirements?
- Likewise, has the organization properly answered the question concerning the quid pro quo disclosure requirements?
- Likewise, has the organization properly answered the question as to the receipt of nondeductible gifts?
- Likewise, has the organization properly answered the question as to the payment of tax because of legislative or political campaign activities?
- Likewise, has the organization properly answered the question as to its involvement in any excess benefit transactions?
- Likewise, is the organization properly reporting its related income, unrelated income, and income shielded from taxation by statute?
- Likewise, does the organization control one or more organizations?
- Likewise, is the organization the owner of one or more disregarded entities?
- Likewise, has the organization received any funds to pay premiums on a personal benefit contract?
- Likewise, is the organization properly reporting compensation arrangements?
- Likewise, is the organization properly reporting any transactions with insiders?
- Likewise, is the organization engaging in any transactions with noncharitable organizations?
- Likewise, is the organization properly calculating its public support ratio (if applicable)?
- Likewise, is the organization properly reporting information about contributions to it?
- Likewise, is the organization filing a copy of the annual information return with one or more states?

§ 9.28 DISCLOSURE REQUIREMENTS[187]

- Has the organization (if required to do so) made a copy of its application for recognition of exemption available to those who request it?
- Is this practice ongoing?
- Is the organization's application posted on the Internet?
- Does the organization have copies of the application available to timely respond to requests for it?
- Is there any basis for application of the harassment campaign exception?
- How is the organization responding to the question on Form 990, Part VI, question 18, with respect to its application for recognition of exemption?
- Has the organization made one or more copies of its annual information return available to those who request it or them?
- Is this practice ongoing?
- Are one or more of the organization's annual information returns posted on the Internet?
- How is the organization responding to the question on Form 990, Part VI, line 18, with respect to its annual information return?
- Does the organization receive charitable contributions?
- Is the organization in compliance with the charitable gift substantiation requirements?
- Is the organization taking the position that it is providing goods or services in consideration for contributions?
- If so, is it providing a good faith estimate of those goods or services? How is that estimate amount determined?
- By what means is the organization providing written acknowledgments of gifts?
- In this context, how is the organization treating donors' understandings and expectations?
- Does the organization receive quid pro quo charitable contributions?
- Is the organization in compliance with the quid pro quo contributions disclosure requirements?
- How is the good faith estimate amount determined?
- How is donative intent being determined?
- How is the organization responding to the question on Form 990, Part V, line 7b?
- If the organization is not a charitable entity, is it in compliance with the rules concerning disclosure of nondeductibility of contributions?

---

187. See § 8.9.

- Is the organization in compliance with the IRS's safe-harbor rules?

- If not, how is the organization complying with these rules?

- How is the organization responding to the questions on Form 990, Part V, lines 6a and b?

- Is the organization working with its donors to be certain that they are in compliance with the rules requiring disclosure to the IRS of certain gifts of property?

- Is the organization properly completing Form 8283, Section B, Part IV?

- Is the organization receiving copies of Form 8283, Section B in a timely fashion?

- Is the organization disclosing dispositions of contributed property to the IRS by means of Form 8282 in a timely fashion?

- Has or is the organization consuming or distributing contributed property in furtherance of its exempt purposes?

- Has or is the organization transferring contributed property to another charitable organization?

- Is the organization working with its donors to be certain that they are in compliance with the rules requiring appraisals of certain gifts of property?

- Does the organization offer to the public services or information that are available to the public without charge from the federal government?

- If so, is the organization in compliance with the rules requiring disclosure of that availability?

- Has the organization received or is it now receiving any funds to pay premiums on one or more personal benefit contracts?

- Has the organization paid or is it paying premiums on one or more personal benefit contracts?

- How is the organization responding to the questions on Form 990, Part V, line 7f?

- Is the organization involved in one or more tax shelters?

- Is the organization involved in a listed transaction?

- Is the organization involved in a reportable transaction?

- Does the organization file an unrelated business income tax return (Form 990-T)? If so, is it properly publicly disclosing that return?[188]

§ 9.29 CONSIDERATIONS FOR LAWYER CONDUCTING LEGAL AUDIT

- How are you [the lawyer] advising your clients as to applicability of the commerciality doctrine?

---

188. See *Law of Tax-Exempt Organizations* § 27.7.

- How are you determining which persons are insiders and/or disqualified persons with respect to tax-exempt organizations?

- In application of the contributions substantiation requirements, how are you advising clients to treat expectations and understandings?

- How are you, in your practice, applying the private benefit doctrine?

- In establishing a tax-exempt organization, how are you treating exempt functions performed by one or more founders personally?

- When clients obtain appraisals of property, are you evaluating the accuracy of the appraisals?

- Do these appraisals take into account future events that may impact the valuation?

- If the intermediate sanctions penalties are being applied, is revocation of tax exemption also being attempted? If so, how are you evaluating the standard for the revocation?

- When clients obtain opinions as to the reasonableness of compensation, are you evaluating the reports to determine whether all of the relevant factors have been taken into consideration?

- In advising charitable organizations as to the federal tax rules concerning lobbying, are you making distinctions between organizations that are advocating the merits of a studied issue and those that are selling an assumed conclusion?

- Also, as to the lobbying rules, are you differentiating between legislative issues that are highly public and controversial and those that are not?

- When applying the private inurement, intermediate sanctions, and/or self-dealing rules, are you also applying the private benefit doctrine?

Index